England and Germany. Studies in theological diplomacy

STUDIEN ZUR INTERKULTURELLEN GESCHICHTE DES CHRISTENTUMS
ETUDES D'HISTOIRE INTERCULTURELLE DU CHRISTIANISME
STUDIES IN THE INTERCULTURAL HISTORY OF CHRISTIANITY

Herausgegeben von/edité par/edited by

Richard Friedli
Université de Fribourg

Walter J. Hollenweger
University of Birmingham

Hans Jochen Margull
Universität Hamburg

Band 25

Verlag Peter D. Lang
FRANKFURT AM MAIN · BERN

S. W. Sykes (ed.)

ENGLAND AND GERMANY.
STUDIES IN
THEOLOGICAL DIPLOMACY

Verlag Peter D. Lang
FRANKFURT AM MAIN · BERN

CIP-Kurztitelaufnahme der Deutschen Bibliothek

England and Germany : studies in theolog.
diplomacy / S. W. Sykes (ed.). - Frankfurt am
Main ; Bern : Lang, 1982
  (Studien zur interkulturellen Geschichte des
  Christentums ; Bd. 25)
  ISBN 3-8204-5854-9
NE: Sykes, Stephen W. [Hrsg.] ; GT

ISBN 3-8204-5854-9
© Verlag Peter D. Lang GmbH, Frankfurt am Main 1982

Druck und Bindung: fotokop wilhelm weihert KG, darmstadt

CONTENTS

LIST OF CONTRIBUTORS

I.U.DALFERTH

Is Hochschulassistent and assistant to Prof. Dr. E.Jüngel at the University of Tübingen, where he teaches systematic theology. He is also currently stellvertretender Leiter of the Institute of Hermeneutics. He has edited Sprachlogik des Glaubens (1974), and translated (together with J.Kalka) F.P.Ramsey's Foundations: Essays in Philosophy, Logic, Mathematics and Economics (1978). In 1981 he published Religiöse Rede von Gott and co-edited with Prof. Jüngel, K.Barth's Fides Quaerens Intellectum.

A.O.DYSON

Is Samuel Ferguson Professor of Social and Pastoral Theology at Manchester University. Previously he was Principal of Ripon Hall (1968-74), Oxford, Canon of Windsor (1974-77), and Lecturer in Theology at the University of Kent (1977-80) where he taught the history of modern European theology. His writings include Who is Jesus Christ? (1969), The Immortality of the Past (1974), and We Believe (1977).

J.W.ROGERSON

Is Professor and Head of Department of the Department of Biblical Studies, University of Sheffield. From 1964 to 1979 he taught Old Testament and Intertestamental Studies at the University of Durham, and has written several books, including Myth in Old Testament Interpretation (1974), and Anthropology and the Old Testament (1979). He is currently preparing a book on Old Testament interpretation in Britain and Europe in the 19th and early 20th centuries.

R.MORGAN

Is Lecturer in New Testament at the University of Oxford. From 1967 to 1976 he taught in the Lancaster University Department of Religious Studies. He has edited The Nature of New Testament Theology (1973), and co-edited (with Michael Pye) The Cardinal Meaning: Essays in Comparative Hermeneutics (1973) and Ernst Troeltsch: Writings on Theology and Religion, (1977).

S.W.SYKES

Is the Van Mildert Professor of Divinity at the University of Durham.
From 1964 to 1974 he was Fellow and Dean of St. John's College, Cambridge,
and University Lecturer in Divinity. He has written three books, Friedrich Schleiermacher (1971), Christian Theology Today
(1971) and The Integrity of Anglicanism (1979), co-edited (with
J.P. Clayton) Christ, Faith and History (1972), and edited Karl
Barth, Studies of his Theological Method (1980). In 1980 he
published the first volume, co-edited with Derek Holmes, of New Studies
in Theology.

D.RITSCHL

Has been Professor of Systematic Theology at the University of Mainz
from 1970, after holding appointments in Austin, Texas; Pittsburgh; and
Union Theological Seminary, New York. Among his works are Christ
our Life (1960), Die homiletische Funktion der Gemeinde
(1959), A Theology of Proclamation (1960) Nur Menschen,
Zur Negerfrage in den amerikanischen Südstaaten (1962), Memory and
Hope (1967), Athanasius - Versuch einer Interpretation
(1974) and Konzepte, Gesammelte Aufsätze Bd. I. (1976)

The studies contained in this book are to be thought of as contributions towards the eventual writing of a thorough and detailed history of the theological relations between England and Germany (1). The point of such a history, as of these essays, would be to help those who regularly read the theological literature of the other's nation to a fuller appreciation of the differences and similarities of each other's traditions. The presupposition obviously is that foreign literature is, indeed, foreign and in need of elucidation.

At once the student of English and German theology comes upon the fact that these two nations have been, for several centuries, mutually impinging upon each other's scholarship and thought. This establishes the existence of what I have called "theological relations", a concept which deserves a certain clarification. The basis of it is, as outlined above, simple enough; namely that, in the course of his search for theological wisdom, the citizen of one nation lights upon and reads the literature of another, either in its original language or in translation. If there exists a practical community of scholarship between the two nations involved, the difficulties which may arise are likely to be minor. If, however, the nations have developed on different lines, so that educational, legal, political, economic and ecclesiastical structures and traditions are plainly distinct, then the problems of interpretation and reception may begin to be of importance. If one adds to this situation the presence of an ideology which insists that cultural differences are ineradicable because rooted in the peculiarities of the two languages, the divergences quickly transform themselves from being problems to be overcome into matters of national pride, and mutual incomprehension is taken to be the normal and desirable state of affairs.

"Theological relations" in a context such as that between England and Germany, which manifests all the differences mentioned above together with the complicating factor of a history of rival national ideologies, presents the theologian with a peculiar challenge. What value, he must ask himself, does he place on understanding "foreign" literature? Does it matter if what a theological work means in its own land is something other than its reception in another? Is it realistic to attempt to enter fully into another environment, or must one be content with "feeling at home with strangeness"? These, among others, are the questions which the elucidation of "theological relations" eventually imposes. But at the very least they set out from a conviction that the present situation is far from satisfactory.

There is abundant evidence in contemporary theology that neither English nor German patterns of theological education include introductions to the modern church history of the other nation. German students are not well served in respect of basic information about the English reformation, or

English deism or the Evangelical or Oxford movements. English students, even if they may have some knowledge of major German theologians from Luther to Bultmann, would be very hard pressed to put them in any kind of church historical context. The theological structures, when communicated, tend to emerge from a void, teutonic thunderbolts from an inscrutable Lutheran heaven. (And even well-educated theologians have been known to speak as though Barth himself was a Lutheran - or even a German!).

The absence of a basic framework makes the matter of interpreting theological work from each other's countries extraordinarily haphazard. Small wonder that some theologians have shown themselves very reluctant to allow their work even to be translated into the other language. As Gerhard von Rad put it in 1965, when voicing his own doubts about the issue of a translation:

> Theological writings are like others - their roots are often more exclusively bound up than we are aware with the country and language in which they were written, for a specific country and language always imply as well a specific mode of thought (2).

Those, however, whose work is read in the other country, either in the original tongue or in translation, deserve to be understood by reference to the history of the immediate discussion of which they are part. Such understanding permits a deeper level of critical apprehension, and, in the end, promotes a more searching self-appreciation.

In this book the essays are concerned not with the institutional history of the churches in England and Germany, important though that is, but with certain selected aspects of the history of theological thought. We have limited ourselves primarily to protestant theology, mainly because it is for obvious reasons in protestantism that national divergences have become most marked. We have further limited ourselves, within the British Isles, primarily to England. There is obviously more to be said once Scotland has been taken into account, with its different ecclesiastical, educational and legal traditions. The history of relations between two countries can only ever be part of a much larger history; but where, as in the case of relations between England and Germany, there is so much to be elucidated, it cannot be a bad thing consciously to limit oneself to a few major topics.

By any criterion Luther makes a massive impact upon the separate development of English and German theology. We have, mercifully, moved beyond the days when a British scholar would have to write a book entitled, Martin Luther: Hitler's Cause - or Cure?, and open the book with a quotation from a great nineteenth-century admirer of Luther, Julius Hare; "the most unfounded charges against Luther have found acceptance with many, who catch them up with a parrot-like volubility in repeating ugly words" (3). However, the caricature of Luther as the great irrationalist has its contemporary exponents; and English theologians, self-consciously proud of a long tradition of natural theology (in one or other of its forms), may well be tempted to dismiss not merely Luther but much German theology also as anti-rational, if they fail to consider how Luther himself argued about the relation between philosophy and theology. In the long history of the reception of Luther this argument has been frequently simplified and distorted. But the tradition seems also to have contained the seeds of its own regeneration; and Dr. Dalferth, with proved acquaintance with the most recent work in English-language philosophy of religion (4), argues the case for Luther's importance as a point of reference in the contemporary debate about the status of religious language.

No less major, and no less in need of careful elucidation, is the varying impact of the European Enlightenment in England and Germany. The usual model here, a triangular one in which "enlightenment" was exported from England to France, from to Germany, and from Germany back to England, leaves much unexplained. What is meant by "enlightenment"? Why did the movement, if that it is, take root differently in different countries? Why did England, an exporter in the seventeenth and eighteenth centuries, need to become an importer in the nineteenth? The essays of Professor Dyson, Professor Rogerson and Mr. Morgan separate out the issues and clarify the complexities. No one studying the theological history of the seventeenth, eighteenth or nineteenth centuries in England or Germany can avoid the impact of ideas from the other country. Yet the reception of these ideas invariably entailed their transformation, consciously or unconsciously. There are genuine divergences in the philosophical environment in which "enlightened" opinions become fashionable. Then, on closer examination, it appears that the activity of biblical criticism in each country manifests the signs of these divergences. The articulation of Christian doctrine, moreover, is responsive not merely to the philosophical and biblical, but also to the ecclesiastical climate of opinion, and this latter plays an important role in each country in creating a different sense of what is acceptable, and what is not.

Together with these three essays should be taken the discussion of the role of nationalism and the national character hypothesis in the deteriorating theological relationships of the nineteenth and twentieth centuries, contained in my essay of theological diplomacy, here published in English after earlier publication in German. It would, after all, be absurd if no one were to advert to the fact that Germany and England fought two wars of unparalleled violence, scope and sophistication, to the accompaniment of all the manipulative techniques of national propaganda. On both sides the normal exchange in theological education was ruptured, and it is possible to detect signs that the habit of estrangement is still repeating itself. The problems of a Christian theology are manifestly common to the post-war churches of the West; why, then, should it be the case that one speaks with so much less assurance, if at all, of a European theology than a Latin American one? Or should all theology be, or at least aim to be, merely catholic?

That this question has its own acute contemporary relevance is clear from the two essays relating mainly to the modern climate of opinion in which theology is written. Even a superficial acquaintance with the modern Church of England will reveal the acute problem of its stance viz-à-viz protestantism. Anglicanism dominated the Universities of England for centuries, and stamped its own imprint on the structures, procedures and assumptions of theological education widely outside its own borders, at least until very recently. (Distinguished non-Anglican theologians in English Universities are still likely to be thought by Germans to be Anglican, principally because they participate in a certain indefinable community of scholarship deriving from this imprint). How is Anglicanism to be explained? That is the theme of my own essay on "Anglicanism and Protestantism".

Professor Dietrich Ritschl of the University of Mainz speaks of the contemporary situation in German theology out of an unrivalled personal knowledge of the Anglo-Saxon world (Scotland, North America, and the continent of Australasia, in addition to England). He well knows the indebtedness of the whole English-speaking world to the achievements of German theological scholarship; but sees those achievements from the standpoint of their total environment. Inevitably a close inspection of the present is resistant to the pressure for schematization. A plurality of themes and possibilities, of conscious directions and historical accidents, impose themselves on the observer, forcing him to the most modest of conclusions.

There is a lesson in this modesty for the whole work of comparison opened up by these studies. Far from confirming the grandiose generalisations of those who would fit the theology of one nation into some national typology, close and careful study of both past and present yields a great variety of factors at work in shaping a nation's theological output. This very variety may cause students of theological relations great difficulty. But the same variety is a source of hope for those who wish to promote transnational interaction, for it means that the present difficulties are not the outworking of some intractable fate or destiny; but, rather, that by hard and patient work at particular points, misunderstandings can be elucidated and mutually profitable exchange fostered, ad maiorem gloriam Dei.

Footnotes

1 Versions or drafts of chapters 1-6 of this book were read at the 1978 Annual Conference of the Modern Churchmen's Union, at Culham College, nr. Abingdon, Oxford, under the chairmanship of the present editor.

2 G. von Rad, Preface to the English Edition of Old Testament Theology, II (Edinburgh, 1965), p.ix

3 Gordon Rupp, Martin Luther, Hitler's Cause - or Cure? (London, 1945), p.9, quoting from Julius Hare's Vindication of Luther (1852). On the reception of Luther in England see "Luther in England", ch.2 of Gordon Rupp's, The Righteousness of God (London, 1953). The signs of "quickening interest in Luther in England" there referred to have not matured, and studies of Luther must be admitted to be largely restricted to the works of Professor Rupp and Professor James Atkinson.

4 See Dr. Dalferth's translation of the basic essays of the modern English writers on philosophy of religion, Sprachlogik des Glaubens (München, 1974).

THE VISIBLE AND THE INVISIBLE:
LUTHER'S LEGACY OF A THEOLOGICAL THEOLOGY

by

I. U. Dalferth

O. Introduction

In the days when the Modern Churchmen's Union was founded, Adolf von Harnack remarked in assessing Luther's role in the history of doctrine: "A philosopher may be able to find the means of showing the doctrines of the Greek church to be profound and wise, but no philosopher will be capable of acquiring any taste for Luther's faith" (1). This was a noble way of putting it, and few of those who think of Luther as irrational and dismiss his influence as inimical to any sound consideration of present day theological issues have left it at a matter of taste or distaste.

For example, in his Gifford Lectures, R e a s o n a n d B e l i e f , published in 1974, Brand Blanshard, one of the very few philosophers who have actually attempted to examine Luther's teachings in recent years, comes to the much stronger conclusion, that "it is hard to see how any reflective and humane person can acquiesce in such a theology" (2). Luther's teachings he finds to be wrong on all accounts, and the "only way to make them plausible is to surrender to a kind of theology that respects neither logic nor ethics" (3). That it was so much "more effective immediately than ... the Erasmian coolness that will probably have the last word" he explains as being due to the "Lutheran temperament"; "Luther 'thought with his blood'; for good and evil he was a soothing pot of passion" (4); and Blanshard goes as far as to hold that because of his "frank, withering, philistine scorn for 'the harlot reason' ... Luther was deficient in mere loyalty to truth" (5).

This goes far beyond noting, as Harnack did, the strangeness and in many respects medieval and pre-Copernican character of Luther's thought; and it no doubt supports the widespread opinion that Luther was an irrationalist whose influence has been harmful and who has 'no word to speak to our time' (6). Now whatever one may think of the soundness of Blanshard's presentation and assessment of Luther, it at least makes perfectly clear, that the difficulty of understanding Luther is not simply due to the historical gap between his time and ours. No doubt, he is one of the great and therefore ambivalent figures, whose impact on the course of history has been decisive; but the real problem which he poses only begins to emerge when we move beyond the general problem of understanding a thinker living and expressing himself in a world very different from ours, by noting that Luther has achieved his impact by speaking as a theologian. "Luther's characteristic standpoint", as P.S.Watson put it, "is quite strictly and exclusively theological. It is not, for instance, philosophical or psychological; and his thought is inevitably misinterpreted if it is approached from such angles" (7). This, of course, can not mean that his thought is not open to philosophical criticism. But such criticism will miss the point if it does not take into account the theological motive and justification of Luther's critique of reason. For his often quoted "scorn for the harlot reason" is intimately bound up with his thoroughgoing attempt to work out a strictly theological theology (8) which distinguishes between "Physica" and "Theologica" (9) and thus is not confusing metaphysical, psychological and theological issues as did the various "philosophical" theologies of his time. This, I dare say, is no less provocative and challenging to most of our ways of doing theology than it has been in his time.

Luther has been remarkably ineffective in his attempt to reform theology; and the history of the reception of his thought shows that his critical attitude towards reason has found a much wider audience (10) - in philosophical as well as in theological circles - than his reasons for it or his positive theological programme. But it is the latter which justifies us in taking a more than merely historical interest in Luther. He has a lot to contribute to such hotly debated questions of present day theology as the difference between theology and philosophy or religious studies; the experiential foundation of theological statements; the problem of creation and natural knowledge of God; the central role of christology and eschatology in Christian theology etc. But more important than these contributions to particular topics is his general approach to theology which, by basing theology exclusively on the experience of faith, tries to establish it as a strict alternative to any speculative or metaphysical account of reality. This, I think, is of lasting significance. For just as, to use a modern example, logic had to be disentangled from ontological and psychological considerations before it could progress in the way it did since the time of G.Frege, so theology has to be established as a subject in its own right independently of meta- physical, psychological or whatever considerations; and this - as Luther has attempted to show - will be possible only by basing it firmly on faith and the experience of faith. Yet just as ontological considerations have reoccurred in logic in recent years, albeit in a rather different form, so the concentration of theology on faith can be expected to have consequences for ontological, psychological and other issues, albeit in a different form. The call for a theological theology, therefore, is not to be misunderstood as a call for a theological isolationism; it only wants to get the priorities straight.

In what follows I shall not talk about the manifold receptions of Luther's thought in, and influences on, German protestant theology (11). Rather I shall turn immediately to Luther himself and try to elucidate some aspects of his conception of theology which I think cannot be neglected in our own attempts at theologizing. Of course, I in no way wish to pretend that Luther has given the final answer to all or even most theological problems; and therefore I have no qualms in being selective and in stressing certain strands in his thinking more than others. I am not interested in a balanced picture but in making a point, namely that Luther offers a coherent and consistent conception of theology which provides a noteworthy alternative to much present-day theologizing.

To show this, at least in outline, I shall draw upon a number of texts (13) spread over some 30 years, during which his thinking underwent major changes. And yet there is a basic unity, as I hope to show by concentrating on 3 theses of Luther, namely

(1.) that theology is fundamentally different from philosophy and all other subjects;
(2.) that this difference is due to their different subject-matter in so far as philosophy has to do with the visible things of experience and reason, while theology treats of the invisible things of faith;
(3.) and that the subject-matter of theology is to be explicated as knowledge of God and man in their specific relations.

1. The difference between philosophy and theology

1. The intellectual climate in which Luther was brought up was that of late medieval nominalism. In Erfurt he was trained in the via moderna, the Ockhamist way of thought. Thus it comes as no surprise that from the very beginning of his theological career we find him expressing a very critical attitude towards the role of philosophy (which according to the understanding of the time includes every sort of knowledge obtained by the natural faculties of sensual experience and reason) in theology. There is a fundamental gap between philosophy and theology, natural knowledge and faith, reason and revelation, and as early as 1509 we find him severely criticizing those who rely only on reason in theological matters (14), and the "shameless nonsense that Aristotle does not disagree with the Catholic truth" (15).

This, of course, is directed against the great scholastic synthesis of Aristotelian philosophy and Christian faith, which was most notably achieved by Aquinas and subsequently propagated by the via antiqua in its Thomist form. Thomas had constructed an impressively comprehensive and harmonious intellectual system, which integrated in a highly balanced form biblical tradition, neoplatonist thought as represented by Pseudo-Dionysius and Proclus, and Aristotelian philosophy. He thus managed to overcome the prima facie tension between philosophy and theology, reason and revelation, nature and grace by combining the Aristotelian idea of s c i e n t i a , i.e. of a science of necessary and evident knowledge, with the Augustinian idea of faith seeking to become knowledge (16). The price he had to pay for introducing the Aristotelian notion of science into theology was that he had to construe theological knowledge as necessary knowledge which lead to obvious difficulties in coping with the intrinsically historical and contingent nature of the Christian faith. But he arrived at an harmonized account of philosophy and theology by invoking the principle that "since grace does not destroy nature, but perfects it, the natural reason must serve faith" (17), so that although revelation and Christian faith are beyond reason, they are not contrary to it. He set out to justify this claim with the help of the Aristotelian ontology of e s s e in a detailed and complex argument by showing that our pre-revelational concept of God coincides with the God known through revelation. His whole system is designed to bear witness to the fact that the God of reason is identical with the God of revelation, and it is above all Aristotle's philosophy which provides the means for establishing this fundamental identity.

For a number of reasons (which we have no time to go into) this unified system, with its smooth harmonization of rational and theological knowledge, soon came under attack. The more the Aristotelian concept of knowledge was elaborated, and the more one became aware of the contingent nature of Christian faith, the more obvious it became that theology could not be called a science in this sense; it simply could not live up to the standards of evident knowledge, for it was neither a matter of immediately evident truths of reason nor sufficiently grounded in direct observation and the inferences therefrom (18). God in his p o t e n t i a a b s o l u t a could quite well have ordained everything in a very different way, and it was only by his p o t e n t i a o r d i n a t a that things were as they were. This in itself was difficult to accomodate with a science of necessary knowledge; but it placed theology squarely outside the realm of philosophy or science. So one in fact was presented with the dilemma of either replacing the Aristotelian concept of science by some other theory which allowed to hold a coherent view of reality comprising both rational and theological knowledge, or sticking to the Aristotelian conception and give up the attempt at a unified and comprehensive system of rational and theological knowledge. The v i a m o d e r n a , having no comparably effective theory of science at hand, clearly opted for the second way out. It firmly maintained and even elaborated in detail the Aristotelian concept of science (19), but tried to escape the conclusion of leaving theological matters utterly incomprehensible by proposing an epistemological dualism between philosophy and theology, couched in terms of a double logic, or a double mode of knowing. Thus although it stressed the antithesis between theology and reason because of the completely different subject of theology which was only given on the authority of revelation, this did not stop it from making an intensified and formalist use of reason in theological matters by showing both the implications and consequences of revealed truths and the impossibility of justifying them in any other way than by reference to authority. Under the proviso of a double epistemology, double truth, and a specific l o g i c a f i d e i distinct from ordinary logic (20) one thus managed to combine a thoroughly Aristotelian approach to science in the realm of natural knowledge, a strictly "irrational" view of the truth of the Christian faith, and a free and unhindered use of reason in each of the two realms in its own way.

2. This, in a very rough outline, is the background against which Luther's early outbursts against the use of reason, philosophy and especially Aristotle in theology are to be understood. They are neither evidence for a general irrationalist tendency nor can they be attributed to reformatory leanings at this period already (21). They rather show his dissatisfaction with a certain way of doing theology which no doubt was an important part of the process by which he arrived at his own conception of theology. It was not so much reason but its use in theology by the schoolmen which he criticized because, as he came to see, it implied an inadequate and misplaced understanding of faith.

In his own theological thought he in fact attempted to overcome not only the Thomist attempt of understanding reality with the help of the doctrine of analogy as a unified ontological system which managed to apply the same standard of truth to both matters of reason and faith only by construing a higher order reality of grace supplementing and perfecting the natural order, but also the nominalist conception which conceived reality as consisting of two realms to which different standards of truth, modes of knowing, and uses of reason apply. He undertook to show that neither a unified theologico-metaphysical system which tries to verify theological truth-claims by incorporating faith in a general ontological scheme as one of its orders, nor a metaphysical dualism which adds faith as a separate realm of truth to the otherwise selfcontained realm of natural truth, really has grasped the essence of the Christian faith and the nature of its truth-claims, and accordingly fails to provide an adequate model for theology. Luther's critique of reason is a corollary of his insistence on the unavoidability and irreducibility of f a i t h in theological matters. Faith can in no way be arrived at or be replaced by reason, for, as he puts it in his S h o r t   C a t e c h i s m , "I believe that I cannot of my own reason and strength believe in or come to Jesus Christ my Lord" (22). This claim was based on the biblical insight that there is no other way of verifying Christian truth-claims than by faith and that faith cannot be grounded in anything except itself. It is the irreplaceable nature of faith which requires a theological theology that is strictly distinct from any metaphysical or psychological enterprise.

Throughout his career Luther never changed in his critical attitude towards the role of reason in theology (although he could hail it as the "most excellent of all things" in its own field, the affairs of this world (23)). But it was only when he had developed his distinctively biblical approach to theology that he could give a justification for it which went far beyond and was very different from the nominalist position of his teachers.

That Luther is not simply echoing the nominalist position becomes quite clear in his D i s p u t a t i o   c o n t r a   s c h o l a s t i c a m   t h e o l o g i a m

19

(1517). This disputation for the first time made public his critique of scholastic theology which was, as he saw it, buried under a load of philosophical speculation. It is characteristic that he attacks both schools:

"43. It is an error to say that no one can become a theologian without Aristotle.
44. Indeed, no one can become a theologian unless he becomes one without Aristotle.
45. To state that a theologian who is not a logician is a monstrous heretic, is a monstrous and heretical statement."

And he continues 'against the recent dialecticians', i.e. philosophical theologians:

"46. In vain does one fashion a logic of faith ...
47. No syllogistic form is valid when applied to divine terms.
48. Nevertheless it does not for that reason follow that the truth of the doctrine of the Trinity contradicts syllogistic forms.
49. If a syllogistic form of reasoning holds in divine matters, then the doctrine of the Trinity is demonstrable and not the object of faith."

Quite clearly Luther is not speaking here as an adherent of one school attacking the other. He is rather criticizing a general way of doing theology common to the whole of traditional theology irrespective of the differences between its competing schools. Both the rationalist attempt to adapt theology to Aristotelian logic and the fideistic attempt to "fashion a logic of faith" that is different from ordinary logic commit the same fallacy, namely to try to make demonstrable what is an object of faith. But to neglect the difference between articuli sciti and articuli crediti is to confuse matters of philosophy and theology, reason and faith. This confusion effectively blocks any genuine theological understanding of faith. Matters of faith are such that they do not simply conform to the syllogistic forms of philosophical reasoning, and yet this does not mean that the truth of faith contradicts logic. It is obvious that this is to say that faith is not only another field of enquiry but something different in kind which is neither subject nor contradictory to philosophical reasoning. This is what the schoolmen have failed to grasp.

This critique of the scholastic solution of the problem of the relationship between theology and philosophy is the outcome of Luther's work as a biblical scholar and the discovery of the Augustine of the antipelagian writings that went along with it (25). It begins to appear in outlines in his Dictata super psalterium (1513-1515) (26) and becomes fully worked out in his lectures on Romans (1515-1516), Galatians (1516-1517) and Hebrews (1517-1518) (27). It was Luther's exegetical task as a professor of biblical theology which provided him not only with the arguments to attack both the harmonizing metaphysical theology of the via antiqua and the rationalizing fideism of the via moderna, but also with the reasons for his critique of reason.

3. It was while he struggled to achieve a proper understanding of the writings on which he had to lecture by paying close attention to the biblical modes of speech, the structure of the arguments of the biblical writers, and the way they used language to express their faith, that Luther became increasingly aware that this could not be done in terms of the theology and hermeneutic principles of the schoolmen (28). They operated with categories and employed a philosophical terminology which, when applied to scriptural exegesis, completely confused the issue at stake. Because they read the bible in the light of a metaphysical or philosophical universe of discourse (29), designed to solve problems which for Luther had not even begun to be theological ones (30), they were not able to see the distinctive character of biblical discourse and thus failed to grasp its subject-matter in an unconfused way or to give a proper account of Christian faith.

A famous case in point of the fallacy of using the terminology and criteria of intelligibility of philosophical discourse to elucidate theological discourse is the term "righteous" as e.g. used in Aristotle's Nicomachian Ethics and in St. Paul (31). "Righteous" in the New Testament sense must not be construed in the sense of suum cuique, nor is "to be righteous" in the biblical universe of discourse the result of righteous actions. Thus "righteousness" in its theological as opposed to its moral sense cannot be understood as one of the virtues which men can acquire as a habit (32) by doing right, for if it were to be understood in this sense nobody ever could be called righteous because no man is able to do what is right, i.e. pleases God. But those who believe in Christ are called righteous in the New Testament. So given the premises we have either to conclude that this is not true, or that "righteous" has to be understood in a different sense. It was Luther's exegetical discovery that it has to be understood passively (33), i.e. as "having been made righteous", "having been justified", and this quite apart from any moral righteousness which one may or may not have acquired, for no number of morally right actions can stop man from being a sinner. Christians are called righteous in the New Testament not because they have managed to become righteous by their actions, or close to righteous, or because they have at least done what was in their power to do, but rather because they live of a gift to which they have contributed nothing whatsoever because it is utterly beyond their power to achieve it, to produce it, to maintain it, or freely to dispose of it. In the above mentioned disputation of 1517 Luther put this in his usual very succinct way: "40. We do not become righteous by doing righteous deeds but, having been made righteous, we do righteous deeds" (34). What is needed in order to understand the New Testament properly is therefore "a new definition of righteousness" (35), a very careful distinction of righteousness in the Christian sense from all other sorts of righteousness used in other areas of human discourse (36). And this applies to all other terms as well (37). Whenever we apply a term which is defined in some other, e.g. philosophical, context to the scriptures, we are bound to misunderstand them (38); and if we attempt to construe the scriptural meaning in its terms we can be sure of producing confusion. Only by clearly distinguishing between the biblical realm of discourse of faith and the philosophical realm of discourse of reason we shall be saved from reading problems into the scriptures which are not theological and from overlooking the genuine theological problems by concentrating on the wrong issues (39).

The fundamental distinction between philosophy and theology which Luther had inherited from nominalism thus became increasingly grounded on exegetical facts: it proved to be necessary in order to secure a proper understanding of the scriptures. This shift in the justification of the distinction involved a growing awareness of the specifically linguistic quality of the Christian faith. Faith is intrinsically assertive and necessitates confession which has resulted in a particular kind and tradition of discourse which it is theology's task to elucidate. The (normative) grammar of this discourse, however, is not to be found in philosophy but in the basic confessional documents of the Christian faith, the biblical writings (40).

It is important to notice that this does not entail the conclusion which some latter day linguistic philosophers have drawn. Although Luther distinguishes sharply between the philosophical and theological universe of discourse and insists that the same terms may be used in both fields with different meanings, indeed, will have different meanings insofar as all words acquire new meaning in Christ without, however, simply loosing their old meaning (41), he is not left with two separate universes of discourse, each with its own kind of logic and with mutually unintelligible languages. Instead we can understand their different meanings by paying close attention to their grammar, their actual way of employment; and this becomes possible precisely because the same language is used in both universes of discourse.

The specific theological meaning of terms like "righteousness" etc. which Luther defends against philosophical misreadings is thus not something mysterious which is only accessible to e.g. allegorical interpretation. It is rather, as he stresses at the beginning of the Operationes in Psalmos (1519), the grammatical meaning which is the truly theological meaning (42). That is to say, the theological import of a term is not so much determined by its dictionary meaning but rather by the specific grammatical structure, linguistic environment, and situative context of its employment (43). It is therefore misleading and wrong to infer from its typical meaning in a specific universe of discourse its actual meaning in another; instead we have to find out in each case in which sense it is used by studying the grammatical structure of the texts involved. Thus the distinction between philosophy and theology does not entail different languages and mutual incomprehensibility; on the contrary, just because the same language is used in both universes of discourse everyone who knows the language can come to see that it is used to talk about different subjects.

Philosophy and theology, then, are fundamentally different. The difference shows in two universes of discourse in which the same language is used to talk about different subjects. The subject-matter of theology is neither a subject treated also by philosophy, only differently or inadequately, nor simply an additional subject alongside that of philosophy which requires its own special "logic of faith". But if it is different and yet not simply additional to philosophy, what, then, is theology talking about?

2. "Philosophia habet visibilia, theologia vero invisibilia."

In order to answer this question we must look more closely to how Luther positively characterizes their different subject-matters.

Philosophy, he says, always talks about the visible and apparent things and about the conclusions which it can derive from those (44). The subject-matter of philosophy (in the wide sense mentioned) comprises everything that can be experienced by the senses and that can be inferred from experienced reality. It is the realm of knowledge accessible to the natural faculties of man, his senses (sensualitas) and reason (ratio), and it includes everything that belongs to the visible, apparent, present, and temporal things (visibilia, apparentia, praesentia, temporalia) (45). On the other hand, it is utterly unable to treat of the invisible, non apparent, future, eternal, and spiritual things (invisibilia, non apparentia, futura, aeterna, spiritualia) which are the subject-matter of theology and accessible to faith only.

This account of the difference between philosophy and theology seems to have strongly Augustinian overtones, but it is not understood by Luther in any neoplatonist sense (46). He used this terminology not only in his early Dictata super psalterium (1513-1515) but throughout the formative years of his theology, e.g. in the Disputatio Heidelbergae habita (47), or the Operationes in Psalmos (48), and even as late as 1539 he couches the distinction between philosophy and theology in the same terms: "Philosophy treats of the things that can be known by human reason. Theology treats of the things which are believed, i.e. which are apprehended by faith" (49). Or even more concisely: "Philosophy has the visible things, but theology the invisible as subject" (50). This sounds very traditional but it takes on a completely new meaning insofar as in his understanding invisibilia does not refer to an unchanging world behind the flux of visible things which can only be reached by the exercise of reason abstracting from everything that is experienced by the senses and concentrating on the intelligible structure beyond the experienced surface of reality. Nor is it a second and independent realm of truth besides the realm of the visible and apparent things, which only together constitute the whole of reality. Though different, philosophy and theology neither supplement nor contradict each other (51). Rather theological truth "is not something contrary to, but something outside, inside, above, below, within, beyond all philosophical truth" (52). The plethora of prepositions makes it perfectly clear that whatever the proper subject-matter of theology is, it is neither of a higher order nor of a different order than the visible, but rather altogether different in kind and yet to be found in and amongst the visible.

But then what is this invisible within the visible which is the proper subject-matter of theology? In his Disputatio Heidelbergae habita (1518) Luther answers first by refuting the most natural answer that springs to mind. For example, Thomas Aquinas states the subject of theology to be God and everything else insofar as it is related to God (53). Thus although God is invisible we can know of him through his effects in the world by infering the invisible God from his visible effects as their origin and cause. But this is not the sort of invisibility which Luther understands to be the subject-matter of theology (54): "That person does not deserve to be called a theologian who looks upon the invisible things of God as though they were clearly perceptible through those things which have been created" (55). Theological reflection of this sort will inevitably result in what he calls a theologia gloriae, a metaphysical system (56). The God who is the subject of this sort of theology is a result of speculative argument and not the living God of the Bible. It is an abstract entity, a theoretical postulate which may be needed to secure the coherence of a metaphysical system and is inferred by going from the visibilia of this world to the invisibilia beyond it. Yet inferential reasoning and postulation will never lead to knowledge of the invisible things of faith. "That wisdom which sees the invisible things of God in works as perceived by man is completely puffed up, blinded, and hardened" (57). There is no way from the world of experience to God and for this reason reason is incompetent as a guide to matters of faith. There is only one way to get to know the invisibilia of faith, and that is by starting from the place where they become accessible; but this they become only for the one "who comprehends the visible and manifest things of God seen through suffering and cross" (58). Suffering and cross, however, are not as such intelligible as the visible and manifest things of God; they take on this quality only for faith. Because faith comprehends the cross of Christ contrary to what it appears to be to reason as the place where God has become visible and manifest, it is said to have to do with things that are not seen (Hebr. 11,1). The invisible things of God, however, become visible to faith in such a way that it notices that God is hidden in the cross of Christ; and it is for this reason that Luther characterizes the revelation of God as God's hiddenness under his contrary. For natural reason there is nothing but the cross; and no account of God's revelation will be adequate which does not come to terms with God's continued and obvious invisibility and absence as far as experience and reason are concerned. Thus that God has revealed himself in Christ does not mean that he has become one of the visible things of our general experience; it rather means

24

that one particular visible thing proves to faith to be more than what it appears to be to reason. That is, God is revealed by becoming discernible as hiding under something which is contrary to him, i.e. the cross of Christ; but only faith discerns God's presence in what is nothing but his absence to reason.

Luther's account of God's revelation seems to be highly sophisticated; in fact, however, it is very realistic in giving full significance to the fact of God's continued invisibility in our world of experience and by showing the irreplacable importance of faith for theology. He thus bases theology firmly on a christological conception of the invisibility of God that is only accessible to faith; for only faith will discern the visible reality of the cross as concealing God. This allows him to use the traditional formulation of the difference between philosophy and theology in a new and precise sense: Only where theology restricts itself to treat of the invisible things of faith in this christological sense, it will avoid getting mixed up with philosophical speculation. To avoid such confusion is essential if theology wants to say "what is actually the case" (id quod res est) and not call "evil good and good evil" as the theology of glory does (59). For the invisible reality discerned by faith is "what is actually the case" because it is what will be the case even if it now looks as if it were not; it is an eschatological reality which from the point of view of the visible world is at best a possibility; a possibility, however, which has an ontological priority over our present world (60). To talk of this eschatological reality under the conditions of our present world is possible only in the form of assertion, parable, and metaphor all of which are characteristic of the language of faith.

Luther's christological understanding of the invisibilia of theology was new and challenging; yet it was not something he had thought up for himself but which forced itself on him by his biblical exegesis. When he started to read the scriptures as the history of God's dealings with his people (61) he was forced to abandon the traditional exegetical and hermeneutical principles of allegorical interpretation because he realized that this only produced a speculative philosophical conception of the invisible things meant by the biblical texts. Instead he stressed increasingly the literal analysis and grammar as the key to the proper understanding of the invisibilia of faith; and this in turn made abundantly clear how easily familiar terms in the biblical writings were misunderstood if one construed their textual meaning according to a dictionary meaning established in some other universe of discourse. Yet Luther did not stop at noticing the differences in meaning but went on to the theological task of mapping out the structure of the biblical universe of discourse. He found it to be thoroughly christocentric and it was for this reason that he so vigorously insisted on a christological grammar of theological discourse (62).

It may be objected that his christocentric approach to the scriptures is as allegorical or at least typological as the traditional exegesis which he rejected. However, his reconstruction of biblical discourse and its subject-matter was by no means arbitrary. Rather it was based on a principle that has been neglected since the rise of the historical-critical method but which deserves to be taken seriously as modern developments in hermeneutics and text linguistics show. If a text is understood formally as an ordered set of instructions communicated between a speaker and a hearer who partake in the same linguistic repertoire, then in order to understand it properly it is not enough to analyse its grammatical structure or even to go beyond it to the situation of its origin and the intentions of the speaker or writer; it is also necessary to take into account its r e c e p t i o n , or rather series of receptions, by the (various) hearers or readers, or as Luther's calls it, its u s e (u s u s). The importance of this use-aspect is obvious in the very notion of scriptures which we apply to the biblical writings: They are not simply records of historical events or a collection of texts like the works of Plato but texts with a very specific use in the Christian community. Uses, however, are manifold and many uses are actually abuses. It is therefore important to have the notion of the r i g h t use of a text in order to be able to judge on its proper understanding. It was Luther's hermeneutical insight to start from such a notion of the r i g h t u s e o f t h e s c r i p t u r e s which he specified in terms of the characteristic situation of their proper reception. This normative situation is the situation of the experience of faith, for only faith, as Luther says, is the right use of the scriptures (63). Thus Luther's hermeneutical principles which he used to reconstruct the biblical universe of discourse were designed to elucidate not simply the texts but the r i g h t u s e o f these texts; and they were derived from the particular situation of the experience of faith which is constituted by the preaching of the gospel and leads to the confession of Jesus as Christ (64).

The invisible things of faith, then, in virtue of which theology is fundamentally different from philosophy, are given in the experience of faith which expresses itself in prayer, confession, preaching, worship etc., and only in this form they are accessible in the world of visible things. It is for this reason that theology cannot be without texts, and above all the texts of the bible which are the fundamental and normative confessional expressions of the Christian faith.

Yet what exactly is the subject-matter of a theology which concentrates strictly on the Christian faith as it is articulated in the confessional texts of the bible and repeated throughout the history of the church in the confession that Jesus is Christ?

3. The subject-matter of theology

1. It is no surprise to find Luther's most explicit and condensed answer to this question again in a thoroughly exegetical context, namely in his E n n a r r a t i o P s a l m i LI of 1532. This famous passage which amounts

to a definition of the specific character of the invisibilia of faith and theology deserves to be quoted in full (65):

> "Divine wisdom in its proper theological sense is knowledge of God and man; and this is knowledge of God and man in such a way that in the last resort God is referred to as the one who justifies and man as the one who is a sinner, so that the proper subject of theology is man who is guilty and lost and God who justifies or saves. Whatever is asked outside this field or subject is plainly error and vanity in theology because we do not expect in the holy scriptures anything about matters of possession, the health of the body, or the welfare of the state. All these are created things which are given in our hands ... Theology therefore does not pertain to this life but belongs to another life than which is Adam's" (66).

2. The first thing to be noted about this passage is that the task of theology is described as that of obtaining knowledge of God and man. Theology is a certain way of cognoscere (ידה) which according to its biblical understanding, as Luther stresses, means to experience, to feel, to become aware of something (67). It is not a speculatio or cogitatio but grounded in genuine experience, and its subject-matter is not "some sort of speculation or an idea which the mind thinks up for itself" but something given in a "true feeling, a true experience" (68): the experience of faith. Yet what is this all-important and fundamental faith?

Luther always stressed that faith is trust (fiducia), confidence in the object of faith, not just propositional belief. For example, in his Larger Catechism Luther states that "to have a God is nothing else than to trust and believe in Him with all our hearts" (69). Trust, however, is a general anthropological phenomenon or, as Ebeling puts it, "the basic human situation" (70), because man must have something to rely on, to trust and to believe. But if "whatever ... thy heart clings to ... and relies upon, that is properly thy God" (71), then there is no man without a god and without faith.

Trust, then, is a necessary criterion for faith; but is it sufficient? Here we have the root of the "natural knowledge of God" which Luther was prepared to admit. Reason, according to him, not only knows that God is but "so far reaches the natural light of reason that it takes God to be benign, merciful, and indulgent" (72) - more than even Aquinas allows for. It is precisely the general human phenomenon of trust and confidence which Luther took to be evidence for this far reaching natural knowledge of God since it shows that "every man sets up as his god that from which he hopes to obtain good, help, and comfort" (73). For example, "whoever is confident and boastful because he has great skill, cleverness, power, favour, friendship, and honour, he also has a god" (74). Thus to have a god in this sense need not be to have the right God. Trust as a phenomenological manifestation of faith is not a sufficient criterion of the true experience of faith. For, as Luther says: "If the faith and trust are right, then thy

God is also the right God, and, again, if thy trust is false and wrong, then thou hast not the right God" (75). How can we decide on whether our trust is right or wrong?

Perhaps the intensity of trust is a criterion. "Question and search well thine own heart; then wilt thou learn whether or no it depends on God alone. If thou hast such an heart as to expect nought but good from Him, expecially in thy needs and necessities, and to be ready to let everything go which is not God, then thou hast the only true God. Again, if thy heart depends on other things, and looks to them for good and help rather than to God, and, instead of seeking Him, flies from Him when things go ill, then thou hast but another idol" (76). So the criterion for true trust is that it has only one object in which it puts complete and unshakable confidence (77). Yet obviously trust may be complete and single minded without having the right object or indeed without having any object at all. As Nietzsche remarked: "strong faith proves only its strength, not the truth of what is believed" (78). An adequate account of Christian faith, therefore, needs more than a phenomenology of trust. Trust as a general human phenomenon may show that we cannot live without something like a god. But contrary to what Luther thinks it does not follow from this that we all have some (even weak) natural knowledge of God. He believes it to show that reason "knows that there is a God. But who he is or which God he is it does not know ... So reason plays blind man's buff with God and makes mistaken identifications and clutches here and there by calling God what is not God and again by not calling God what is God. None of which it would do if it either did not know that there is a God or on the other hand knew who or what God is" (79). But it is obviously mistaken to conclude from the fact that everybody has a god in which he puts his trust either that there is a God in which everybody puts (or aims to put) his trust or that everybody knows such a God to exist. "Natural knowledge of gods" is not "natural knowledge of God" but only man's natural inclination to idolatry caused by his inability to live without trust, and this is not enough to support natural theology.

We must therefore specify the o b j e c t one has to trust in order to have right trust. Yet knowledge of the right God, as Christians claim, can only be obtained from the v e r b u m D e i itself, i.e. from God's self-presentation to man in Jesus Christ. The right God is, formally speaking, the subject of the address of which Christians have become aware since Pentecost in their experience of Jesus as Christ. Christian faith, therefore, is the believer's relationship to God through Christ manifest in his trust in Jesus as Christ; or as Luther often says, it is f i d u c i a i n f i l i u m D e i vel fiducia cordis per Christum in Deum (80). Because of God's relationship to him, Christ so relates us to God that we, though mortal beings, live in the enduring community of the immortal God. Luther described this as the "happy change" in which Christ "took upon him our sinful person, and gave unto us his innocent and victorious person" (81) so that we shall live and not die.

To have this relation of faith to Christ is to know Jesus as the son of God; and this knowledge finds expression in the confession "Jesus is the Christ". It is in confessions of this sort that the invisible things of faith are present and accessible in our world of experience; and they are the data on which theology has to build. Yet this has important implications for the type of knowledge (c o g n i t i o) theology is said to be. For confessions of faith assert propositions like "Jesus is Christ" as true whose truth cannot in principle be shown to obtain in the visible world of general experience. And theology makes truth-claims based on the experience of faith which are distinguished from "speculations" or "ideas which the mind thinks up for itself" not because they can now be shown to be true (while the others cannot) but only because they are based on this experience of faith which gives good reasons for making these claims and maintaining that, eschatologically, they are and will ultimately be shown to be true. Of course, these claims have to be semantically meaningful and to secure this is one of the most important tasks of theology. But if their truth is questioned what can be done at best is to show that they are at least possible and not downright false; in consequence, since demonstration and verification of their truth in this world are impossible, the only way of validating the making of Christian truth-claims is by narratives of the experience on which they are based; hence the indispensable function of narrative in Christian theology.

Thus authentic theological knowledge can never be presented as a system of verified or rationally guaranteed claims but of truth-claims which are asserted on the basis of faith; and the only mode in which theological knowledge of the invisible things of faith can be maintained in the visible world is the mode of confessional assertions. It is for this reason that Luther makes his debate with Erasmus in D e   s e r v o   a r b i t r i o turn decisively on the assertive character of the Christian faith: "Do away with decisive assertions, and you have taken away Christianity" (82) - a point well worth considering in view of certain developments in the philosophy of religion in recent years.

3. But what is the content of these truth-claims of theology? Luther answers that they articulate k n o w l e d g e   o f   G o d   a n d   m a n . It is important to realize the conjunction and its implications. Luther does not simply hold that theology asserts knowledge of both God and man. What he stresses is rather that theology will not be able to assert anything true of God apart from his relations to man, and v i c e   v e r s a . The subject-matter of theology is the field of relations between God and man and every theological statement which purports to make a truth-claim about the i n v i s i b i l i a of faith will have to talk about these relations and will only be true if the relation which it asserts in fact holds. Talk of God as such, therefore, does by no means imply that it is theological; indeed, as Luther says in commenting on Aristotle's notion of God, it is characteristic of philosophical theologies to talk of God in "isolation": "That God is a being separate from creatures, as Aristotle tells us, truly existing and viewing creatures within himself - but is this of any concern to us? This is how the devil also understands God and knows that he truly exists. But when we speak in

theology of the knowledge of God, then God must not be known and understood as abiding within himself, but as he comes to us from without, so that we clearly grasp that he is God for us" (83). To talk theologically about God (84), then, is to talk of God exclusively in terms of his relations to man; and the relations in question are real relations in the sense that they are constituted by God's saving actions towards us.

It may be objected that even if theology talks theologically about God in this way it must in principle be possible to have at least one statement which is exclusively about God, i.e. that he exists. This, of course, is true but it does not conflict with Luther's insistence on the conjunction of God and man in theological knowledge. For we have to understand him as specifying the universe of discourse in which it is theologically meaningful to talk about God (and about man!). This means, firstly, that the concept of God, which the existential statement claims to be instantiated, is to be defined with reference to this universe of discourse and not to be introduced into theological discourse from some other discourse. But even then the existential statement "God exists" is not so much a theological proposition in itself but rather a presupposition of any theologically meaningful talk of God. How are we to understand this existential presupposition if it is not to be in conflict with Luther's specification?

Very roughly, I think, we can say the following. To assert "God is F" is to presuppose that "God exists" is true and to assert that God has the property designated by "F". But to assert "God exists" is to assert something quite different, namely a real relation between the speaker and God such that they both belong to the same universe of discourse. In asserting God's existence I locate him and myself within a common reality by taking him to be related to me not only by logical or intentional relations (e.g. knowing, believing) but by real ones such as speaking, hearing, acting (85). So "God exists" is true only if the speaker and God belong to the same universe of discourse, i.e. have real relations to each other. But then this existential statement is not in conflict with Luther's insistence on the conjunction of God and man but rather underlines the fact that proper truth-claims about God will always be truth-claims about his relation to man. And the often voiced misgiving that "God exists" is not "really" a religious statement is due to the fact that although it asserts a real relation it does not specify it as a particular action of God towards the speaker and thus leaves open the precise nature of this relationship.

4. If Luther's definition is thus understood as a specification of the domain of theological discourse, one could still object that it is restricting the traditional wide and all-comprehensive domain of talk of God to the rather more limited domain of his relationship to man. But this again would miss the point. For has theology not always stressed the relations holding between God and everything in the world including man, who is not only part but the most important part of creation? The answer usually given is that Luther proposes a change of focus from God the Creator to God the Saviour. But this has to be taken with a pinch of salt. For what he is

proposing is rather that we have to understand what "creator" means by reference to the universe of discourse constituted by the real relations between God and man; and as these are God's saving actions, the term "creator" will have a soteriological meaning, or, to put it differently, creation itself will have to be understood as God's saving action.

The difference between Luther's approach and traditional theology may become clearer if we remember the problem of the invisibility of God. Luther's insistence that it is the conjunction of God and man which defines the universe of theological discourse in its proper sense, is not to be mis-understood as if he were advocating that theology should talk about the re-lations between the invisible God and man as opposed to the whole world. Rather his definition specifies the domain of theology as the field of real relations between both the i n v i s i b l e God and, as it were, i n v i s i b l e man. For theology, as we have seen, is distinguished from philosophy by having as subject the i n v i s i b i l i a of faith and not the v i s i b i l i a of common experience. If, therefore, it is characterized as knowledge of God and man, this cannot mean that it is knowledge of God as belonging to the i n v i s i b i l i a and man as belonging to the v i s i b i l i a , for this would be precisely the confusion of theological and philosophical issues to which Luther was so much opposed. It rather is knowledge of both God and man as i n v i s i b i l i a , or, in other words, as known and asserted by faith.

That this is indeed how Luther wanted his definition to be understood is brought out by the more detailed way in which he specifies the subject-mat-ter of proper theology: Theology is not simply talk of God and man in their relations, but rather talk of man a s g u i l t y a n d l o s t and of God t h e j u s t i f i e r o r s a v i o u r . These qualifications not only make explicit the "soteriological" character of the real relations which structure and constitute the domain of theological discourse; they also leave no doubt that b o t h terms of these relations belong to the i n v i s i b i l i a of faith. That man is a sinner and lost is no more a matter of the visible world and of common experience than is God, the saviour: no philosophical, psycho-logical, anthropological or comparable account of man will ever be able to show him to be a sinner. It is no doubt possible to show certain, if not all, men to be morally corrupt, and some more so than others; but this will never be enough to call them sinners in the theological sense. Moral cor-ruption comes in degrees, but sin does not and there is no proportionality between moral corruption and sin; to assume this would again confuse the visible with the invisible, philosophical or moral with theological issues. To know man as sinner is to know him c o r a m d e o and this is an intensly personal knowledge which is expressed adequately only in I-statements ("I am a sinner") and at best approximately in generalizing theological state-ments about man as sinner (85). It is, in other words, knowledge of faith, for only faith discerns how utterly different I am from what God wants me to be. However, from this point of view the whole man, and everything he does, including not only his morally evil but also his morally best actions, are to be judged as sinful (87).

Thus Luther's account of the subject-matter of theology has to be understood strictly in the light of the visibilia/invisibilia distinction; but understood in this way it offers an internally consistent theological position which is full of theologically interesting implications, and, in consequence, problems. Let me show this finally first with respect to theological anthropology or the doctrine of man, and secondly with respect to the doctrine of creation.

5. Luther has sometimes been accused of starting the anthropological approach in theology because of his stress on the essential relationship between talk of God and talk of man. But this would be true only if he had not distinguished between the visible and the invisible and tried to talk theologically about man (88). Indeed, "from Luther's point of view it looks rather as if it was scholastic theology which, although it defined God as the subject of theology, has given much too much weight to man in theology" (89). Scholastic theology attempted to construe a unified view of man in terms of a complicated and comprehensive psychology designed to integrate the theological account of man as sinner and believer with a general theory of the soul, the faculties and the actions of man. It thus started from "the philosophical knowledge of man which defines man as a rational animal and so forth" (90) and based its theological considerations on the same definition. However, the complicated structure of the various conceptions of the schoolmen show that instead of realizing the futility of the attempt, they sought to overcome the fundamental difference between philosophical and theological matters by ever greater complications. But according to Luther all the effort spend on a psychological grounding of theological talk about sin, grace, justification etc. is utterly misguided because it fails to distinguish between the visible and the invisible. This does not mean, as we have seen, that these theological phenomena are not matters of experience. But the philosophical knowledge of man as a rational animal is "a matter of science, not of theology ... a theologian discusses man as a sinner. In theology, this is the essence of man. The theologian is concerned that man become aware of this nature of his, corrupted by sins" (91). So the attempt at a unified philosophico-theological anthropology is a "category-mistake" if there ever was one.

But does this not leave us with two totally distinct views of man, one which defines him on the basis of the "visible" and experienced reality as animal rationale while the other (theological) one conceives him on the basis of the experience of faith as "the sinner who is saved by God" or, as Luther puts it succinctly in his Disputatio de homine (1536), as "homo iustificatur fide" (92)? And has a theology which is based on the visible/invisible-distinction anything meaningful to contribute to life in this "visible" world? Does it not champion a privatized faith, which has been so characteristic of a certain conservative Lutheran tradition (Liefoth, Vilmar, Stahl), and a split between man as a Christian and man in the world?

There are two questions to be distinguished. One is the relationship between the two accounts of man and thus between man as member of the visible world of experience and man as known by faith and treated in theology; this is the ontological question. The other is the problem of the Christian existence in the world; this is the moral question (93). I confine my comments to the first problem.

The problem of the relationship between the philosophical and theological account of man becomes most pressing in the case of the Christian. For how is his Ego as natural man related to his Ego as believer? Luther answers that it is as if "two men fight against each other in one and the same man" (94). The Christian has lost his Ego-identity by acquiring the Ego of faith (95). He now exists in a "double" way, as simul iustus et peccator, as Luther puts it. He is no longer just the "visible" man as defined by philosophy, but he is not yet wholly the "invisible" man discerned by faith; he is rather both at the same time for he is still "in fieri, non in esse", he is still in the making ("noch jhm bau") (96), and this will only come to an end at the resurrection.

The theological account of man thus asserts the essential nature of man, i.e. what he will be in the end; yet this assertion will only be shown to be true eschatologically. However, not only the resurrection but also the reception of the word of God and thus faith is an eschatological event. Faith, therefore, claims to know the true reality of man as hidden under the contrary of human life in this world. This reality, invisible to reason, is created by God who justifies by giving the gift of faith. Faith is not the imparting of additional powers to man but "a work of God within us, which transforms us and makes us born again from God" (97). The justification of the sinner, accordingly, is not simply a change of direction of an otherwise continuous life-story but a total break, or better, a new creation which constitutes the reality of man which theology asserts. Man in this life, as Luther says, is only the materia of what he is supposed to be and will be in the future life (98); but insofar as he has faith he is already partaking in this future form by being related to Christ. For "faith makes of you and of Christ as it were one person, so that you cannot be divided from Christ, but cling to him as though you were called Christ, while he says: I am that sinner, because he clings to me" (99). So the identity of the Christian in the last resort rests on the identity of Christ as both man and God.

The ontological problem, then, of the relationship between the reality of man as described in the philosophical account of man and the essential reality of man which is discerned by faith as hidden and concealed under the contrary of his visible life and asserted in theology can only be solved in both a christological and eschatological way. What faith asserts about man is intelligible only if grounded in a coherent doctrine of Christ; and it will be a defensible truth-claim only on the basis of a consistent eschatology.

6. Luther has frequently been credited with an overemphasis on God the Saviour at the expense of God the Creator and there is, no doubt, some truth in this. But his account of the subject-matter of theology has important implications for the latter doctrine as well. We are, by the powerful convention of our religiously impregnated culture, accustomed to talk of the world as creation as if this were a fact and usually fail to see that in doing so we are not describing the world as it presents itself to experience and reason but express theological judgments. No argument, for example, which talks of the world as creation in its premises and of God the creator in the conclusion will ever convince anybody who does not already believe the world to be created and the creator to be God. In identifying the world with what is meant by "creation" we fail to distinguish between the visible and the invisible and thus confuse philosophical and theological issues. Creation is no more a straightforward description of the world than is sinner of man and it is in no way part of natural (philosophical) knowledge that the world has a creator (100). Thus if we talk theologically of the world as creation we can do so only by noting the enormous difference between the world as it is and how it should be as God's creation. And if faith confesses the world to be created it can do so only by asserting this contrary to our general experience; it then asserts a reality hidden and concealed in the experienced world which is its contrary.

Yet if the world cannot be simply identified with creation and is distinguished from it as is the visible from the invisible, one of the favorite procedures of traditional natural theology is impossible. For many of the (cosmological) arguments of natural theology rely on the inverse form of a doctrine of creation which does not observe the distinction between the visible and the invisible. They start from a misconceived and undialectical identification of the visible world with creation and are therefore doomed to failure. The same applies to the specific version of natural theology of later Lutheran theology that points to the "orders of creation" and identifies these with the lex natura, or even conceives them to be an "original revelation". Here we have amongst Lutherans a failure to observe Luther's distinction between the visible and the invisible, the world as it is and what it should be like as creation.

But, again, does this not leave us on the one hand with a world which has nothing to do with God, and on the other hand with a creation which is talked about in theology but which has nothing to do with the world in which we live? How, if at all, is the experience of faith which discerns the world as creation related to our general experience of the world? Are we not forced into a position similar to that of Ritschl, Harnack, Hermann, or Troeltsch which - using the apparatus of Kant's philosophy - proclaims on the one hand the autonomy of the natural orders of this world, and on the other hand the "value-judgment" that it is created? Luther's position is more subtle, and so is his influential doctrine interpreted in many different ways of the two kingdoms or regimes which is bound to be misunderstood if not seen in relation to his conception of the world as creation.

He not simply identifies the world and creation but again remains consistent in his use of the distinction between the visible and the invisible; yet he not allows them to fall apart either but relates them eschatologically. To maintain an eschatological relationship between the world as it is now and as it will be as creation is not to propound a version of the contemporary complementarity theory because it does not leave it at two alternative and irreducible descriptions of one and the same phenomenon placed in different frames of reference, but rather points to the dynamic process of their integration on a more adequate level. Hegel has formulated this process in his theory of A u f h e b u n g : a phenomenon that is known in itself in an isolated and thus necessarily incomplete way, gets new significance without loosing its original content by being viewed in its wider context; but looked at in this way it is both reduced to and preserved as a factor or element of a more comprehensive pattern which brings out its true nature more adequately. Yet even from this the eschatological relationship differs decisively, because viewing the world as an element of the more comprehensive creational pattern which relates it to God involves, not only its preservation in a more adequate context, but its transformation into a more adequate form; and this is not an epistemological but an ontological process which exceeds the intrinsic possibilities of the world and is effected only by God who by transforming the world into his creation establishes the eschatological relationship between "that what is the case" ("id, quod res est") and "that what is not yet but will be the case" ("id, quod futura nondum est") (101).

The world as it is, as Luther puts it, is only the matter (materia) out of which God is going to form his creation (102), that is, the visible world is on the way of becoming creation by being transformed by the invisible reality of God's actions which can be discerned by faith as present and yet hidden in it. In Genesis 1 we have, according to Luther, not the story of the creation tout court but rather an account of the beginning of creation, i.e. of the first act of creation which instituted the world as the matter of God's creation (103). And as man in this life (in hac vita) is nothing but the matter for his future form (materia ad futuram formam) (104) so the world is still waiting, and waiting desperately, to acquire the full form of creation (105).

It is this distinction between the world as matter and creation as the eschatological form of the world which theology has to observe in talking of God as the creator, if it wants to avoid confusing theological and philosophical issues (106). This obviously is itself a theological distinction, for only faith will assert both that the world is not simply what it appears to be but the matter of something which is still in the making, and that, contrary to appearances, its eschatological form of creation is already being realised by God's transforming actions in this world, inaugurated by the resurrection of Jesus and continued by the presence of the eschatological reality of faith in this world. For faith the presence of this new reality is signalized and sealed by the proclamation of the gospel, and experienced in the sacraments of baptism and eucharist; and this experience enables it to discern in the world a parabolic quality, forshadowing its future perfection as God's creation (107) without pretending that this can be read of the visible world.

To look at the world in this way as the m a t t e r of its future form as creation is decisive for the way nature and worldly matters are to be treated in theology: they are no more, but also no less, than the m a t t e r which God has chosen to transform into his creation. As such they "pertain to this life" and are within the province of man's reason to order and to govern at the best of his abilities without him attempting either to confer a special religious quality on them as allegedly God-given orders of creation or to pretend that they are totally at his arbitrary disposal. Luther's examples are very telling. It is not theology's task to tackle problems of property and possession, of health, of political and social order. Theology has nothing to say as to "what we should eat, what work we should undertake, how we should rule our family, how we should till the soil" (108). These are all problems to be solved not by theologizing but by the proper use of our reason and appropriate actions. For all these things "were put into man's hands", given into our responsibility, and "need no other light than the light of reason" (109).

To treat the world as the m a t t e r of creation in theology - and this includes all aspects of the natural world and our life in it - means for example (a) that theology has to oppose all attempts of either tolerating the present reality of the visible world as definite and ultimate, or (b) of confusing the visible world of our experience with its invisible eschatological form, or (c) of trying to embody and bring about this future form in our visible world and thus reduce it to an, as yet, unrealized possibility of the world as it is. Theology, therefore, is opposed to a life without hope; to all versions of a metaphysical account of reality which blur the fundamental distinction between the world and God, the present but temporary reality of the world and the future and ultimate reality of the creation; and finally to all attempts at either identifying the kingdom of God with any political or ecclesiastical institution in this world or of trying to bring it about by political or any other human means. It is not our task to transform the world into creation (110); this is the sole work of God and all attempts to do this by our own human means will only result in a more inhuman world. Our task is rather to live as God's c r e a t u r e s and cultivate the matter of God's creation to the best of our human abilities, so that our aim can only be a more human world. (It is this distinction which Luther's doctrine of the two kingdoms is supposed to safeguard.) By stressing this, theology makes plain that we are neither God, nor a mere accident of nature, but God's creatures who are responsible to him for how we treat the matter of his creation. Thus we take seriously both the matter-aspect of the world and of ourselves and our status as God's creatures if we live a responsible h u m a n life. For - and this sums up the whole of Luther's theological enterprise - "we must be human and not God. This is the sum of it; it will never be otherwise ..." (111).

A theology, then, which observes the distinction between the visible and the invisible in the sense explained, "does not pertain to this life but belongs to another life than that which is Adam's" (112); but this in no way entails that it ignores or shuns the visible world of our experience. For by drawing attention to the m a t e r i a -aspect of this world and by pointing out how the future life is hiddenly present in our reality, and where it can be found and experienced (and where not!), it will have a good deal to say on matters of property and possession or of political and social order, whenever these take on inhuman forms by neglecting their man-made preliminary status and by assuming an ultimacy which is only appropriate to God's final creation.

Footnotes

I thank Dr. E.Booth, O.P. for his helpful comments on an earlier draft of this paper.

1 A.v.Harnack, Lehrbuch der Dogmengeschichte III (Berlin, [4]1910), 875.

2 B.Blanshard, Reason and Belief (London, 1974), 177.

3 Op. cit., 184.

4 Op. cit., 185.

5 Op. cit., 186.

6 R.Marius, Luther (London, 1975), II.

7 P.S.Watson, Let God Be God! An interpretation of the theology of Martin Luther (London, 1947), 23.

8 This is not Luther's phrase, as far as I can see. He talks, however, of a "cognitio Dei Theologica" (cf. WA 40/2, 327, 37). The term is used by G.Ebeling, Luther. Einführung in sein Denken (Tübingen, 1964), 82 to characterize Luther's theology. The English edition of this book Luther. An Introduction to His Thought. Transl. by R.A.Wilson (London, 1970) translates: "true theology" (op. cit., 79). - References are usually only given to the Weimar Edition of Luther's works (WA), even where I have consulted (and sometimes used) the translations of the Philadelphia Edition of Luther's Works.

9 WA 40/2, 327, 18.

10 Cf. Ebeling, op. cit., 20.

11 Cf. H.Bornkamm, Luther im Spiegel der deutschen Geistesgeschichte; mit ausgewählten Texten von Lessing bis zur Gegenwart (Göttingen, [2]1970). There is, however, another history to be written of the effects which Luther's theological thought should have had, but did not have in German theology. It would be misleading, to say the least, to restrict the relevance of his theology to the various ways in which it has been understood and misunderstood. Much of what he taught as a theologian has proved to be remarkably ineffective and some of the effects which the receptions of his teachings have had do hardly accord with his theology. The true relevance of his thought, therefore, is to be judged above all with reference to its ability to prove itself to be relevant for us now and for any future time. Cf. E. Jüngel, Zur Freiheit eines Christenmenschen. Eine Erinnerung an Luthers Schrift (München, 1978), 11 ff.

12 Cf. R.Weier, Das Theologieverständnis Martin Luthers (Paderborn, 1976).

13 L.Grane, Modus Loquendi Theologicus. Luthers Kampf um die Erneuerung der Theologie (1515-1518) (Leiden, 1975) is right in stressing that one has to interprete Luther's thought "aufgrund von konkreten Textzusammenhängen" (op. cit., 199). I shall therefore concentrate on a number of texts in which Luther explicitly reflects on the proper understanding of theology.

14 Cf. WA 9, 46, 16 ff.

15 WA 9, 27, 22 ff.

16 Cf. B.Hägglund, Theologie und Philosophie bei Luther und in der occamistischen Tradition. Luthers Stellung zur Theorie von der doppelten Wahrheit (Lund, 1955), 22 ff.

17 Thomas Aquinas, Summa theologica I q.1 a.8 ad 2.

18 Cf. B.Lohse, Ratio und Fides. Eine Untersuchung über die ratio in der Theologie Luthers (Göttingen, 1958), 27 f.; Hägglund, op. cit., 29 ff.

19 Cf. Hägglund, op. cit., 24 ff.

20 Cf. Hägglund, op. cit., 43 ff.

21 Cf. O.Scheel, Martin Luther. Vom Katholizismus zur Reformation Bd.1 (Tübingen, 1917), 192; Lohse, op. cit., 25 f.

22 M.Luther, Kleiner Katechismus, BSLK (Göttingen, [6]1967) 511, 46-512, 1.

23 M.Luther, Disputatio de homine (henceforth DH), in: G.Ebeling, Lutherstudien II, Disputatio de Homine. Erster Teil: Text und Traditionshintergrund (Tübingen, 1977), Prop.8; 24.

24 WA 1, 226, 14-25.

25 Cf. Grane, op. cit., Chap.1; G.Rupp, The Righteousness of God. Luther Studies (London, 1953), 122, 160.

26 Cf. Lohse, op. cit., 30 ff.; G.Ebeling, "Die Anfänge von Luthers Hermeneutik", in: Lutherstudien I (Tübingen, 1971), 8 ff.

27 Cf. Lohse, op. cit., 43 ff.

28 Grane, op. cit., 174ff.; Ebeling, Anfänge op. cit.

29 WA 55/2, 13, 13-20: "hii sunt, qui Scripturam ad suum sensum torquent et sua propria statuta meditatione cogunt Scripturam in eam intrare et concordare, cum debueri fieri ediuerso". Cf. WA 55/2, 69, 6-11.

30 WA 56, 371, 12-16: "Quando sapiemus et videbimus, quod tam preciosum tempus tam vanis studiis perdimus et meliora negligimus? Semper agimus, vt sit verum in nobis, quod Seneca ait: 'Necessaria ignoramus, quia superflua didicimus, Immo Salutaria ignoramus, quia damnabilia didicimus'".

31 WA 56,172, 8-11: "Et dicitur ad differentiam Iustitie hominum, que ex operibus fit. Sicut Aristoteles 3. Ethicorum manifeste determinat, secundum quem Iustitia sequitur et fit ex actibus. Sed secundum Deum precedit opera et opera fiunt ex ipsa".

32 For Luther's attitude towards the scholastic distinction between habitus acquisitus and habitus infusus cf. Ebeling, Luther op. cit., 89 f, 153 ff.

33 WA 40/1,45, 24-27: "Haec est nostra theologia qua docemus accurate distinguere has duas iustitias, activam et passivam, ne confundatur mores et fides, opera et gratia, politia et religio. Est autem utraque necessaria, sed quaelibet intra suos fines contineri debet". Cf. WA 40/1, 48, 25-33.

34 WA 1, 226, 8-9.

35 WA 2, 503, 34 ff.

36 WA 40/1, 45, 9-11: "sine ista distinctione non poterimus servare nostram theologiam vel statim fiemus Iuristae vel ceremoniales; Christus obscuratus, nemo potest consolari. Ideo bene disce istas 2 iusticias". Cf. WA 40/1, 46, 19-21.

37 WA 39/1, 231, 1-4 [A II]: "Omnia vocabula fiunt nova, quando transferuntur ex philosophia in theologiam". Cf. op. cit., 231, 1-11 [A I]; 231, 18-29 [A III]; 231, 18-27 [B] .

38 WA 39/1, 229, 8-24 [A]: "una quaeque ars habet suas terminos et sua vocabula, quibus utitur, et ea vocabula valent in suis materiis. Iuristae sua habent, medici sua, physici sua. Haec si transferre ex suo foro et loco in aliud volueris, erit confusio nullo modo ferenda. Nam tandem obscurat omnia ... Cum vocabula physica in theologiam translata sunt, facta est inde scholastica quaedam theologia". WA 39/1, 229, 23-26: "Si volumus uti philosophicis terminis, müssen wir sie erst wohl zum Bade führen; neque tamen sine periculo utemini". Cf. op. cit., 229, 35-230, 29.

39 Cf. WA 56, 354, 19-22; WA 55/2, 13, 13-20; WA 56, 334, 14 ff.: "Modus loquendi Apostoli et modus metaphysicus seu moralis sunt contrarii". WA 56, 371, 12-14.

40 Cf. Luther's program of a Grammatica Theologica (WA 5, 32, 19). - S.Raeder, Grammatica Theologica. Studien zu Luthers Operationes in Psalmos (Tübingen, 1977), 34 ff, 55, 305.

41 Jüngel, op. cit., 43 ff.; Weier, op. cit., 50 ff.; WA 39/2, 94, 17 f.: "omnia vocabula in Christo novam significationem accipere in eadem re significata". Cf. WA 39/1, 229, 6-24.

42 WA 5, 27, 8: "primo grammatica videamus, verum ea Theologica".

43 Jüngel, op. cit., 45.

44 WA 3, 508, 1-3: "philosophia semper de visibilibus et apparentibus, vel saltem ex apparentibus deducta loquitur". Cf. W.Joest, Ontologie der Person bei Luther (Göttingen, 1967), 79 ff, 95 ff.

45 Cf. Joest, op. cit., 95.

46 So A.W.Hunzinger, "Luthers Neuplatonismus in der Psalmenvorlesung von 1513 bis 1516", Lutherstudien I (1906) and E.Seeberg, Luthers Theologie. Motive und Ideen I. Die Gotteserfahrung (Göttingen, 1929), 116, 145, 155, 209. CF. W.Link, Luthers Ringen um die Freiheit der Theologie von der Philosophie (München, ²1955), 208. This is criticized by Rupp, op. cit., 141 f, 144; Ebeling, Anfänge op. cit., 19 f.; Joest op. cit., 99 f.

47 WA 1, 354, 17-20.

48 WA 5, 69, 11-14.

49 WA 39/2, 6, 26-28.

50 WA 39/2, 15, 8 f.

51 WA 39/2, 27, 31 f.: "non sunt contrariae ... sed sunt diversae".

52 WA 39/2, 4, 34 f. - Similarities to N.Cusanus are pointed out by Weier, op. cit., 56 f.

53 S.th. I q.1 a.7 crp.

54 Cf. Grane, op. cit., 146 f.; WA 1, 614, 17 ff.

55 WA 1, 354, 17 f.

56 WA 1, 614, 17-20: "Theologus vero gloriae ... est qui non cum Apostolo solum crucifixum et absconditum deum novit, sed gloriosum cum gentibus, ex visibilibus invisibilia eius, ubique presentem, omnia potentem videt et loquitur".

57 WA 1, 354, 23 f.

58 WA 1, 354, 19 f.; cf. WA 1, 362, 5-24: "Quia enim homines cognitione Dei ex operibus abusi sunt, voluit rursus Deus ex passionibus cognosci et reprobare illam sapientiam invisibilium per sapientiam visibilium, ut sic, qui Deum non colerunt manifestum ex operibus, colerent absconditum in passionibus ... Ergo in Christo crucifixo est vera Theologia et cognitio Dei ... Patet, quia dum ignorat [sc. Theologus gloriae] Christum, ignorat Deum absconditum in passionibus".

59 WA 1, 354, 21 f.

60 E.Jüngel, "Die Welt als Möglichkeit und Wirklichkeit. Zum ontologischen Ansatz der Rechtfertigungslehre", EvTh 29 (1969) 417-442.

61 Cf. J.Pelikan, Luther the Expositor, Luther's Works, Companion Volume (Saint Louis, 1959), 89 f.

62 WATR 2, No. 1353: "Summa theologiae lectio est Christum posse agnoscere" (cf. No. 2459), for "Christus est subjectum theologiae" (WATR 2, No. 1868; cf. WATR 1, No. 561).

63 M. Luther, Von der Freiheit eines Christenmenschen, L. E. Schmitt (ed.), Neudrucke deutscher Literaturwerke des 16. und 17. Jahrhunderts Nr. 18 (Tübingen, ³1954), 40 (henceforth FC).

64 Cf. my "Luther on the experience of faith", Heythrop Journal 21 (1980), 50-56.

65 Cf. G. Ebeling, "Cognitio Dei et hominis", in: Lutherstudien I (Tübingen, 1971), 255 ff.; Weier, op. cit., 83 ff.

66 WA 40/2, 327, 11-328, 9.

67 WA 40/2, 326, 10 f.: "Es gilt nicht disputirn. Agnosco significat proprie: fülen".

68 WA 40/2, 326, 34 f.; cf. WA 40/2, 327, 26 ff.; 328, 30 ff.

69 WA 30/1, 133, 2 f. = Luther's Primary Works together with his Shorter and Larger Catechisms. Transl. into English. Ed. with theological and historical essays by H. Wace and C. A. Buchheim (London, 1896), 34 (henceforth LC).

70 Ebeling, Luther op. cit., 254.

71 WA 30/1, 133, 7 f. = LC 34.

72 WA 19, 206, 12 f.

73 WA 30/1, 134, 37 f. = LC 36.

74 WA 30/1, 133, 35-134, 1 = LC 35.

75 WA 30/1, 133, 5 f. = LC 34.

76 WA 30/1, 136, 19 ff. = LC 38.

77 This is how Ebeling seems to read Luther's account of faith and trust. For if, as Luther says, "to have a God is nothing else than to trust and believe in Him with all our hearts" (WA 30/1, 133, 2 f. = LC 34), then "one only needs to conjugate faith through all situations which fall within the range of its definition, and as we do it to bear in mind that what is meant is really faith and not having something, or better, only the kind of having which is pure faith. Every pseudo-faith and every pseudo-God will quickly be unmasked by this sharp criterion" (G. Ebeling, Wort und Glaube II (Tübingen, 1969), 303). Yet it is significant that the outcome of this via negativa suggested by Ebeling is pure faith (cf. Ebeling, Luther op. cit., 255) and not right faith. Pure faith, however, is not faith in anything but simply faith, "the radical degree to which the situation of faith is maintained" (ibid.). It is hard to see how the selfexamination suggested could ever lead to a positive assurance of right faith or to anything but an empty concept of faith. - From some such understanding of Luther

one can trace a clear line to both Schleiermacher's account of faith as the awareness of one's absolute dependence, the source of which one cannot describe but only name as "Absolute Causality" (cf. F. Schleiermacher, T h e C h r i s t i a n F a i t h, (Edinburgh, 1928) § 51), and to Feuerbach's assertion that the mystery of theology is really anthropology.

78 F. Nietzsche, M e n s c h l i c h e s, A l l z u m e n s c h l i c h e s. Erster Band. Nietzsches Werke. Kritische Gesamtausgabe, ed. G. Colli and M. Montinari. Vierte Abteilung. Zweiter Band. (Berlin, 1967) 32.

79 WA 19, 206, 32-207, 10.

80 WA 40/1, 366, 24 f.

81 WA 31/2, 435, 11 ff.

82 WA 18, 603, 10-12, 22-24, 28 f.; 605, 32-34.

83 WA 43, 240, 23-28.

84 Cf. WA 40/2, 327, 27.

85 This relational view of existence is also hold by Kant as is shown by R. Campbell, "Real Predicates and Exists", M i n d LXXXIII (1974), 95-99.

86 Luther was sceptical in principle about the possibility of theological generalisations. He called it one of the characteristic mistakes of a rationalising theology that it is "faciens ex particulari universalem, more sapientiae suae" (WA 18, 673, 28-33).

87 WA 2, 410, 35-38; WA 39/1, 116 f.

88 WA 40/2, 327, 17 f.

89 Ebeling, Lutherstudien II op. cit., 35.

90 WA 40/2, 327, 17 f.

91 WA 40/2, 327, 18-22.

92 Cf. DH, Prop. 32.

93 Luther has treated both questions and their relationship in his treatise on T h e F r e e d o m o f t h e C h r i s t i a n P e r s o n, showing that the first is to be answered in terms of a (theological) account of f a i t h, the second in terms of a (theological) account of l o v e.

94 FC 38.

95 Cf. Jüngel, Zur Freiheit op. cit., 26 f.

96 WA 39/1, 252, 8 ff.

97 WADB 7, 10, 6 f.; cf. WA 39/1, 90, 11-91, 10.

98 DH, Prop. 38.

99 WA 40/1, 285, 5-7.

100 DH, Prop. 14.

101 WA 56, 371, 28-31: "Igitur optimi philosophie, optime rerum specu-
latores fueritis, Si ex Apostolo didiceritis Creaturam intueri ex-
pectantem, gementem, parturientem i.e. fastidientem id, quod est,
et cupientem id, quod futura nondum est".

102 DH, Prop. 36.

103 DH, Prop. 37, 40.

104 DH, Prop. 38.

105 Cf. Joest, op. cit., 350 f.

106 WA 56, 371, 3-6: "philosophi oculum ita in presentiam rerum
immergunt, vt solum quidditates et qualitates earum speculentur,
Apostolus autem oculos nostros reuocat ab intuitu rerum presentium,
ab essentia et accidentibus earum, et dirigit in eas, secundum quod
future sunt".

107 Chr. Link, Die Welt als Gleichnis. Studien zum Problem der
natürlichen Theologie (München, 1976).

108 WA 40/2, 328, 22-24; cf. WA 10/I, 1, 531, 6-11.

109 Cf. Joest, op. cit., 230 f.

110 Cf. WA 18, 754, 1 ff. We are co-operatores but not co-cre-
atores Dei! - Cf. M.Seils, Der Gedanke vom Zusammen-
wirken Gottes und des Menschen in Luthers Theologie (Gütersloh, 1962), 83, 136 ff.

111 WABR 5, 415, 45 f.

112 WA 40/2, 328, 18-29: "agitur ... de futura et aeterna vita, de Deo
iustificante, reparante ad vivificante et de homine a iusticia et vita
prolapso in peccatum et aeternam mortem". Cf. WA 40/2, 328, 30-33.

THEOLOGICAL LEGACIES OF THE ENLIGHTENMENT:
ENGLAND AND GERMANY

by

A. O. Dyson

My allotted theme requires me to attempt some indications and explanations of the similarities and differences between English and German theological developments in the period of the Enlightenment and into the 19th
century. It is assumed (in my view justifiably) that such a comparative
study can in some measure deepen our understanding of theological presuppositions, issues, and methods in the two countries today.

Many historians of ideas have attempted to capture the essence of the Enlightenment in a single phrase. Their characterisations have been varied
and sometimes conflicting. Thus the Enlightenment has been described as
the age of reason, of rationalism, of optimism, of human autonomy, of
secularisation, of inquisitive scepticism, of scientific humanism, of
atheism, of a new form of religious faith, of the aristocracy of the spirit,
of a resurgence of humanistic values, of the fruition of the Renaissance,
of the rise of modern paganism, of the recovery of nerve, of the inversion
of the Middle Ages, of the transformation of culture, of the rise of the modern world, of the application of laws and principles to society, of the omni-
competence of criticism, of the perseveration of Christian values and traditions. In fact, some evidence can be found to support each of these descriptions, for the Enlightenment was a rich and diverse phenomenon. It
does not lie within the scope of this paper to set forth the arguments for
and against these different characterisations, but it is as well, at the outset, to indicate my consent to three general judgements about the Enlightenment, not least because they point to my dissatisfaction with the
standpoint of many Christian commentators that the Enlightenment was an
unfortunate interlude in the history of Christian thought and that it was essentially hostile to the interests of Christian theology.

First: much of the content of this paper bears witness to my conviction
that the period of the Enlightenment marked in many, but not all, respects
a momentous and irreversible break with Western Europe's political,
social and religious past. I subscribe, therefore, to Dietrich Ritschl's
view that "the Enlightenment constitutes a more important change than
Augustine or the Reformation in the history of the church and theology" (1).
Second: I also hold the opinion that it is principally in the Enlightenment
that there first arose certain acute problems and striking possibilities
which were passed to 19th and 20th century theology, and which have been

partly confronted but by no means mastered. Thus I share Troeltsch's well-known point of view that it is to the Enlightenment that we must turn for the origins of modern theological culture (2). Third: I take the view that on balance the Enlightenment was more concerned to reconstruct religion than to destroy it. Thus I sympathise with Cassirer's conclusion that "the strongest intellectual forces of the Enlightenment do not lie in its rejection of belief but rather in the new form of faith which it proclaims, and in the new form of religion which it embodies" (3). On the basis of these three judgements - whose justification cannot be rehearsed here - I argue that the Enlightenment marks the decisive t e r m i n u s a q u o for the analysis of modern theological developments.

While this may be the case, it must nonetheless be asked whether a comparative study of Germany and England represents a fertile theme. A good deal of scholarship concerned with the Enlightenment has been bedevilled by generalised judgements about England, France and Germany, as if it were clear that there is one Enlightenment taking three broadly similar forms. Though it is true that many of the movements of ideas transcended national boundaries, there is in my view no doubt that fundamental differences can be found which were of capital importance for subsequent developments in the three countries. While my aim in this essay is precisely to indicate the possible origins of such differences between England and Germany and to assess their respective effects, it is by no means easy to arrive at stable conclusions. Partly this difficulty arises from our tendency to concentrate upon those aspects of the period which are easily intelligible to us and to ignore those aspects which are alien. Partly the difficulty resides in the absence of firm scholarly conclusions about certain key movements in the period, e.g., the character of the late Enlightenment in Germany. In the case of England, much of the relatively scant literature suffers from repeated dependence upon secondary material. I shall, however, begin by commenting briefly upon the different circumstances in the two countries which provide the setting for their respective Enlightenments. I shall then offer an account of the main theological developments in each country.

In England the onset of the Enlightenment was not sudden. The aftermath of the Stuart Restoration of 1662 reflected, on the one hand, a powerful appeal to the past, a gravity of learning, a dignity of spirituality, a concern for reason and a deference to authority. On the other hand, it was a period in which significant intellectual changes could be initiated and developed. Calvinism and religious enthusiasm waned in the Church of England. With the settlement of 1689, the relations of church and state were stabilised with the church definitely subordinated to secular interests, in a manner which both reflected and encouraged indifference and toleration. The latitudinarian theologians steered a middle course between Laudian authoritarianism and the later rationalism. Stillingfleet, for example, was suspicious of mysticism and of excessive dogma; he favoured an ethical and practical faith. Sprat and Glanvill were not unnerved by, and could seek to accommodate, the growing influence of science. In the background,

Newton's outlook was remarkable for combining a stringent method of observation and experiment, with a far from shallow theism. But these tendencies were also bound up with the increasing importance of philosophical empiricism with some of its roots in the scepticism of Bacon and the materialism of Hobbes. It found its first culmination in John Locke. The Cambridge Platonists are sometimes incorrectly regarded as an anomalous group in this intermediate period. In fact they show many typical symptoms in their mistrust of dogma and enthusiasm, in their twinning of reason and virtue, their relative anti-ecclesiasticism, and their emphasis upon life rather than doctrine. In this overall context religion was, as one writer has put it, "detheologised and defanaticised".

The situation in Germany was in many ways radically different. The Thirty Years War had left the country at a low ebb - politically, economically, morally and religiously. The religious character of much of this conflict had caused dissatisfaction and weariness with religion. The dominant Protestant Orthodoxy, recently described as the "wastes of a narrow, smug and sterile Aristotelian scholasticism", had yielded a theological inertia in which the intellectual aspect of faith was exalted, in which no attention was given to the new philosophy and the new science, in which sophistry and polemic were at a premium, and in relation to which the control of the churches by the states gave little scope for religious toleration. Thus, whereas in England we may speak of a steady and sober prelude to the Enlightenment, in Germany the change was much more sudden. "Hence the 18th century brought Germany all the successive intellectual developments of modern times belatedly and at once - the humanistic renaissance, the coming of science, the commercial revolution, the national feeling and the political absolutism of the territorial state" (4). But it is important not to conclude from this that the profound upheaval of the German Enlightenment is also a sign of its hyper-radical tendencies. I shall argue that in major respects the English Enlightenment was more radical but that the German Enlightenment was more intense and theologically productive.

Probing a little more deeply the setting in both countries, I will mention six factors which may help to account for some of the differences of religious sensibility and intellectual outlook.

First: German national feeling was not, as in England, indifferent to religious tradition at this time but was closely allied to it. The earlier movement of German mysticism and what has been called "the individualistic and deeply emotional Lutheran faith" were treasured traditions and were, in significant respects, brought to life in and before the Enlightenment by Pietism in the years c.1675 to c.1750.

Second: whatever the criticisms to be made of Protestant Orthodoxy, it is not sufficiently noted that it was a strong and coherent doctrinal tradition such as English Protestantism had never really known since the Reformation. Whereas the English Enlightenment concerned itself to no small extent with the bases and grounds of revelation and reason, the German Enlightenment had to come to terms with actual doctrinal questions, whether by reducing them, eliminating them, or understanding them afresh.

Third: though Pietism was partly a revival of an earlier German tradition of religious experience, it was also in other respects (and this is not widely appreciated) itself a manifestion of Enlightenment self-consciousness, both as precursor and exemplar. It is in this sense that we must interpret Pietism's individualism, its lay consciousness, its appeal for religious toleration, its stress on the primacy of the will over the intellect, its concern for the moral life, its preoccupation with the content rather than the authority of the Bible, and its recognition of other autonomous areas of life. Although Pietism hardened only too quickly into its own orthodoxy, it did provide a stimulus for the German Enlightenment to embrace a much deeper concept of human life and religious experience than was possible in England.

Fourth: although, as we shall see, Lockean empiricism and Newtonian science did make notable inroads into German thought at various points in this period, the fact that they never assumed a dissolvent and dominant role must in no small measure be attributed to the influence of Leibniz in Germany. In Leibniz' debate with Locke and in his correspondence with Samuel Clarke, we gain the sense of an opposition between "the two sets of underlying assumptions about knowledge, the presuppositions that were to be sharpened but not fundamentally questioned in the tradition of British empiricism, and those that Leibniz embedded deeply in the classical German philosophy. These differences in intellectual attitude and premises ... have persisted in the two national traditions to this day" (5). Randall expands this point as follows: "It is clear that Leibniz is here expressing a quite different conception of knowledge and science from that of British empiricism. Knowledge is not for him the passive effect of experience, describing and reproducing it in a copy, but an active organisation and interpretation of experience - a conception that has remained characteristic of the German tradition" (6).

Fifth: a differentiating factor which has perhaps been underestimated concerns the place of science. Not least because of the professionalisation of philosophy in the German universities, speculative philosophy held its ground against the new science until well into the 19th century. In England the new science developed primarily at the expense of speculative philosophy. Thus the energing gulf between theology and the new science, which was to have a powerful impact on English thought in the 19th century, was never as readily apparent in Germany. "... Protestant theology had been carefully prepared by Leibniz for harmony with science and its implications. But the new science never in Germany, as in France and England, completely superseded a decaying metaphysical tradition. It was merely incorporated into one still vigorous; and it was assimilated after a century of criticism had already weakened its claims to exclusive validity. Germans at no time felt that natural science explained everything, or that its methods were alone valid" (7).

Sixth: already in the period of Orthodoxy, German theology had exhibited a strongly scholastic character, which was only reinforced by the advent of Wolffian philosophical theology - itself of a scholastic type. This scholastic character of theology may in no small part be attributed to the strength and multiplicity of universities in Germany in the 17th and 18th centuries, each partly reflecting and encouraging rivalries, academic and non-academic, between the small states. Further, we have to recognise the phenomenon of each major new intellectual movement in Germany producing, and then being nurtured by, its own university. This had two notable consequences. First: theology became a F a c h and a liberal profession earlier and, to this day, more completely, than in England (8). Second: theological "schools of thought" in Germany have carried an institutional meaning which they have not had in England. In the scholastic university setting, each school of thought is pressed to its limit and generates its academic antithesis elsewhere, as well as producing extreme anti-scholastic reactions outside the universities, which are themselves eventually brought under scholastic control. In this context, it is noteworthy that nearly all the main theological protagonists in the German Enlightenment were holding university professorial appointments. In England the proportion is not more than a third. Thus we may have to reckon with a difference, in Germany and England, between what Claude Welch has called "scientific" and "folk" theologians. This points to a different style and intention for the theological enterprise. In England the driving force has been not so much "completeness", or "rigorous systematisation" or "philosophical interconnections", as a more immediate relation to "the life of a church congregation", to "social needs", to "the national community", or to "the conflicts within the Christian community" (9).

I turn now to theological developments in both countries during the Enlightenment proper.

In England the period between 1690 and 1750 may usefully be characterised as one of rational theology, so including both orthodox and deist thinkers who often shared similar assumptions, even if they came to different conclusions. There is no straightforward chronological development over the period, though the dispute between orthodox and deists probably reached its peak between 1720 and 1740. The rational impulse lost its dynamic around 1750 and the causes and consequences of this must be examined. It is misleading to suppose that the religious debates of this period were exclusively concerned with theological questions. There was an impatience with the alleged bigotry and intolerance of organised Christianity; a preoccupation with morality and the public good; a suspicion that much of the system of traditional Christianity was superstitious in character; a concern for freedom of opinion; an appeal to cool and deliberate reason as a guide to thought and life; a detestation of atheism. Many of these concerns were shared, more or less, by thinkers reflecting a wide range of religious opinion. In one way or another most were disposed to take up a new attitude towards the received Christian claim that there are natural theological truths which can be discerned by reason and revealed theological truths which can be apprehended only by faith. This meant a challenge to the inherited basis of religious authority and a questioning of received theological method. Different tendencies may be briefly illustrated.

Though Tillotson attempts to combine supernaturalism and rationalism, he avers that nothing is to be accepted that does not approve itself to reason. Samuel Clarke argues that natural religion is good and true as far as it goes, but needs to be supplemented by revelation, which in turn may not contradict natural religion. Blount sees religion as consisting almost wholly in morality. Tindal argues that God demands no more from men than the practice of virtue. For Locke, essential Christianity is in harmony with natural religion. For Toland and Tindal, Christianity does not transcend natural religion but is an instance of it. For Collins and Woolston, revealed religion is unnecessary and even opposed to reason. And the context of this overall discussion is often a fierce and relatively uninformed debate about the Biblical writings.

In particular, the course and outcome of the deist controversy provides an apt means of appraising the value of a roughly hundred year long consensus in English orthodox theology in the significantly new intellectual milieu initiated by Newton. This broad consensus may be summarily stated as follows. The traditional Christian doctrinal scheme, based upon an inerrant Scripture and only secondarily upon tradition - central to this scheme being a supernaturalism proved by appeal to miracle and prophecy - could successfully withstand the negative criticism of reason and could in fact be confirmed by rational proof. While some theologians might be more or less interested in this or that part of the doctrinal scheme, while some theologians might be more interested in morals than in doctrine, and while some theologians thought that the truths of the Christian religion could not only be confirmed by but could actually bearrived at by reason, nonetheless the consensus which I have described represents the broad point of view to which most orthodox theologians in the period would have subscribed. In many respects it offered an encouraging picture for Christian faith. For it presented, apparently, a positive and satisfactory reconciliation between the old faith and the new scientific view of the world. The effect of the deist controversy was to reveal the hollowness of that reconciliation. It is of course a commonplace to remark (as I have already done) that the deists shared many of the presuppositions of the orthodox, and that the concept of reason entertained by both groups was not able to withstand the acids of Humean scepticism. But that only served to confirm the problematic nature of the orthodox consensus. For if the orthodox were not equipped to deal with the deist onslaught on, to some extent, shared ground, then even less were they able to withstand a far more searching brand of criticism.

By and large the English deists have not received particularly sympathetic treatment from historical theologians. Leslie Stephen's tart and dismissive attitude to the deists, summed up in his phrase "ragged regiment", has been uncritically reproduced by a number of later writers. Certainly some of the deists were responsible for scurrilous pamphleteering and crude polemic; certainly they relished gleefully the exposure of doctrinal divisions within the orthodox camp; certainly the positive doctrines which they sought to substitute were vague and inconsistent. But I judge it is correct to assert that the small number of active deist writers in the early 18th century probably represented a much larger body of silent opinion, so that the critique which they offered is not to be regarded as the tendentious mockery of an anomalous group, but as a body of much more widely held ideas which were deeply subversive of orthodox Christianity of the time. The commonly held view is that in due course the orthodox ousted the deists. If this is meant in the sense that the orthodox won the short-term debating points by virtue of weight of numbers and more assured scholarship, then a limited but by no means assured case can be made. Perhaps more probably the case can be argued that in the short term neither side won, but that the public became bored and the controversy died a natural death in its extreme form. But even if we take the former view, then as William Neil has remarked, "it is of little moment that on paper the victory went to orthodoxy" (10). For on any longer-term view of the matter it must be conceded that the deist critique had not really been answered. There is abundant evidence to show that, in the remainder of the century, the credibility of a rational proof of Christian truth became ever more doubtful, that again and again the orthodox could do no more than demand assent to the authority of Scripture at the cost of a sacrifice of the intellect, that the new initiative of Butler (where it was understood) was widely held to fuel the deists' fire, that William Law's mystical fideism only served to disengage orthodoxy further from the reality of the issues raised by the deists, and that the immaterialism of Berkeley (not to be appreciated for many decades) had the same effect.

In what ways did the deists offer a decisive challenge to the orthodox consensus described above?

First: the deists challenged the received doctrine of the inspired and literal authority of the Bible as the direct word of God. They expounded instead the thesis that the Bible was the work of many hands, uneven and contradictory, so that, if the Bible is inspired, it is so only in parts. The orthodox did not possess the necessary scholarship to set this kind of challenge in a wider perspective and to elaborate a more sophisticated version of Biblical authority. Although textual and philological criticism of an expert kind had been making rapid strides, historical criticism was hardly in evidence. Nor did historical criticism receive from the deists the stimulus which it did in Germany.

Second: the deist notion of "natural religion", in fact shared by a number of the orthodox, never proved a satisfactory basis for doctrinal construction since the deists never really said what it consisted in and where it could be found. For even if many deists were willing to assert that Jesus' moral teaching lay at the heart of this natural religion, it was never clear whether that teaching was to be regarded as unique or final. Nevertheless, in a negative way, "natural religion" did provide an important if vague criterion by which to evaluate the current beliefs and practices of the church. Using this criterion, the typical deist conclusion (though there were others) was that the gap between the original simplicity of natural religion and the complexity of doctrinal orthodoxy could be explained by reference to the corrupt and deceitful machinations of priests and like agencies. Orthodoxy's obligation to offer a satisfactory response to this kind of charge could only be discharged with the help of a model of doctrinal change and development which would include some clear criteria for doctrinal criticism. But this was not forthcoming.

Third: one of the central supports of the orthodox consensus was provided by the claim that the truth of Christianity was confirmed by its perfect and socially beneficial morality. The deists challenged this argument in two different ways. First, there were those who accepted Christianity as embodying a worthy morality but argued that this morality was not peculiarly Christian. In other words, Christian morality, where it has not been perverted by priestcraft, is no more than a republication of the morality of the religion of nature. Second, some went further and argued not only that Christian morality was not peculiar to Christianity, but that in fact Christian morality was far from satisfactory. In this more radical attitude, e.g., in Mandeville, we can see evidence of a conflict between the alleged unrealism of the Gospels and the economically productive self-interest which is apparently a contributor to the common good in an economically competitive society. But in the question about the particularity of Christian morality there are signs of the deists attempting to work out, however inadequately, the implications of the vast amount of material which was becoming available about non-Christian cultures. Again the orthodox apologists lacked a framework with which to deal with these kinds of considerations. It was not sufficient to repeat Cudworth's gentle argument that in some sense all were Christians so that "the prospect was opened up for these religious English humanists that some day in another sphere they might have converse in the groves of Academe with Cicero, Seneca, and Plutarch, perhaps even with Socrates himself" (11).

Fourth: an aspect of deism rarely noticed concerns the psychology of religious behaviour. An outstanding treatment of this theme is found in John Trenchard's Natural History of Superstition (1709). Since the deist judges that all religion except the simple religion of nature is false, it was important to show the origins of this degeneration of natural religion. As noted above, it was common to attribute this degeneration to the subterfuge of the disciples and the scheming of wicked priests. But Trenchard undertakes to deal with what he believes are more fundamental questions, namely "to examine into the frame and constitution of our own Bodies, and search into the causes of our passions and infirmities" (12). In Trenchard and Lord Shaftesbury we see early examples of the projection theory which later assumes so important a role in Feuerbach and Nietzsche, but which here takes the form that men had projected their own foul moods into their gods. This attempt to offer a naturalistic explanation for religious fanaticism and enthusiasm can of course also be applied to other phenomena on which the Christian claims about revelation are buttressed. This approach was symptomatic of the Enlightenment's sense of the complexity of the human person as far more than a passive object of divine action. It required, but did not receive, of the orthodox some fundamental remodelling of the

the supernaturalist scheme which could picture a transcendent God working immanently in and through the admitted complex autonomy of the human person.

Fifth: in one way or another the deists constantly challenged the historical particularity of Christianity. This challenge derived from the deist premise that, if Christianity is true, it is true because it is the republication of the religion of nature which is everywhere and at all times the same. The impact of Newton's account of a vast universe controlled by changeless laws fitted ill with the idea that the Author of this universe should reveal himself to Moses - "an obscure man of a benighted race on a petty planet" (13). Thus the deists judged it contrary to both reason and morality that one group of men should have been selected as the recipients of divine revelation. The deists' constant and conscious disparagement of the Jews only served to heighten this sense of irrationality and immorality. Warburton's reply to this kind of argument in The Divine Legation of Moses (1738), on any count a book both remarkable and perverse, reveals the orthodox inability to respond to this instance of the profound question about the relationship between incidental facts of history and necessary truths of reason except by a blow-for-blow dialectic.

In looking at the deist controversy as a whole (14), it is clear that both sides held in common the view that the truth of Christianity as a divine revelation was in principle and without remainder testable by reason. The orthodox believed that in practice totally satisfying proof could be found. The deists believed that totally satisfying disproof could be found. If the debate is couched in these terms, then the deists were victorious. Inevitably the orthodox, given their position and given the intellectual equipment which they had inherited and which they had themselves forged, were not competent to ask the different question "what grounds should be adduced in favour of Christianity if it is not a phenomenon totally subject to proof or disproof?". A very different approach of this kind could not be broached without a far richer concept of reason than that provided by Locke and without the help of the kind of historical sensibility which 18th century English theology never knew.

Positively, however, the deist outlook represented, however confusedly, the Enlightenment's belief in the capacity of the human faculties to understand and master the world - a belief which must not be lightly ridiculed when we reflect upon the practical achievements of Enlightenment man. For many reasons, supernatural sanctions and the authority of tradition were losing their hold. Adequately to grasp the deeper implications of the deist movement, I suggest that we have to explore Cassirer's contention (noted above) that nothing less than the elaboration of a new form of religious faith was at issue, which would be congruous with a new self-understanding and self-consciousness on man's part. This new form of religious faith would evolve from the premise that religion has its roots in man - a proposition denied by the traditional doctrine of original sin whose truth was everywhere called into question in the Enlightenment. It is true that the contours of this more profound enterprise were lost sight of amid much that was trivial and negative in the period of English theology here under consideration. There was a lack of major creative theological figures, and the theological and philosophical assumptions were too limited by far to broach such an enterprise. This poverty and superficiality brought its own reward at the hands of Humean scepticism. That the English theologians were unable to carry forward, correct, enrich and historicise these fumbling steps in rational theology in fact led to the postponement of the task for several decades, when the external circumstances turned out to be even less propitious. The evengelical revival, whatever it did for religion, had nothing to contribute to the fulfilment of the theological task bequeathed by the failure of 18th century rational theology.

I turn now to a consideration of the German theological Enlightenment or Aufklärung, where I shall concentrate on the period from 1730 to 1780. By way of introducing this analysis, I am disposed to question McGiffert's judgement that "in England evangelicalism followed rationalism and crowded it off the field, in Germany rationalism followed pietism, instead of being followed by it, and hence its development went on unchecked for a much longer time" (15). I have already indicated that English theological rationalism was much more the victim of deism and empiricism than of evangelicalism. In Germany the term "rationalism" is inadequate to describe the theological Aufklärung once the Wolffian philosophy had lost ground. In any case, to speak of German rationalism following pietism is to misunderstand the relationship between the two movements. Instead I shall argue that, after the demise of the Wolffian philosophy, the Aufklärung developed, mainly from intrinsic resources, a standpoint which in important respects anticipates and is in continuity with the subsequent Romantic and Idealist movements, and that, in this regard, the fortunes of German theology in the later 18th century are profoundly instructive for later developments. Thus my objections to McGiffert's formulation are not trivial; they touch instead on crucial differences between English and German theology in this period.

I will now comment briefly on the first part of this period. No exact subdivisions can be marked out as the different tendencies recur at different stages. In the first place, however, we have to note the work of several theologians articulating an explicit dissatisfaction with the theology of late Orthodoxy, but showing a definite suspicion of Wolff's philosophy because of its apparent subordination of the religious interest. These theologians include Turretin, Werenfels, Stapfer, Wettstein, Lemker, Raubach, Weissmann, Budde and Pfaff. They show unease about the Orthodox theory of biblical inspiration and profess a concern for grammatical and literal exegesis. From this quarter arise some of the early rebuttals of the English deists, e.g., Pfaff on Collins and Lemker on Woolston.

Partly parallel to the above tendency is a movement showing more or less conscious dependence on Wolff's philosophy. It includes such theologians as Canz, Büttner, Bülfingger, Carpov, Reinbeck, Reusch, Ribovius, Schubert and, perhaps most significantly, S.J.Baumgarten. They argue for an harmony between reason and revelation, though with the implication that revelation is testable by reason. There is much that is reminiscient of Locke, Tillotson and Clarke. If, however, reason is in principle judged to have a decisive voice in the affairs of faith, in practice these writers (like Wolff) do not much pursue particular doctrinal implications. They thought that their brand of rational supernaturalism offered sufficient defence against the deist challenge - of which they were well aware. But they were mistaken. For their point of view depended upon the demonstration that the content of revelation did successfully meet the tests of reason. In fact the detailed deist arguments to the contrary showed the need for a far less generalised defence.

The middle third of the century manifests abundant evidence of the influence of the English deists in Germany. Their writings were made known by translations and commentaries from the pens of orthodox and deists alike. For example, in 1741 J.L.Schmidt, himself a deist, translated the principal works of Tindal, including Christianity as Old as Creation. In 1755-6 H.G.Schmidt's translation of Leland's View of the Principal Deistical Writers was published. Between 1745 and 1782 translations of about twenty English originals appeared. Among the German deists, of whom Reimarus is of course outstanding, there is evidence of the continuing influence of Locke and Wolff, though put to more radical use than heretofore. Reimarus' celebrated fragments "On the Resurrection Narratives" and "On the Intentions of Jesus and His Disciples" (published by Lessing in 1777 and 1778 respectively) utilise these philosophical resources in telling fashion. In particular, Reimarus puts to consistent use Wolff's two criteria of "necessity" and "freedom from contradiction". Reimarus seeks to show that the orthodox claims about revelation are invalidated by the copious contradictions in the gospels and by the fact that Christian origins do not require a miraculous explanation.

In this context it is clear that a more satisfactory alternative to deism than a modified Orthodoxy or a Wolffian rationalism was required. For Reimarus was claiming to demolish all orthodox theories of revelation and of Scriptural religion in favour of a religion based wholly on reason and nature. We have seen that the ultimate English response to a similar state of affairs was either to reaffirm a literalist approach to Biblical authority, or sharply to separate reason and faith in favour of faith. The most significant German response was on different lines. This was the work of a group of theologians, the neologists, whose principal publications fall mainly in the 1760s and 1770s. This group includes Semler, Spalding, Töllner, Ernesti, Michaelis and Jerusalem. The aim of these writers was to evolve methods of internal and external criticism leading to an historical reevaluation of the contents of revelation and dogma, and culminating in the exclusion of doctrines which were deemed irrational and/or morally indefensible. It must be admitted immediately that the achievement of these writers did not match their intentions. For this reason there has been a tendency to give the neologists credit for their pioneering work in historical-critical Biblical study but to diminish their work as historical and systematic theologians. In fact their overall intention, as I have described it, means that the two aspects of their work are inseparable, and that if the purely methodological aspect is separated out, it loses its point. In any case I want to argue that the significance of the neologists as systematic and historical theologians has been to some extent obscured through the critical treatment meted out by their illustrious contemporary Lessing, and by the somewhat misleading categorisation of the neologists in Karl Aner's highly influential study Die Theologie der Lessingzeit (1929). For example, both Lessing's and Aner's evaluations are apparently taken at face value in H.E. Allison's largely admirable Lessing and the Enlightenment (1966). Aner and Allison virtually repeat Lessing's charge that the neologists combine reason with the concept of revelation but reject its content. So there is attributed to the neologists a "shallow rationalism", "an ungainly hybrid, which is neither philosophically sound nor religiously meaningful", and an "inconsistent and superficial compromise" (16). To accept without more ado these charges as legitimate would be to ignore Lessing's own vital interest in the matter. For his criticism is a way of pressing his own case for a theory of revelation not tied to historical facticity. In fact the neologists were attempting the much more difficult task of producing a rationally criticisible theory of historical revelation. It is not so much therefore that they retain the concept of revelation but reject its content, as that they retain both the concept and the content in principle, but in practice make the received content open to historical criticism. Unlike Lessing, the neologists were determined to hold together both rational-historical criticism and historical revelation.

Thus the neologists, who have been described as the "real theological innovators in Germany" at this time, differed markedly from the Wolffian theologians and developed positive theological outlooks in several important respects.

First: they rejected Wolff's abstract concept of reason, which was an unhappy alliance of empiricism and rationalism, confusing the ground of knowing with the ground of being, as they also rejected Locke's sensationalism, in favour of a richer view of reason as empirical and ethical, but also as intuitive and productive. In a later section I shall put this approach within the wider context of the Aufklärung's distinctive treatment of reason. Granted this account of reason, the neologists also rejected Wolff's dualism of theologia revelata and theologia naturalis. Instead they wanted to affirm religious truth as somehow at one and the same time "revealed" (i.e., historically manifested) and "rational" (i.e., appropriable but not discoverable by reason). Thus religious claims are open to historical, philosophical and ethical criticism.

Second: much of the deist critique of Christian origins, and much of the orthodox defence, lacked any sound grounding in historiographical method. It was an atomising approach which, incidentally, recurs in Strauss' Life of Jesus. Several of the neologists made a notable contribution to the development of modern secular historiography in their approach to

Christian origins and the later tradition. I shall make some general observations about the basis of this approach at a subsequent stage. Their scientific procedures struck a decisive blow at the long-standing theory of Scriptural authority. For Semler, Michaelis and others the Bible is seen as a collection of documents written at different times in response to particular circumstances. This of course challenged the notion that the Biblical documents have a timeless and absolute meaning. Thus Michaelis' Mosäisches Recht (1770-5) argues for the relativity of all the Mosaic legislation to the circumstances in which it was formulated.

Third: whereas Wolff had in principle allowed for the critical role of reason in relation to the contents of revelation, but had in practice (and with ecclesiastical caution) neglected such a task in favour of more abstract epistemological issues, the neologists developed not only historical but doctrino-ethical criticisms of dogma. A classical instance is to be found in Töllner's Der tätige Gehorsam Jesu Christi untersucht (1768) which, on moral and doctrinal grounds, rejects Anselmian satisfaction theory. Töllner argues that Jesus' active obedience, which is His only representative action for men, is the expression of the ethical character of Jesus' genuinely human relationship to God.

Fourth: perhaps most significant of all, the neologists devote considerable attention to the phenomenon of positive religion. This marks an aspect of the general Enlightenment outlook, not only to the need for an historical and practical attitude to life, but also to the active and autonomous character of human existence. It is thoroughly in line with the neologists' arguments when Cassirer argues, in a more general context, that in the Enlightenment "religion is not to be a matter of mere receptivity; it is to originate from, and to be chiefly characterised by, activity" (17). This goes a long way to account for the neologists' rejection of traditional doctrines, especially those of Augustinian origin, which run counter to this view of immanent autonomy, e.g., original sin, predestination, the damnation of the heathen, vicarious sacrifice and the eternity of divine punishment. Thus the writings of the neologists abound in attempts to elaborate an understanding of religion which is both historical and spiritual. Michaelis goes to extraordinary lengths to characterise the kind of primitive culture which can give rise to the kinds of mythical expression which he finds in the Bible. On this kind of approach Michaelis argued for the concept of religion not, like d'Holbach, as contagion sacrée, not as a social prop, but as an inborn drive. (Here Michaelis clearly departed from Locke who rejected the innate idea of God, though of course the view that religion is primary and natural to man was held by the early deists). But Michaelis developed a much more sophisticated model of religious evolution and development. For example his argument modestly to extend the traditional Biblical chronology reflected his search for a framework which can incorporate the idea of slow spiritual change. Mosheim, similarly, regarded the Church as a human creation expressing a general religious impulse in forms determined by different times and places. Like Michaelis, Mosheim postulated a basic religious drive in human nature which preceded experience. History reveals a constant conflict between spiritual, ecclesiastical and human elements in which this conflict is worked out. Mosheim is seeking a non-supernaturalist doctrine of spiritual causation which is contained in experience and which is found in interaction with all sorts of other factors. Likwise, Semler sees religion as a universal force in constant change. It is neither complete nor immutable. It must expand with man's consciousness and meet the needs of every age. In each religious manifestation there is a tension between forms and spirit which gives birth to new understanding. If historical forms mirror prevailing conditions of life, religious forms also shape human values. As the history of religion is seen as process, so God's revelation is interpreted as a function of human development in history. Here lies, for the neologists, the close relationship between history, spirit, dogma and exegesis (18). For dogma, seen as an objectification of religious belief, and when appropriately interpreted, could point to the vital religious element within a dynamic process of history, and thus pave the way for a living perception of religion in the present. If the neologists rejected supernaturalism, their understanding of spirit as both historical and autonomous was held to defy logical analysis and thus to be incapable of naturalistic reduction.

I want to conclude this section on the German A u f k l ä r u n g by some more general remarks on two aspects which are central to the distinctive German development which the neologists represent: - historiography and philosophy.

First: it was once a commonplace to judge the Enlightenment to be an unhistorical era. This judgement has now been thoroughly and properly revised. The thinkers of the A u f k l ä r u n g had inherited a model of historical understanding which has been described as an unstable mixture of classical, medieval and humanist elements circumscribed by and crammed into the traditional Christian interpretation of universal history. This approach denied any qualitative change in history and so closed the future to intellectual enquiry. By the end of the 17th century this kind of historiography had already been partly called into question because it was incapable of dealing with the intricacies of political life. At the same time, given the philosophical climate, historical interpretation of any kind was under a cloud because of its apparent inability to attain to objectivity. Thus for Christian Wolff history is a lesser science which should confine itself to finding out the facts and should eschew interpretation. In this context a number of Enlightenment thinkers set out to produce a new model of historical explanation which could make history into a discipline which spoke to the problems of contemporary life. Dissatisfied with a narrowly empirical historiography, yet wary of polemical and dilettante history, they were especially concerned with questions of method. In particular this meant an effort to find analytical modes which would integrate an individual occurrence within a wider matrix of relations, instead of explaining events by reference to one prior specific intention or to an immediately preceding event. Rather, events must be seen in their relationship and connection with each other, not however in static juxtaposition but in a way which relates past, present and future. The actual methods evolved were: to consider succession or process; to consider spatial relations by cross-sectional analysis. In fact this points to an exceedingly difficult task. For the historian is apparently to study a past epoch both in and for itself and as a determinant of the present. Nonetheless this analysis of developmental and structural relations was commended and essayed under the name of "pragmatic history".

This method was from the first applied to religion. In a culture which, as I have suggested, was neither indifferent nor widely hostile to religion, there was nonetheless a common revulsion in the Aufklärung to religious persecution and polemic, an impatience with dogma, and the concern for a reshaping of religion in accordance with Enlightenment ideals. The pursuit of this task of reconstruction could be assisted by pragmatic history. After 1750 there were a number of attempts to use pragmatic history to explain the relationship between dogma and religion. Thus, if religion is an elemental drive taking different historical forms, dogma is a necessary but ephemeral objectification of this temporal religious belief. It was assumed that by this kind of analysis religious consciousness itself could be expanded. On this view history was seen to be useful - to broaden vision, to prepare the way for an enhanced future. So history, thus understood, becomes the starting-point for all enquiries into the science of man.

Second: the distinctive philosophical development in Germany was crucial. A good deal of the 18th century was dominated by debates between rationalists and empiricists. It is therefore misleading to attribute too powerful an influence to Wolffian philosophy. Wolff may perhaps best be seen as the last representative of neo-scholasticism. His reductive systematisation of Leibniz produced results in some respects reminiscent of earlier English rationalism. But from the earliest stage, Wolff's rationalism was subjected to empiricist criticism, in part deriving from the impact of Newtonian science in Germany. Thus Rüdiger insisted that observation was the sole source of knowledge and later Maupertius expressed doubts about the existence of an intelligible world lying behind experience. But what is distinctive of the German philsophical development was the refusal to allow rationalism to be replaced by empiricism. Under the recurrent influence of Leibniz we find, at the philosophical level in Euler and Crusius, at the psychological level in Tetens, and of course most fully in Kant, an attempt creatively to reconcile, or, rather, to integrate, rationalist and empiricist tendencies by locating the observational a n d the explanatory power of reason w i t h i n the structure of experience. Such an integration has powerful implications for the possibility and character of theological reasoning.

I have sought to show that neither the scholasticism of Wolff, nor the imported British empiricism, nor the sceptical historiography of the deist Reimarus are typical of the Aufklärung. Further there is no need to designate such figures as Lessing, Herder and Hamann as representatives of a C o u n t e r - Enlightenment boldly reversing an earlier straightforwardly rationalistic tradition (19). As in Crusius, Euler and Lambert, and then in Kant, so in the new secular and theological historiography, the starting point of knowledge is experience - but not experience reducible to sensation. Thus the deeper sense of historical reality and of the historical evolution of religion (Lessing), the appeal to a doctrine of the whole man (Hamann), the intellectual intuition of faith in God (Jacobi), and the integration of monism and individuality leading to a view of history as the intelligible expression of nature and God (Herder), served to reinforce and enrich, rather than to contradict, the tendencies of the A u f k l ä r u n g , bringing philosophy, religion and historiography together in powerful combination.

In conclusion I will offer some brief observations concerning the relationship between the Enlightenment in England and Germany and subsequent developments in the two countries. I do not subscribe to a genetic fallacy which would trace a l l subsequent developments to a source in the Enlightenment nor do I underestimate the generalised and over-simplified character of the hypotheses which which I put forward. They do however represent possibilities which deserve further exploration.

My principal hypothesis can be formulated as follows: from the Enlightenment, German theology received a powerful and positive impulse which enabled it comprehensively, vigorously and critically to explore the meaning of Christianity in the modern world, but that English theology responded to the Enlightenment essentially by way of retrenchment and hesitation, and so found itself less able and confident to meet the penetrating challenges of the 19th century, and that, when it did so, it was often on the basis of resources directly or indirectly, but tardily, derived from the German development. I shall expand this principal hypothesis with several supplementary hypotheses.

1. That the German Enlightenment gave a strong impulse to the recognition that man is a being set in, and part of, an historical world, and that in consequence all theological assertions about man must locate transcendental claims in the context of human historicity.

2. That the German Enlightenment gave a strong impulse to, and provided a conceptual basis for, the pursuit of biblical and historical hermeneutics, thus recognising that all acts of historical interpretation are profoundly marked by the standpoint and attitude of the interpreter.

3. That the view of productive reason derived from the German Enlightenment gave to theology an understanding of its task as c o n s t r u c t i v e , revealing the theologian less as a reflector and analyst of a past tradition, but as the builder of a continuing tradition.

4. That the German Enlightenment's structure of a precarious balance between productive reason, historical understanding and religious sense later broke down in favour of either an unhistorical moralised biblicism or an immanent historical materialism.

5. That the German Enlightement's impulse towards the recognition of human historicity contained an underlying tendency towards relativism and nihilism. As Iggers has observed: "The third basic weakness of German

historicist doctrine was contained in its philosophy of value. This weakness was the most serious, because it involved the core of historicist theory, the ideas that objective truths and values exist, that they are manifested in certain persons and in institutions that have developed historically, and that history is the sole guide to the understanding of things human. But in the course of the nineteenth-century the theological and metaphysical assumptions upon which this philosophy rested increasingly lost their credibility. Historicism thus came to be confronted by ethical nihilism as the logical consequence of its position that all values and cognitions are bound in their validity to the historical situation in which they arise" (20).

6. That the character of German theology, as a public discipline, stamped by and deeply indebted to the presuppositions of culture, has in practice made theology vulnerable to domination by changing philosophical and other fashions.

7. That the inbuilt critical character of theology derived from the German Enlightenment has created a sharp and unavoidable tension between church and theology, in particular between the certitude of faith and the variability of critical findings.

8. That the more narrowly empiricist character of English philosophy since the Enlightenment has led to a gulf between theological and philosophical enquiry, often offering in practice a choice between a philosophical theology uninformed by biblical and dogmatic material, and a self-contained biblicism without philosophical foundations.

9. That the English Enlightenment's adhesion to pre-critical Scriptural authority has greatly confined English theology to the task of recovering an historical (especially Biblical) past in which the presuppositionful character of historical interpretation has been inadequately acknowledged.

10. That the powerful tradition of productive reason deriving from the German Enlightenment suppressed an encounter with the challenging questions posed to theology by science.

11. That the predominantly church-centered character of English theology since the Enlightenment has meant only a limited degree of systematic theological involvement in wider cultural issues, though its less strongly intellectualist character has brought it closer than German thought to questions of worship and spirituality.

Footnotes

1 D. Ritschl, "Johann Salomo Semler: The Rise of the Historical-Critical
   Method in Eighteenth-Century Theology on the Continent", in Introduction to Modernity, ed. R. Mollenauer, 1965, p. 109.

2 In, e.g., Protestantism and Progress.

3 E. Cassirer, The Philosophy of the Enlightenment, 1951,
   p. 135 f.

4 J. H. Randall, The Career of Philosophy, Vol. 2, 1965, p. 51.

5 Randall, op. cit., p. 41.

6 Randall, op. cit., p. 48.

7 Randall, op. cit., p. 53.

8 L. W. Beck, Early German Philosophy, 1969, pp. 7 ff.

9 C. Welch, Protestant Thought in the Nineteenth Century,
   1972, p. 242 f.

10 W. Neil, "The Criticism and Theological Use of the Bible 1700-1950",
    in The Cambridge History of the Bible: The West
    from the Reformation to the Present Day, ed. S. L.
    Greenslade, 1963, p. 243.

11 In F. E. Manuel, The Eighteenth Century Confronts the
    Gods, 1959, p. 60.

12 Manuel, op. cit., p. 74.

13 R. N. Stromberg, Religious Liberalism in Eighteenth-
    Century England, 1954, p. 56.

14 See G. V. Lechler, Geschichte des englischen Deismus,
    1841.

15 A. C. McGiffert, Protestant Thought before Kant, 1919,
    p. 251.

16 Allison, p. 94.

17 Cassirer, op. cit., p. 164.

18 See G. Hornig, Die Anfänge der historischen-kritischen
    Theologie, 1961.

19 See the valuable discussion in F. W. Kantzenbach, "Die Spätaufklärung",
    T LZ, 102, 1977, pp. 337-347.

20 G. G. Iggers, The German Conception of History, 1968,
    p. 270.

PHILOSOPHY AND THE RISE OF BIBLICAL CRITICISM:
ENGLAND AND GERMANY

by

J. W. Rogerson

Are the results of biblical criticism in any way affected, or even determined by philosophy? About seventy years ago, an answer to this question
was given by no less a person than Julius Wellhausen. Looking back over
the previous century, and mindful that some of the early pioneers in biblical criticism such as Vatke and Strauss had been self-confessed hegelians,
Wellhausen wrote:

> Philosophy does not precede, but follows [biblical criticism] , in
> that it seeks to evaluate and systematise that which it has not it-
> self discovered. The authors of the two great theological works
> of 1835 [Strauss's Life of Jesus and Vatke's Biblical
> Theology] were hegelians, it is true. But that which is of
> scholarly significance in them does not come from Hegel. Just
> as Vatke continues and completes the work of de Wette, so
> Strauss continues and completes that of the old rationalists. The
> particular value of the Life of Jesus lies not in the philo-
> sophical introduction and conclusion, but in the middle part,
> which is by far the largest section of the book (1).

Wellhausen's opinion contains much that would be endorsed by biblical scholars today. He holds that biblical criticism is a philosophically neutral
method of discovery. In cases where it can be shown that philosophy has
affected the work of a biblical scholar, the philosophy can be disentangled
from the results of the biblical criticism, and the latter can then stand in
their own right. The example of Vatke's Biblical Theology is an excellent one in this connection (2). Vatke had argued, on hegelian grounds,
that in the religion of the Old Testament, the prophets had preceded the
law. Graf and Wellhausen had then upheld this point of view by arguments
based upon the content of the Old Testament itself (3). On the other hand,
it is debatable whether Wellhausen was correct to describe Strauss as continuing the work of the rationalists, and Vatke as continuing that of de Wette.

The purpose of this paper is to argue that biblical criticism has, in fact,
been far more influenced by philosophy than is allowed by Wellhausen's
statement. It is readily conceded that the position that will be defended may
differ from that of Wellhausen more by way of definition than by substance,
and thus it is important that at the outset, the scope of my argument should

be clearly set out. If biblical criticism is defined as the investigation of the literary processes which brought the books of the Bible to their extant form, together with a critical evaluation of the history and culture of ancient Israel and Judaea so as to interpret biblical material in its original historical and cultural setting, it is difficult to see how philosophy, even defined very broadly, can affect such investigations. Surely, the reconstruction of the history of Israel, or of the apostolic period, involves the use of an historical method unaffected by philosophy. Further, the conclusion, based upon the alternation of the divine names and other criteria in the 'Flood' narrative of Genesis 6-9, that this narrative is a combination of two originally separate written accounts, is something else that in no way depends upon philosophy. It is true that a book such as H. Palmer's The Logic of Gospel Criticism has argued that the generally accepted cases for some standard conclusions in critical New Testament scholarship involve logical fallacies, but this is a case of the use of philosophy in a narrow sense to test hypotheses, rather than to propose new ones (4). Again, some conservative writers have held that where philosophical influence upon a theory such as the Documentary Hypothesis can be urged, then the whole theory is discredited (5). None of this, however, seems to me to be compelling, and I am happy to agree that in many of its technical procedures, biblical criticism is not affected by philosophy. What is affected, however, by the general philosophical climate combining with different religious traditions, is the possibility and the character of biblical criticism. Had it not been for the different philosophical climate in Germany in the period, say, 1770 to 1840, compared with Britain, combined with distinctive emphases of Lutheranism, biblical criticism would not have made such great progress in Germany in this period, as against practically no progress in Britain (6). Moreover, when biblical criticism finally found acceptance in Britain in the 19th century, it did so in the context of a different philosophical climate and religious tradition compared with Germany, with the result that it played, and continues to play, a different role in Britain. The phrase 'philosophical climate' is, of course, vague, so I must spell out that I understand the important philosophical questions in this regard to be the following: what is the source of knowledge, and what part does the perceiving subject play in knowledge of the external world and of God? Are there truths of reason independent of sense experience, from which deductions can be made about God and about such things as meaning in history? What is religion, and where is it to be located in human knowledge and experience?

In the course of the argument, some enormous generalisations are going to be made, and it is only fair to indicate some of the respects in which my account of British and German theological thought is oversimplified. Against the account that will be given of the reception of biblical criticism into Britain in the early 19th century must be put the position that has been argued in Elinor Shaffer's book 'Kubla Khan' and The Fall of Jerusalem, where it is shown that in Unitarian circles at the end of the 18th and the beginning of the 19th centuries, German biblical criticism was known and appreciated to a considerable extent (7). However, although these Unitarian circles influenced Coleridge, and later Browning and George Eliot, they do not seem to have had any noticeable affect upon the Established Church or the main Dissenting bodies. If, however, ignorance of German biblical criticism in Britain in the early 19th century was not as great as my account will tend to suggest, it is also true that in Germany itself, biblical criticism had a less easy passage than will be implied. Within protestantism, German theological thought in the period 1770 to 1840 had many differing and complex strains. Rationalism competed with neologism, supranaturalism and pietism; there were various theologies based upon types of German speculative philosophy, which came up against conservative reactions which themselves were grounded in different fundamentals (8). Again, in the study of key scholars in this period such as Semler, Strauss and even Wellhausen in a later period, a considerable secondary literature has sprung up in the attempt to evaluate these scholars and to determine their presuppositions. There is a 'Semler problem', a 'de Wette problem' and a 'Strauss problem', to each of which a series of lectures could be devoted, and in regard to which the position that I shall outline could be challenged.

It may well seem that the above paragraph, containing as it seems to, the thousand qualifications that ought to lead to death, is sufficient proof of the futility of the position that this paper argues. However, I am convinced, not withstanding the qualifications that it is right to make, that the general position that will be presented is correct. I hope to demonstrate this in a book before too long. It was one of the most knowledgable historians of philosophy and theology in Germany and Britain, Otto Pfleiderer, who pointed out that in England in the early 19th century, no philosophy comparable to that in Germany had penetrated the educated classes or exercised a determining influence on their thought, and he concluded

> It seems to me that we have here the explanation of the remarkable
> fact that the Church life of England, until within the last decade,
> has remained almost untouched by the vast progress of scientific
> thought of the educated classes, and that wherever the two came
> into contact, such a violent collision is the consequence that popular
> feeling is shocked, and not a few despair of the possibility of any
> mutual understanding (9).

I

The philosophical climate of British theology in the late 18th and early 19th centuries was a Lockean sort of supernaturalism. The important thing about it for our purposes was that it regarded knowledge as something that came from outside of man, as the external world impinged upon the perceiving subject in the form of sense impressions. It distrusted theories about innate ideas from which, for example, the existence of God could be deduced. If there were such a thing as divine revelation, this, too, came from outside of man, and it was to be recognised by the supernatural evidences that supported it. Since some of these evidences, such as miracles and the fulfilment of Old Testament prophecy in the New Testament, were contained in the Bible, the latter was therefore an unassailable book so far as orthodox believers were concerned (10).

Of course, there was controversy in England about reason and revelation, and this took its sharpest form in the attacks of the deists upon the Bible. At one end of the spectrum of opinion were those who held that revelation was above reason. In the middle, there were those who held that there was revelation but that it was to be, and could be, approved by reason. At the opposite end of the spectrum were those who were prepared to attack the Bible, especially the Old Testament, for failing to come up to the standards of that natural religion which reason could discover in the world around it. However, what was common to all parties was the view that revelation was information or doctrine that had been communicated through an external medium, the Bible. The deists may have attacked the Bible, but they did not deny that the New Testament at least revealed truths of natural religion such as the oneness of God, the immortality of the soul, and punishments for the wicked and rewards for the righteous. These controversies did not lead to anything resembling biblical criticism in the sense of a radical probing into the sources behind the biblical traditions with a view to their interpretation in ways that might differ significantly from a surface reading of the biblical story. At the close of the 18th century, Paley could still write his Evidences of Christianity in which the main evidence for the truth of Christianity was the New Testament miracles (11). He was not prepared to accept Old Testament history entirely uncritically; on the other hand, he did not regard the acceptance of occasional errors or exaggerations in the Old Testament as entailing the view that the whole of the Old Testament was to be regarded as false. The theological-philosophical climate of England in the period 1770-1840 can be summarised by saying that Christianity consisted of truths conveyed by revelation, approved by reason, accepted by faith, and put into effect by moral conduct and by worship and prayer. Since the Bible was a principal source of that revelation, its substantial trustworthiness was to be, and could be defended, even though slight doubts could be entertained about parts of the Old Testament.

The achievements of English biblical scholarship in this period fall well into the scheme just outlined. One of the most eminent of 18th century biblical scholars in this country was Bishop Lowth, whose lectures on the poetry of the Old Testament have deservedly become a classic. Of greater interest for present purposes is his new translation of Isaiah, of 1779 (12). Scholars of Lowth's day were well aware that in places, the Hebrew text of the Old Testament was corrupt. Scholars such as Benjamin Kennicott scoured libraries for Hebrew manuscripts that might contain readings different from those of the traditional text, and scholars were prepared to use other Semitic languages including Arabic to suggest alternative meanings for obscure Hebrew words. They also resorted to conjectural emendation. But all this was done without questioning the divine authority of scripture.

After describing the many blemishes in the traditional Hebrew text of
Isaiah, Lowth assured his readers that

> If it be objected, that a concession, so large as this, tends to inval-
> idate the authority of Scripture; that it gives up in effect the cer-
> tainty and authenticity of the doctrine contained in it ... this ... is
> a vain and groundless apprehension. Casual errors may blemish
> parts, but do not destroy, or much alter, the whole (13).

In cases where conjectural emendation was used, Lowth was prepared to
allow the judgement of the reader to be the final court of appeal and to decide

> whether the conjectural reading ... be more agreeable to the con-
> text, to the exigence of the place, to parallel and similar passages,
> to the rules and genius of the language, and to the laws of sound
> and temperate criticism (14).

Literary criticism in the sense of the detection of sources went no further
than allowing that editors may have written the opening verses of prophetic
books, especially if the opening verses were in the third person, followed
immediately by verses in the first person.

In the early 19th century, in spite of all that was being achieved in biblical
criticism in Germany, things had not altered greatly. When Pusey studied
the Old Testament in Oxford in 1823, Lloyd, the Regius Professor of
Divinity and later Bishop of Oxford, was lecturing on works such as Moses
Lowman's Civil Government of the Hebrews (1745[2]) and
Hebrew Ritual (1748), and Sumner's Records of the Creation
(1816), a work that defended the Genesis account of creation against recent
geological discoveries, and which stressed the harmony between the biblical
account and that of natural religion (15).

Apart from the contribution of the Unitarians mentioned by Elinor Shaffer,
several German works on the New Testament had been translated into
English in the period 1793 to 1825, notably J.D.Michaelis's Introduction to the New Testament and Schleiermacher's Critical
Essay on the Gospel of St. Luke. But how little anything of biblical criticism was penetrating deeply can be seen from a work which caused
such a commotion when it was published in 1829, that the publisher had to
suspend its issue. I refer to H.H.Milman's History of the Jews (16).
What offended Milman's readers was a mildly rationalising treatment of
the miraculous (e.g., the plagues in Egypt were natural occurrences),
together with commonsense observations, such as that it is unlikely that
Sarah was twice in danger and that therefore the second account is a dupli-
cate; or the observation that the events recorded in the last five chapters
of the book of Judges may well have happened before the period of the
judges. What strikes a modern reader, however, is that the book is little
more than a re-telling in the author's own words of the biblical story accompanied by moralising observations. No use of the critical studies already provided, say, by de Wette, is made, and the modern reader cannot

but notice how shallow the treatment of the history of Israel is, for all that the rationalising may have given offence to Milman's original readers.

The same can be said, to a lesser extent, of A.P.Stanley's Lectures on the History of the Jewish Church of 1863. The author pays tribute to Ewald, and to the 'silent effect' of the latter's great History of Israel. Not without reason, Stanley regards Ewald as far too dogmatic; but although his own work is immensely learned in the sense that it shows a vast knowledge of ancient Jewish and Graeco-Roman writings, as well as the latest discussions of the topography of ancient Israel, one misses the radical penetration of the texts, and the insights into the historical process familiar from German criticism. The reason for this, I suggest, is to be found in the philosophical-theological context in which scholars such as Milman and Stanley worked. Even 'advanced' theologians such as Stanley and the contributors to Essays and Reviews still regarded revelation as the communication of 'external' truths and doctrines, especially through the Bible. They upheld the claims of reason and historical enquiry, and therefore welcomed cautiously what was going on in Germany. But it is arguable that their position was at root only a more sophisticated version of that common in the 18th century: Christianity is based upon an external revelation which is to be approved by reason. Of course, by 1860, reason has become more sophisticated and has many more facts at its disposal; but there is still a deep-seated reluctance to use reason to question the Bible in such a way as to disturb its status as external revelation. When biblical criticism begins to be accepted in England, it occasions no fundamental change in the general philosophical-theological position of the churches, neither has it to this present day - a point to which I shall return.

Above, the philosophical-theological climate of Christianity in Britain in the period 1770 to 1840 was characterised as consisting of truths conveyed by revelation, approved by reason, accepted by faith, and put into effect by moral conduct and by worship and prayer. The philosophical-theological climate in protestant Germany in which biblical criticism originated and progressed can be characterised, in contrast, as follows. It is personal experience of a liberating God, who can be glimpsed in the deepest feelings of the human soul and in the processes of history, and whose reality is confirmed in the biblical record of God's dealings with his people, which record is also a means whereby God becomes a living reality to the believer. This view is derived not from the empirical philosophy of Locke, but is connected with a philosophy that can be traced through Schleiermacher, Fries, Schelling and Hegel to Kant, Wolff and Leibniz. It seeks knowledge and truth not only in what comes from outside of the perceiving subject, but especially in what is within, whether this be in human reason, the sense of obligation, or feelings of absolute dependence. On the one hand, this view is nourished by the various forms of pietism with their stress on personal experience for all that these movements were abhorred by biblical critics; on the other hand, there is a hostility to metaphysics in the sense that we live in one world, part of which is unseen but whose ex-

istence affects what is seen. The German philosophy of this period, especially after Kant, prefers not to speculate about unseen worlds, except
insofar as they can be discovered in the depths of the human soul and in the
processes of history. If English theological thought of the period regards
revelation as external truths largely contained in the Bible and backed by
external evidences, the German thought that I have in mind sees revelation
in the disclosure of a saving God, the Bible being the record of that disclosure, the evidences being sought in the human spirit.

The first of three German examples designed to illustrate the point just
made is J.S.Semler, whose most important writings date from the 1760s.
Amid the uncertainties involved in interpreting his thought - uncertainties
not a little contributed by Semler's obscure written style - two facts stand
out clearly (18). First, although Semler abandoned the pietism in which he
had been brought up, and in whose context he was a student in Halle, he
never gave up his conviction that at the heart of religion was the sort of
personal experience which gave inner certainty, and dispensed with the
need for external assurance, such as in the doctrine of the verbal inspiration of the Bible. Second, he was convinced of the necessity of an historical
approach to every facet of theology. This led him to study the history of
the text and canon of the Bible, the history of theology especially the Reformation, and the history of philosophy in its relation to theology. These
historical studies convinced him of the futility of rigid theological orthodo-
xies, since there had, in fact, been so many changes in orthodoxy in the
course of the history of the church. He also became a Luther scholar, believing, rightly or wrongly, that the church of his day had misunderstood
Luther, and that Luther had advocated the kind of free enquiry into truth
that Semler himself was now undertaking. Granted Semler's desire for
free enquiry, his point of certainty remained his deep inner conviction of
his knowledge of God.

Semler's position enabled him to become one of the founding fathers of biblical criticism (19). He distinguished between the Bible and the Word of
God, arguing that the Word of God was c o n t a i n e d in the Bible, and was
to be found in those parts of it that spoke directly to a person and assured him
that in Christ, God had acted for his salvation. Quite a lot of the Old Testament could be disregarded as Jewish material, and the Old Testament
contained the Word of God only where it displayed the spirit of Christ. Traditional theories of the authorship of books of the Bible could be questioned.
Whereas up to this period, theologians had equated authority with authenticity,
i.e. the authority of the Bible had been upheld by supposing that its books
had been written by known inspired individuals such as Moses, Joshua,
Samuel, David and Solomon, matters of authorship were now freely inves-
tigated. Of course, when Semler wrote, there was as yet little sense of
history as a process with meaning. Because his writings lack this dimension, he can easily be written off as a sort of rationalist. What he was
doing, however, was to use the methods of rational enquiry in order to free
the interpretation of the Bible from metaphysics and from orthodoxy, so
that its power to enable man to be found by God through its pages would be

unhampered. This work was only possible, however, by his view of the truth of religion as something inward, and by his conviction based upon his historical studies, that this inwardness combined with a spirit of free enquiry was the essence of Luther's own position.

As a second example, I propose to say something about W.M.L. de Wette. Most students know of de Wette only that in 1804 he attempted to demonstrate that the book of Deuteronomy was written in the 7th century B.C., thereby providing one of the major foundations for the later Documentary Hypothesis. In actual fact, the range of de Wette's work and the scope of his influence were enormous. Samuel Davidson, who was one of the pioneers of biblical criticism in Britain, and who was forced to resign from his post at the Lancashire Independent College in 1858 because of his critical views, regarded de Wette as the greatest biblical scholar of the time (20). Rudolf Otto records that Wellhausen said to him of de Wette: 'A clever chap! Why, all that I did in the Old Testament was in his books already!' (21). De Wette wrote not only on the Old and New Testaments and on 'biblical dogmatics' as he entitled one of his books, but he also taught and wrote on ethics. He was deeply interested in aesthetics, and tried his hand as a novelist and playwright (22). The interpretation of de Wette's work is not, however, without difficulty. Professor Smend of Göttingen has argued that de Wette's brilliant early work on biblical criticism, especially the Beiträge zur Einleitung in das Alte Testament in which he demonstrated the lateness of the books of Chronicles as well as of Deuteronomy, and in which he argued that the narratives of books such as Genesis were mythical in such a way as to contain deep poetic and religious truth, came from an early rationalistic period of his life. After this period, Professor Smend thinks that de Wette embraced the philosophy of J.F.Fries, and to a lesser extent, that of Schleiermacher, before entering a third period, in which he became more pietistic and conservative (23). Although I have the greatest respect for Professor Smend's work, my own studies convince me that there is a much greater unity about de Wette's work. Already in the understanding of myth to be found in the early Beiträge, the influence of Fries can be discerned, and it is arguable that in the philosophy of Fries, de Wette found a system by means of which he could articulate what he had already come to believe about truth and religion (24). A factor in his earliest formation was that he attended the Gymnasium in Weimar when Herder was the Superintendent, and it is unlikely that such a sensitive person as de Wette would have been unmoved by the addresses he had heard from Herder. De Wette's friendship with Fries went back to his student days in Jena, where Fries was a Privatdozent, and when de Wette later went as a Privatdozent to Heidelberg, he had Fries as a colleague (25).

From Fries, de Wette learned to regard faith as a kind of knowledge based in reason and not in external metaphysics, transcending empirical knowledge of the world, yet placing it within a religious context of understanding with the help of myths and symbols. Otto has described de Wette's account of reason, which can also be described as inner revelation as follows:

it is the perception of eternal truth itself, independent of our own views, imaginations and thoughts, absolutely non-mediate, lifted above all individual caprice and all possibility of error, in its deepest foundations unseen, and obscure in its origin, constituting as such the central mystery of the reasoning spirit (26).

To this inner revelation there corresponds an outward revelation in history, which is necessary to make the inward revelation fully potential. De Wette, then, in his view of reason and revelation moved from the internal to the external, and saw the essential truth of the Bible not in its external facts or statements, but in the way in which it endorsed and expressed the absolute truths of faith to be perceived inwardly. It was this position, I believe, that enabled him to have the freedom that he did in his use of radical source criticism; and from this position, he could attack rationalist and supernaturalist alike. The rationalist clung to the natural, external world, with only a limited awareness of the range of human experience. The supernaturalist was similarly unaware of the range of human experience, and its potentiality for disclosing truth. De Wette could accept some of the miracles recorded in the Bible, but not on the ground of the external witness which they had, but rather on the grounds of the internal witness of the inner revelation. The supernaturalists, wrote de Wette

> believe in miracles, and conceive them in a natural and material manner. They consider that the laws of Nature are temporarily suspended, that Nature's machine has been differently set. With all their exaltation of Faith they are unable to believe without seeing. And if they had lived in the days of Christ, they would indeed have beheld no marvellous works, for, like the Pharisees, they would have asked for a sign from heaven (27).

The work and thought of de Wette provide ample evidence, in my opinion, that the work of this most brilliant and influential biblical critic stemmed not from straightforward rationalism, but from a sophisticated view of truth and religion expressed through the medium of a post-Kantian philosophy.

As a third illustration of the position being argued, I turn to D.F.Strauss, whose L i f e o f J e s u s of 1835 caused a commotion in Germany, as well as producing shick waves in Britain, when it appeared in an English translation by George Eliot (Mary Ann Evans) in 1846 (28). We have already heard that Wellhausen regarded Strauss as simply completing the work of the old rationalists, once his philosophising introduction and conclusion have been ignored. I am not so convinced that we can separate the critical kernel from the philosophical husk. Strauss himself would have been deeply offended at being called a rationalist, in view of the trouble that he took to demonstrate the shallowness of the work of the rationalists. Rather, we must see Strauss as standing in a philosophical tradition which lays primary stress on inner truth, a truth expressed in antiquity in myths, and a truth completely understood in his day through speculative, hegelian philosophy. For Strauss, myths are 'imaginative symbols,standing not for matters of fact, but for facts of mind, experiences, states of feeling' (29). Historical criticism is unable to disturb the essential truths of Christianity ('essential truths' conceived in a hegelian manner) precisely because these truths are not matters of fact. In other words, we do a disservice to Strauss if we consider him to be a rationalist wolf in hegelian sheep's clothing. No less than Semler and de Wette, he believes that if a modern man is to understand the Bible, he must approach it with a radical criticism which will free it from its metaphysical and historical fetters, so as to release its essential truth, in power. Simply to refute the apparently rationalising parts of the Life of Jesus is to avoid the real challenge that the work presents, namely, whether we can study the Bible at all without first considering what we mean by religion and revelation, and how and where these are to be located in human experience and history.

Although I admit that there is much more to German and British biblical scholarship than the examples that have been given above, I hope that the examples indicate a way of approaching critical scholarship in Germany which was quite different in its philosophical background compared with what was characterised with the English view. In the following section, three examples from more recent scholarship will be taken in order to add cumulative weight to the position being presented, and also to indicate that the differences between Germany and Britain which I am alleging are still of significance today.

II

The scholar who did more than anyone alse to assist acceptance of Old Testament criticism in England was S. R. Driver, who succeeded Pusey as Regius Professor of Hebrew in Oxford in 1883. Driver's Introduction to the Literature of the Old Testament, which went through nine editions from 1891, contains in my opinion the most eloquent and the most shrewd presentation of the Graf-Wellhausen 'Documentary Hypothesis' ever written in English. His Genesis commentary in the Westminster series enjoyed twelve editions between 1904 and 1926, (the 12th edition of 1926 contained additional notes by his son G. R. Driver), and performed the notable function to the author's generation of reconciling Genesis as holy scripture with both biblical criticism and scientific evolutionism. Yet a careful examination of Driver's writings suggests that he accepted and used biblical criticism in the context of a philosophical climate different from that which obtained in Germany. Driver accepts a double theory of the truth of the Bible, according to which its inner or spiritual truths can be distinguished from its outward expression. If the advance of knowledge necessitates the discarding of the outward form, e. g. , the statement of Genesis 1 that the world was created in seven days, this can be done without injury to the spiritual truth which the narrative conveys. Thus

the first record teaches us that God is a Spiritual Being, prior to the world, and independent of it, that the world arrived at the form in which we know it by a series of stages, each the embodiment of a divine purpose, and the whole the realization of a divine plan; that man, in particular, among the other animals, is endowed with a distinctive pre-eminence, signified by the term 'the image of God' (30).

This falls well within my earlier definition of the prevailing English philosophical theology: Christianity is a revelation, approved by reason (which in this case strips off the unacceptable scientific or other form of expression), accepted by faith, and so on. Driver is so much wedded to the idea that the purpose of the Bible is to convey information about the external world, that he is prepared to accept that it informs us about pre-history so far as man's moral experience is concerned. In a remarkable discussion of the 'Fall' in Genesis 3 Driver writes

> All that, as Christian theologians, we are called upon to believe is that a time arrived, when man's faculties were sufficiently developed for him to become conscious of a moral law, and that, having become conscious of it, he broke it ... it is sufficient for Christian theology, if we hold that, whatever the actual occasion may have been ... man failed in the trial to which he was exposed, that sin thus entered into the world, and that consequently the subsequent development of the race was not simply what God intended it to be (31).

Even more remarkably, Driver allows that if the human race arose independently in several centres of the world, then each race independently passed through a similar moral development, each similarly underwent a 'fall' (32). All this is very different from what we find, say, in de Wette or Schleiermacher about creation and the 'fall', where the Genesis narratives, so far from teaching truths about the external world, are rather commentaries on what we know to be true of human existence from reflection upon our status as redeemed persons. Even if the mosaic account of creation could be accepted as 'an historical account communicated in an extraordinary way', writes Schleiermacher, 'the particular pieces of information would never be articles of faith in our sense of the phrase, for our feeling of absolute dependence does not gain thereby either a new content, a new form, or clearer definition' (33).

That different philosophical attitudes can be behind even modern discussions between German, British and indeed American scholars can be illustrated from two examples. The position of Bultmann would be described by many who did not know it intimately as a combination of historical scepticism and existentialism. However, in a recent book entitled The Origins of Demythologising, R.A. Johnson has argued that Bultmann can hardly be understood without taking into account the influence of his neo-Kantian, antimetaphysical teacher, Wilhelm Herrmann (34). Herrmann believed that Luther had delivered theology from metaphysics, and that Kant had worked out the philosophy which would make explicit what was implicit in the theology of the Reformation. This neo-Kantian philosophy combined with the doctrine of justification by faith results in a theology which regards any attempt to make faith or redemption dependent on any humanly-constructed history or metaphysical view of the world, a denial of divine grace, and an assertion of justification by works. Johnson's argument sheds a good deal of light on Bultmann's famous contributions to the Kerygma and Myth debate of the 1940s and 1950s, and his persistent denial that we can derive any metaphysics from the New Testament witness to Jesus. It indicates that while it is possible to discuss Bultmann at the level of whether his use of the formcritical method is valid or not in achieving results for biblical criticism, in fact, as with Strauss's Life of Jesus, there are also fundamental philosophical questions to be faced in considering Bultmann's position as a whole.

The second example is taken from the pages of the Expository Times in 1959-61, and is the debate between Gerhard von Rad and the American Old Testament scholar G. E. Wright (35). The subject of the debate was the interpretation of the patriarchal narratives. Wright accused von Rad of undue historical scepticism. Surely, archaeology had vindicated the historical basis of the narratives, and we could have some idea of the sort of world in which the patriarchs lived, and the sort of persons that they were. We could go some way to recovering the historical acts through which God had revealed himself to the founders of the Hebrew nation. In reply to Wright, von Rad was less certain about the value of the archaeological evidence, and he has the fear that if it is used along with the Bible itself to reconstruct historical events, the result will be a man-made thing which will become a substitute for the Bible as the locus of revelation. If we cannot be sure about the historical accuracy of the patriarchal narratives, we can have confidence in them as Israel's credo, expressing her belief in the reality of God and of his dealings with his people. On the surface of this debate, we have an argument about the merits of an archaeological approach to Genesis whose aim is to confirm the underlying historical accuracy of the patriarchal narratives, versus a literary and form-critical approach which tends to agnosticism about their basic historical accuracy. In fact, behind the use of scholarly methods by von Rad and Wright lie different philosophical-theological positions. In Wright's case, there is the belief that revelation has been in objective historical events that are not beyond the reach of reason as exercised in the historical method. For von Rad, revelation has also taken place in history, but not in objective events within the reach of the historian. Rather, it has been an inward process among an historical community, expressed initially in ancient stories, features of which can be shown to be historically inaccurate, but stories which have nevertheless expressed Israel's experience of God, and which have through re-telling and re-interpretation in the light of new events constituted a witness to the living God in the midst of the historical entity, Israel. It would be possible to show, I believe, that underlying the respective positions of von Rad and Wright are the differing German and English philosophical-theological positions for which this paper has argued.

Let me emphasise once again that I have not been maintaining that philosophy has directly influenced processes of biblical criticism such as the detection of literary sources or arguments about the authorship, date and composition of biblical books. What has been maintained is that these seemingly neutral discovery processes have been carried out in the context of philosophical-theological presuppositions about the nature of knowledge and revelation, the status and nature of religious truth, and the possibility or desirability of metaphysics; and these presuppositions have affected the use of the tools of biblical criticism. It has been suggested that when scholars differ about the results of biblical criticism, they are sometimes differing about philosophical questions although they may be unaware of this. supposing that what has been maintained is true, what follows?

1. Wellhausen wrote 'Philosophy does not precede, but follows biblical criticism '. This certainly seems to be assumed in the majority of departments of theology or biblical studies in universities and colleges, where biblical subjects begin the curriculum, and systematic and philosophical theology follow on later, building on the 'biblical foundation'. I am increasingly convinced that this is a mistake. Only a tiny percentage of students has any philosophical knowledge at the outset of a theological course, and in England, it is likely that their 'natural philosophy' will be a sort of Lockean empiricism combined with belief in an objective supernatural world. Faced with von Rad or Bultmann in their first year, most of them will retreat into an acquiescence of biblical criticism for the purpose of satisfying examiners, but basically, they may well be untouched by biblical criticism. They will not find it liberating, and some may reluctantly be driven into a sophisticated form of fundamentalism, perhaps derived from C.S.Lewis. Those who are ordained may well feel that their academic study of the Bible contributed nothing to their preaching or theology. One way in which this process could be reversed would be by giving the sort of introductory courses to students before they studied the Bible that would bring to light the hidden philosophical questions involved, enabling the students to be more philosophically mature when they begin their biblical studies.

2. At the level of professional scholarship, greater effort should be directed towards the history and method of biblical criticism. To some, this is 'the study of the study', and an evasion of biblical scholarship as such. In Germany, the relevance of such study is better appreciated than in Britain; but there are indications that the tide is beginning to turn in English-speaking scholarship. British scholars have an important contribution to make to the interpretation of German biblical scholarship; for if they cannot always match the profundity and energy of their German counterparts, they can often bring a degree of clarity and impartiality that may be lacking on the German side.

3. The study of the philosophical presuppositions behind biblical criticism will not only help to set it in its context; it will also suggest questions that

have been asked in the past, and ought to be asked today. On reading de Wette's Biblical Dogmatics or Vatke's Biblical Theology, it is difficult not to be impressed by the space which they devote to the discussion of religion in general, its location in human knowledge, experience and history, and its manifestation in non-biblical religions as well as in the religion of the Bible. Modern histories of the religion of Israel appear to assume that the answers to the questions 'what is religion? how is it manifested in human experience and history?' are self-evident (36). At any rate, discussion of these questions is almost wholly absent. But even if we cannot necessarily accept the answers to these questions given by writers such as de Wette and Vatke, are we right to ignore the questions altogether? Can biblical studies continue to ignore the sort of philosophical issues that this paper has tried to raise? Is biblical criticism too important to be left to biblical scholarship?

Footnotes

1   J.Wellhausen, Beilage zur Allgemeine Zeitung, 1908,
    p.354, cited in L.Perlitt, Vatke und Wellhausen, BZAW 94,
    Berlin 1965, p.204, translation mine.

2   W.Vatke, Die biblische Theologie, I Die Religion des
    Alten Testaments, Berlin 1835.

3   K.H.Graf, Die geschichtlichen Bücher des Alten Tes-
    taments, Leipzig 1866; J.Wellhausen, Geschichte Israels,
    Berlin 1878.

4   H.Palmer, The Logic of Gospel Criticism, London 1968.

5   Cp. R.K.Harrison, Introduction to the Old Testament,
    London 1970, pp.505 ff.

6   The period 1770 to 1840 is chosen because of its convenience as a per-
    iod in biblical studies; I do not mean to restrict the philosophical views
    that I discuss to this period.

7   E.S.Shaffer, 'Kublah Kahn' and The Fall of Jerusalem,
    Cambridge 1975.

8   See Franz Delitzsch, Die biblisch-prophetische Theologie,
    Leipzig 1845; S.Wagner, Franz Delitzsch, Leben und Wer-
    ke, Munich 1978; G.Weth, Die Heilsgeschichte. Ihr uni-
    verseller und ihr individueller Sinn in der offenba-
    rungsgeschichtlichen Theologie des 19.Jahrhunderts,
    FGLP 4, 2, Munich 1931.

9   O.Pfleiderer, The Development of Theology in Germany
    since Kant, and its Progress in Great Britain since
    1825, London 1890, p.307.

10 The standard accounts include G.R.Cragg, The Church in the
    Age of Reason 1648-1789, Harmondsworth 1960; Basil Willey,
    The Eighteenth Century Background, London 1940; idem,
    Nineteenth Century Studies, London 1949.

11 See M.L.Clarke, Paley. Evidences for the Man, London
    1974, Ch.8.

12 R.Lowth, Isaiah: A New Translation. References are to the
    New Edition, Glasgow 1822.

13 Isaiah: A New Translation, pp.lxxviii-lxxix.

14 Ibid., pp.lxxxiv-lxxxv.

15 H.P.Liddon, Life of Edward Bouverie Pusey, London
    1893-7, Vol.1, p.62.

16   H.H.Milman, The History of the Jews, London 1829.

17   A.P.Stanley, Lectures on the History of the Jewish Church, London, I 1863, II 1865.

18   For the history of 'Semler Forschung' see the introduction to G.Hornig, Die Anfänge der historisch-kritischen Theologie. Johann Salomo Semlers Schriftverständniss und sein Stellung zu Luther, FSThR 8, Göttingen 1961. Ernst Barnikol has described Semler as 'ein Aufklärungspietist höherer Ordnung, ein Gegner aller orthodoxen wie pietistischen Zwangsreligion, eben auf Grund seiner Privatreligion und seiner Kenntnis der Kirchengeschichte' in 250 Jahre Universität Halle. Streifzüge durch ihre Geschichte in Forschung und Lehre, Halle 1944, p.76. W.Schrader also emphasises the importance of Semler's personal religion, Geschichte der Friedrichs-Universität zu Halle, Berlin 1894, I, p.481.

19   For what follows, cp. Hornig, op. cit.

20   S.Davidson, The Autobiography and Diary of Samuel Davidson, D.D., Ll.D., edited by his daughter, Edinburgh 1899, p.300.

21   R.Otto, The Philosophy of Religion based on Kant and Fries, trs. E.B.Dicker, London 1931, p.152. German original: Kantisch-Fries'sche Religionsphilosophie, Tübingen 1904; see also Perlitt, op. cit., p.222.

22   P.Handschin, Wilhelm Martin Leberecht de Wette als Prediger und Schriftsteller, Basel 1958.

23   R.Smend, 'De Wette und das Verhältnis zwischen historischer Bibelkritik und philosophischem System im 19.Jahrhundert', ThLZ 14, 1958, pp.107-119.

24   See my Myth in Old Testament Interpretation, BZAW 134, Berlin 1974, Chapter 2.

25   See Ernst Staehlin, Dewettiana. Forschungen und Texte zu Wilhelm Martin Leberecht de Wettes Leben und Werk, Basel 1956, p.11. See also de Wette's own account of how Fries's philosophy enabled him to articulate what he had already worked out for himself, printed in Staehlin, p.180.

26   Otto, op. cit., pp.164 ff.

27   W.M.L.de Wette, Theodor, oder des Zweiflers Weihe, Berlin 1822, I, pp.243-4. The English is taken from Otto, p.168. I have not been able to consult the translation by James F.Clarke, Theodor, or the Skeptic's Conversion, Boston, Mass. 1841.

28 See D.F.Strauss, Das Leben Jesu, Tübingen 1835, English translation by George Eliot, London 1846.

29 Willey, Nineteenth Century Studies, p.234. See the important corrective to Willey's account of Charles Hennell and George Eliot in Shaffer, op. cit., pp.230-2.

30 S.R.Driver, Sermons on Subjects connected with the Old Testament, London 1892, p.23.

31 Idem, The Book of Genesis, London 1904, pp.56-7.

32 Ibid., p.57.

33 F.Schleiermacher, The Christian Faith, Edinburgh 1928, para. 40, 2 p.151.

34 R.A.Johnson, The Origins of Demythologising. Philosophy and Historiography in the Theology of Rudolf Bultmann, Suppl. to Numen XXVIII, Leiden 1974. See also P.Fischer-Appelt, Metaphysik im Horizont der Theologie Wilhelm Herrmanns, FGLP 32, Munich 1965.

35 Expository Times, Vol.LXXI, 1959-60, pp.292-6; LXXII, 1960-61, pp.213-6.

36 Cp. G.Fohrer, History of Israelite Religion, London 1973, pp.17-23; H.Ringgren, Israelite Religion, London 1966, pp. 1-4.

HISTORICAL CRITICISM AND CHRISTOLOGY:
ENGLAND AND GERMANY

by

R. Morgan

I

As the Orontes once flowed into the Tiber, so it seems to-day that the Neckar has flowed into the Isis. English theology over the past fifteen years, like Roman Catholic theology on the Continent and in the United States, has quite suddenly come to terms with relatively sceptical conclusions in the historical study of the gospels. After more than a century of polemic and resistance, the methods pioneered in Germany by Strauss and Baur have become broadly accepted in academic theology, even if the debt is rarely acknowledged, and non-specialists remain angry or perplexed.

In the present century the "history of traditons" work first of Wrede and Wellhausen, and then of the form critics developed this rigorously critical approach, and as Germany has emerged from nearly half a century of comparative isolation her partners have again come to appreciate the value of her wissenschaftliche contribution to theology. J.K.Mozley once wrote of "the prestige that had belonged to the great Germans, almost in virtue of their being Germans" before the First War; but he considered, "it is very unlikely, and is certainly not to be desired, that an era of such concentrated attention to the pronouncements and theories of German scholars will return" (1). Desirable or not, in the 1960s English students of the New Testament assimilated the German tradition more thoroughly than ever before and have played a part in creating what is now the most fully international and inter-confessional area of theological study.

If 1963 marks something of a watershed in English religious thought, its symbol must be Honest to God. But so far as the English theological student's perspective is concerned, the more appropriate symbol would be Dennis Nineham's Pelican Commentary on Mark. Most English students still come to theological questions through the historical and critical study of the New Testament. They are now made sharply aware of historical scepticism in what is for many the first theological book that they read. This was not the case for those of us who were initiated into the study of the gospels through the works of such equally distinguished scholars as Vincent Taylor, H.E.W.Turner and C.E.B.Cranfield.

Professional New Testament scholars have of course been discussing German critical work from the beginning of the present century - and even before, as the examples of Lightfoot and Hatch show. But the once formidable language barrier has far from disappeared and the translation industry still provides the best indicator of what is being read widely and forming a climate of opinion. It shows what students are being told to read, and what publishers can sell sufficiently to remain in business. (There has never been much actual profit in publishing German theology in England).

This indicator shows that even during what Mozley described as "the highwater mark of German influence upon British theological scholarship and opinion" (loc. cit.) before the First War, the two countries were already drawing apart again. The gospel criticism of the older liberal Protestants was being cautiously assimilated, but the more radical impulses were not. The widespread failure to understand form criticism after the First War was rooted in an earlier lack of enthusiasm for its history of religions and history of traditions presuppositions. R.H. Lightfoot's Bampton Lectures, History and Interpretation in the Gospels (1935) remained the exception. Dibelius' From Tradition to Gospel (1919) appeared in English in 1934, but was not widely welcomed (see below, p.95 f). Bultmann's classic, The History of the Synoptic Tradition (1921[1] 1931[2]) was not translated until 1963. Equally telling, Wrede's Messianic Secret in the Gospels (1901), the significance of which can scarcely be overrated, was not translated until 1971. Wellhausen's Introduction and commentaries on the Synoptic Gospels were admired by J.M. Creed, but have never appeared in English. Neither has K.L. Schmidt Der Rahmen der Geschichte Jesu. Other classics from this golden age of historical criticism which have only recently become available include J. Weiss Jesus' Proclamation of the Kingdom of God (1892[1], 1900[2]; Eng. tr. of first edition, 1971), and W. Bousset Kyrios Christus (1913[1], 1921[2]; Eng. tr. 1970). To complete the picture, Strauss' Life of Jesus (1835, Eng. tr. 1846) was reissued in 1973 - and at last received favourable reviews.

These books have all decisively contributed to the shape of gospel criticism to-day. This overdue translation is a sign of how rapidly the "Wredestrasse" which in 1956 T.W. Manson could still call "the road to nowhere" (2) could be said by the late Norman Perrin (a former pupil of Manson) in the 1960s to have "become the Hauptstrasse" (3). During this period the American market has become the decisive factor and some Roman Catholic biblical scholarship has caught up with the best of Protestantism (4). In consequence of this new spirit of ecumenical and international collaboration the important German language work on the gospels during the past generation by such writers as Käsemann, Bornkamm, Conzelmann, Kümmel, Schweizer, Tödt, Hahn, and many others, was rapidly translated. All these scholars presuppose the history of traditions methods developed by Wrede, Wellhausen and their successors, which had such little impact in England until the 1960s. English adjustment to the wider critical consensus has been neither painless nor complete, and one may question how much of a consensus exists. But a book like the conservative evangelical symposium, New Testament Interpretation, Essays on Principles and

Methods (1977) edited by I.H. Marshall, shows what a remarkable change of front has occurred.

It would be interesting to trace in detail the change in the climate of opinion about the gospels' historicity during these past fifteen years. It certainly constitutes one important factor in the recently renewed debate about Christology. The question of the relationship of history and dogma has been posed afresh in England in a changed critical as well as a changed philosophical climate from two generations ago.

The most striking difference between this current debate and the otherwise somewhat similar English debate in the first quarter of the present century, is that our Anglican grandfathers were not willing to give up the doctrine of the Incarnation. As J.K. Mozley observed, looking back to this period at the end of his life: "That in Jesus the divine Logos was incarnate, has always been the most firmly held conviction of the English theologian" (5).

This is no doubt an exaggeration. "Always" is a long time, and many English theologians have not been Anglicans. But "from Gore to Temple" (6), the fifty years from Lux Mundi (1889) to the Second War, the doctrine of the incarnation stood at the centre of much Anglican biblical, doctrinal and philosophical theology (7). The concern of this essay with some finally unsatisfactory biblical scholarship ought not to obscure the more creative work done in other departments. If the incarnation is "the basis of dogma" (to borrow Moberley's phrase from Lux Mundi) this is partly because it holds together philosophical and historical thought in doctrinal theology, and partly because it unifies christology and soteriology at the heart of an all-embracing vision of God and the world. In A Study of Religious Thought in England from 1850 (1933) C.C.J. Webb writes of "the central doctrine of our religion, that of the redemption of the whole of human life through the coming in the flesh of the eternal word of God" (p. 187).

If this doctrine is no longer considered central, and is even denied by a few Anglican theologians to-day, its decline is connected with the eclipse of idealist metaphysics as well as with the more sceptical climate in gospel research. The purpose of this essay is neither to revivify idealism (which may well be possible) nor to challenge historical scepticism about the gospels, but nevertheless to clear some of the ground for a modern view of Christianity in which the christological dogmatic formula "truly God, truly man" remains central.

Recent discussions have reminded us of what nineteenth-century theological idealism and also the "modernist" crisis in the Church of England made clear: that the word "incarnation" is used in a variety of ways within Christian theology. It may be used quite formally to refer to the mystery of God's presence in Christ (which is beyond all our conceptualizations), or it may be taken more descriptively as implying something about the mode of that presence. In the latter case it is often taken to refer to the hypostatic union, i.e. to particular patristic (or other) theological interpretations of the mystery, or else to refer to the more mythological narrative expressions of it common in worship. Confusions about "the myth of God incarnate" stem not so much from the ambiguities in the word "myth", as from a failure to distinguish the different levels on which the word "incarnation" may be used. It would aid clarity if instead of speaking of "the incarnation" or even "the doctrine of the incarnation" theologians spoke of "the mystery of the incarnation" to refer to the reality of God in Christ, "the myth of the incarnation" to refer to its narrative expression, "the patristic (or medieval or whatever theology is being specified) doctrine of the incarnation" to refer to particular theological articulations of orthodox definition of Jesus as "truly God, truly man" which requires interpreting in a particular theology, whether that of the Greek Fathers who formulated the definition or some more recent theology developed by later Christians who have inherited the classic definition.

These distinctions, and especially the distinction between the quite formal dogmatic definition of the divinity of Christ and the necessary attempts to make this intelligible in an actual Christology, are necessary if the tangle of interrelated questions is to be sorted out. For example: whether or not such narrative formulations as "he came down from heaven" are necessary or desirable is a serious question. Some protest against treating mythological formulations as historical fact is legitimate even if both protesters and defenders are sometimes blind to the possibility of truth being found outside rationalistic modes of expression. Neither history nor dogma are sufficient in religion, but mythic formulations are in danger of being misunderstood by friend and foe alike when taken out of their proper context in worship and ritual.

The necessity and status of myth in religion is a question which contemporary Christology should not ignore. But a more central question to-day is what kind of continuity with the Christianity of past ages is to be expected. Very different theologians such as E. L. Mascall and T. F. Torrance in Great Britain, who continue to work with the categories of patristic doctrine, obviously expect a more closely defined continuity with the past than those who accept the dogmatic definition but build into their incarnational christologies the results of modern historical research, and consequently use different language from the Fathers and Reformers while reasonably claiming to be expounding the same Christian mystery. Against both these possibilities, such very different neo-liberals as Dennis Nineham and Don Cupitt are prepared to make a definite break with the classical dogmatic formulations. This was an exciting new development in the eighteenth and nineteenth centuries in Germany and was first explored in the seventeenth century in England. It is in full recognition of its strengths as well as its weaknesses that Protestant theologians who have learned from Barth, such as Jüngel (8), Moltmann (9) and Klappert (10), and historically sophisticated Catholic theologians such as Schillebeeckx (11) and Kasper (12) have preferred to develop incarnational christologies in new ways. This brief bibliography contains suggestions how the way formward favoured in this essay can be worked out in a proper Christology.

The point at which nineteenth and twentieth century theology has been faced most dramatically with the problem of continuity with the Christian past has been in the question how important the human historical figure of Jesus is for Christianity. Traditional Christianity, enshrined in the dogmatic formulation "truly man" has always insisted upon this. Logically dubious phrases such as "the fact of the incarnation" and "a historic incarnation" are generally intended to underline this orthodox Christian belief in opposition to some modern emphases upon "the idea" at the expense of the history. We shall find that some modern theology is prepared to abandon the claim that it is in the human historical figure that God is (somehow) to be known. This constitutes a major break with all orthodox Christianity of the past, and (in my view) places a question mark against the whole development which led to it, and provides a stong incentive to return to the tradition.

The traditional claim that God is to be known in and through a human historical figure, implied by the dogmatic formulation "truly God, truly man", itself invites historical research. It also seems to promise that such research will tell us more about God. But that would only follow if Christian knowledge of God in Christ were at least in part mediated through modern historical research. It certainly was and is mediated through history, and nobody who values history can afford to despise modern historical research. But it remains an open question how far if at all this can mediate a knowledge of God. The question leads into the philosophy of history, where the theologian may well have his own opinons. But so long as these are not generally shared by historians he cannot both claim credit for having developed this particular point of contact with contemporary thought and also go away and do history on his own terms. In Western culture today he is compelled to distinguish clearly between historical and theological statements, and this surely undercuts any attempt to derive knowledge of God from modern historical research.

Even if historical research does not mediate a knowledge of God it would he absurd to suppose that such research is quite irrelevant for Christian faith. It could in principle prove very destructive by showing that Jesus was utterly different from what Christians had always thought and quite unworthy of religious veneration. But if historical research is given a positive role in directly confirming belief in Jesus Christ, this belief is likely to be reduced to human historical terms.

It has been necessary to preface the following discussion of some English and some German Christology with a declaration of interest in an incarnational version of Christianity, i.e. one centred on the orthodox Christological definition "truly God, truly man". No attempt is made here to work this out theologically. The English theologians considered below presupposed more of the patristic theology than many to-day would wish to defend. Like the older apologetics they also sometimes confused historical and theological statements. Rightly insisting that Christian incarnational belief refers to a contingent patch of history, they vainly expected modern historical research to confirm their belief. Against this the best way forward would seem to be to combine the characteristically German clear distinction between history and dogma with the English insistence upon the incarnational structure of Christianity. But no attempt will be made here to develop a full Christology. In defending the dogmatic formulation "truly God, truly man" this essay takes it quite formally as no more than a rule which dictates the structure of orthodox belief and invites theologians to make sense of it for their own age. It is epitomized in such biblical phrases as Mt 1.23 "God with us" (naming Jesus) and 2 Cor.5.17 "In Christ God was reconciling the world to himself". Such phrases may be understood in different ways, but they insist that in Jesus we have to do with God himself. However diversely Christians have expressed their conviction they have from the beginning believed that in Jesus they are confronted and claimed by God. Incarnational formulae require theological articulation, but first they direct the theologian to h o l d   t o g e t h e r his Christian doctrine of God with his Christian evaluation of Jesus, and they direct him to h o l d   t o g e t h e r the Christian evaluation of Jesus with the earthly reality of the man from Nazareth.

As it lies beyond the scope of this essay to attempt a theological interpretation of the dogmatic formulation, so there is no intention of showing how such incarnational formulae also help orthodox Christians to h o l d   t o - g e t h e r traditional Christian belief with the sacramental and spiritual (including moral) practice which provides most of its experiential basis. The essential relationship of the dogma to the life of the Christian community (emphasized by O. C. Quick) has been insufficiently considered in the recent debate. But it needs no more than a mention here where the aim is simply to defend the traditional incarnational s t r u c t u r e of orthodox Christianity. Historical study and other contemporary experience is demanding quite new theological explication of the dogmatic formula "truly God, truly man", but that is not our purpose here.

The more immediate purpose of this essay is to clear the ground for such a stance by contrasting two unsatisfactory types of approach to the problems posed for Christology by historical criticism. Both the "orthodox English" and the "German liberal and kerygmatic" approaches seem to be inadequate. But both are strong where the other is weak. Contrasting them should therefore prove instructive, and strengthen the case for a "theological common market" between our two countries.

II

The different philosophical and theological traditions in England and Germany (13) can be presupposed as we consider the impact of the latter in the theologically most sensitive area of gospel criticism.

The rapid development of historical criticism of the gospels in Germany, following the epoch-making L i f e o f J e s u s of D.F.Strauss (1835), coincided with a period in which Anglican theology deliberately resisted German influence (14). Bishop Marsh's translation of Michaelis' Introduction to the New Testament (1793-1801) was the product of a more open era. The young Connop Thirlwall's translation of Schleiermacher's Critical Essay on the Gospel of St. Luke (1825) was not approved and is said almost to have cost him his bishopric. For about fifty years after Pusey's youthful indiscretions (15) the doors of the English Church were fairly firmly bolted against "German rationalism", "anti-supernaturalism", "infidelity" and "poison". George Eliot's translation in 1846 of Strauss' book was considered an anti-Christian act; she also translated Feuerbach. In England it was not taken up and corrected by a Baur, a Wilke or a Weisse; and none of their gospel criticism was translated. It did not lead in this country to a Holtzmann or to the development of a powerful tradition of historical theology such as is found two generations later in German liberal Protestantism. The very few Germanophiles to be found within English university, i.e. Anglican theology, such as Mark Pattison and A.P. Stanley were not biblical scholars, and Jowett avoided New Testament topics after the furore which followed Essays and Reviews (1860). This book, and even more Colenso's work on the Pentateuch (1862), confronted the English church with the problem of biblical inspiration, but did not touch upon the questions raised for Christology by a radical historical criticism of the gospels.

In the 1870s the iron curtain began to be lifted. A group of liberal churchmen sponsored the "Theological Translation Fund" which was intended to make available for English readers the more liberal products of German protestant theology. Two of the earliest titles selected were Baur's Paul (1873 and 1875) and his Church History of the First Three Centuries (1878-9). These are without doubt two of Baur's greatest works, but it is perhaps significant that neither his nor Holtzmann's (much less Bruno Bauer's) gospel criticism was ever translated. The interpretation of Paul has never greatly excited or alarmed Anglicans except where historical reconstructions of the development of the ministry have impinged upon their view of the episcopate (16). The history of the apostolic age could be surveyed coolly except where it involved naturalistic denial of the resurrection (17). But even the "immediately outlying buildings" to "the House of The Lord", namely second century Christianity, seemed to Bishop Lightfoot "to justify the expenditure of much time and labour in 'repairing a breach'" made by "the destructive criticism of the last half century" (18), if the historicity of the gospels was threatened.

That Baur's late dating of the gospels could be used to undermine their credibility was made plain to the English public by the anonymous work Supernatural Religion (1874). The purpose of the author (W.R. Cassels) was to advocate a liberal, non-miraculous view of Christianity. In pursuit of this aim he wished to deny the historicity of the gospel miracles, and used the supposedly late date of the sources as an argument in support of this position. Bishop Lightfoot's reply shows how very closely orthodox belief was still tied to a confidence in the historical reliability of the gospels. He saw in this attack upon the historical credibility of the gospels "an elaborate and systematic attack upon Christianity" as such (19): "I cannot pretend to be indifferent about the veracity of the records which profess to reveal him whom I believe to be not only the very Truth but the very Life" (pp. viii f.). Because the gospels were "the records of the divine life" it was of fundamental importance that they were accurate.

It is not surprising that Lightfoot expended so much time and effort in defending "the authenticity and genuineness of the Fourth Gospel" (20). He argued his case on critical grounds but "could not have you think that I am blind to the theological issues directly or indirectly connected with it" (p. 43) and therefore ended with a "brief confession of faith ... that Jesus Christ is the Very Word Incarnate". He was therefore happy to be able to conclude that "this most divine of all divine books was indeed the work of 'the disciple whom Jesus loved'" (p. 122). The traditional view of Jesus as the incarnate Logos could be held together with one's historical reconstruction, - so long as the Fourth Gospel provided true history. St. John had restricted his Logos theology to his Prologue, but his subsequent historical narrative was congruous with this. Christians too would distinguish the history from the later dogma of the creeds - but it was considered important that they were congruous.

It is in retrospect clear that Lightfoot's claim to have addressed himself to "the theory of the Tübingen school, either as propounded by Baur or as modified by later critics" (p. 42) was only very partially justified. The strength of Baur's criticism of the Fourth Gospel lay not in his assessment of the external evidence and his chronology of second-century Christianity (which proved mistaken), but in his internal analysis of the contents, much of which is still instructive. Lightfoot's linguistic arguments for a semitic origin of the gospel are also still instructive, but fall far short of proving its eyewitness (and therefore historical) character in the christological material upon which his position depended. In attacking Baur's late dating of the gospel Lightfoot had not answered "those who impugn the genuineness of the canonical Scriptures or the trustworthiness of the evangelical narratives" (p. 14).

The consistency of this position has to be felt if the resistance to its destruction (even to-day) is to be understood. The Fourth Gospel presents a clearly Christian view of Jesus. If this is historically accurate, then Christian claims about Jesus as the incarnate Son of God would seem to be scurely anchored in his historical reality. If, however, it reflects subsequent Christian reflexion, and particularly if this is explained as having come into Christianity from the history of religions background, then Christian claims seem to be threatened. If Jesus really was the incarnate Son of God, then it was natural to expect that honest historical research (as opposed to a tendentious rationalism which excluded the miraculous a priori) would reveal this. Wherever the doctrine of the incarnation has provided the lynch-pin of Christianity, amongst followers of Schleiermacher in Germany as well as amongst Anglicans, the historical criticism of the Fourth Gospel has been the most theologically sensitive area of biblical criticism. Only where an alternative centre of Christianity has been found in a Christ of faith more or less independent of the historical reality, whether as an "idea" or in a Pauline-Lutheran theology of the Word, has this criticism posed no problems.

In England the traditional, divine faith-image of Jesus was first shaken by modern historical sensibilities through Seeley's E c c e H o m o , published anonymously in 1865. Within doctrinal theology it was modified by reference to the limitations in Jesus' knowledge by Gore's Bampton Lectures on T h e I n c a r n a t i o n o f t h e S o n o f G o d (1891). As Streeter commented twenty years later: "Those who would forbid us to consider the mind of Christ as that of an historical individual largely moulded by the special environment and the special culture of His own country, virtually forbid us to allow Him a truly human mind at all. What, then, is left of the 'humanity of Christ' - a humanity without a truly human mind?" (21).

At the beginning of the present century one finds in the English theological literature a more obviously human Jesus, based essentially on the Synoptic Gospels. Lightfoot, Westcott and Hort had made a bridge-head for New Testament criticism within the English Church and theology and the meetings of the biblical Revisers' Committee (1870-81) provide a landmark. But the Cambridge trio were thoroughly conservative in matters of gospel criticism and it was not until the next generation that the problems posed for Christology by the historical study of the New Testament became the burning issue for English theology that they had been since the 1830s in Germany. The first quarter of the present century was a period of some importance in Anglican theology and is worth revisiting during the current discussions of Christology.

The influence of German liberal Protestant scholarship, entering England largely through the Williams and Norgate "Crown Theological Library" as well as their weightier "Theological Translation Fund" already noted, swelled to a climax between 1890 and 1910. A key figure during this period was William Sanday at Oxford, who kept English theology informed about what was happening in Germany. Sanday's change of mind about the authorship of the Fourth Gospel is characteristic of the changing climate in gospel criticism. In T h e C r i t i c i s m o f t h e F o u r t h G o s p e l (1905) he had been conscious of swimming against the tide in defending the tradition, but in T h e L i f e o f C h r i s t i n R e c e n t R e s e a r c h (1907) he continued to reject the "Germanism" of E.F.Scott. In D i v i n e O v e r r u l i n g (1920) he admits that he had been "probably wrong" (p.61) and records how impressed he was by von Hügel's essay on the Fourth Gospel in the E n c y - c l o p e d i a B r i t a n n i c a (1910[11]).

Even more significant for Sanday himself was his change of mind on the question of miracles, in the wake of the controversy which followed J.M. Thompson's book on T h e M i r a c l e s o f t h e N e w T e s t a m e n t (1911).

Here, too, an issue which had long been settled for German liberals is causing furious controversy in England during this period. What was at stake was again the historical rootage of the credal dogma of the incarnation. The ecclesiastical political aspects of this case, as of the furore which followed Lloyd George's nomination of Hensley Henson to the see of Hereford in 1918, and even Bishop Percival's appointment of Streeter to a Hereford canonry in 1914 (for which he was "excommunicated" by the Bishop of Zanzibar) reveal a difference between the institutional setting of English and German theology. Anglican clerics were generally more closely tied to the church leadership than German university professors. The Berlin church authorities could prevent Harnack from examining their candidates who were his students, and theological conservatives could block the appointment of outstanding scholars (notably the pupils of Baur, and later some members of the history of religions school) to theological chairs. But once appointed the German professor was relatively free of ecclesiastical pressures.

It would be scurrilous to suggest that the constraints of a professorial canonry at Christ Church ever prevented English theologians form saying what they thought. But their loyalty as church theologians doubtless encouraged caution. Two features of English gospel criticism during this period during which German liberal protestant research was assimilated are particularly striking. Firstly, it was the more moderate continental scholarship, as represented above all by Harnack, which was assimilated. And secondly, there was no question of giving up the doctrine of the incarnation. These two features are worth pursuing further, because they remain characteristic of the English scene right through to the 1960s.

In his Dryden-like satirical poem on Foundations, which he called "Absolute & Abitofhell", Ronald Knox wrote of J.M.Thompson:

> "Who, setting out the gospel truths t'explain,
> Thought all that was not German, not germane."

Knox wrote his satire before the book appeared and in fact it contains nothing by the Dean of Magdalene. But in Thompson's published work there is no sign of the historical scepticism which was by then again rearing its head in Germany. It was not the stringent questioning of a Strauss or a Baur now reappearing in the methods of a Wrede or Wellhausen which he and his friends found "germane", but the constructive liberal efforts to provide on a basis of the earliest sources sufficient historical information about Jesus for religious needs. Sanday found Harnack more important and attractive than Wellhausen (22). Harnack's famous Preface to Die Chronologie der altchristlichen Literatur (1897) which spoke of a "return to the tradition" in critical judgments after the extravagances of historical scepticism, was often quoted with approval. Addressing the clergy of Chichester on the state of play in 1905, Sanday could assert that "the wholesale scepticism of the times of Strauss and Baur has come to an end" (23).

In Germany the liberal Protestant Jesus picture was subjected to two quite different types of historical criticism at the start of the century. Wrede's Messianic Secret in the Gospels and Schweitzer's 'Skizze' translated as The Mystery of the Kingdom of God (1925) appeared on the same day in 1901. Wrede's scepticism was ultimately more damaging to the life of Jesus theology than Schweitzer's presentation of Jesus as an apocalyptic fanatic, and since the development of form criticism after the War his has proved by far the more important book. It is this approach which, allied with the theological objections to the liberal "quest of the historical Jesus" already adumbrated by Martin Kähler (24) brought about the end of an era around 1920.

Neither the sceptical nor the theological critique of liberal Jesus research made an impact in England, and 1920 was in no sense a theological watershed. But the rediscovery of eschatology was influential in this country, and the theological reasons assisting its reception are instructive. Kerygmatic theology attacked liberal theology, and replaced theological interest in the historical Jesus by a new theological centre. Historical scepticism could be exploited in support of this shift to a more Pauline-Lutheran theology. The rediscovery of eschatology, on the other hand, not only kept the life and teaching of Jesus in the central position it had for liberalism, but also seemed to some English theologians likely to remedy the all too human liberal portraits of Jesus by striking a note of mystery and transcendence.

In Germany the weaknesses of Schweitzer's work were readily perceived. Johannes Weiss was better known and more highly respected. But Weiss remained a liberal in theology, and his criticism of Kantian interpretations of "the Kingdom of God" (25) did not imply a total break with contemporary research. Schweitzer was more dramatic and drew more drastic theological consequences from his historical conclusions. His famous book, Von Reimarus Zu Wrede (1906) was translated by W. Montgomery at the instigation of F. C. Burkitt, and entitled The Quest of The Historical Jesus (1910). Burkitt's recommendation carried weight (26), and the book has remained influential. The effect of fusing this new discovery of eschatology with the common liberal picture of Jesus is apparent in B. H. Streeter's essay on "The Historic Christ" in Foundations (1912). Not everyone approved. In his lengthy review article on this Oxford symposium A. C. Headlam found Streeter's essay the "least satisfactory" in the book: "We recognize to the full the importance of taking account of all forms of speculation and of not ignoring any theory that may be presented; but do we really believe that 'the latest from Germany' is to such an extent a final embodiment of truth that we ought to reconstruct our Christian faith in harmony with it?" (27).

The possibilities of this discovery of the eschatological aspect to Jesus were not lost on those who wished to criticize the liberal Protestant picture. G. Tyrrell, the leading Catholic modernist in this country, gave currency to the new views (which were as much the achievement of Loisy as of Weiss and Schweitzer), and Sanday was also attracted. The mysteriousness of this new transcendent dimension seemed preferable to the liberal historians' modernizations which "seek to reduce the Person of Christ to the common measures of humanity" (28). Their brief attempt to jump from the historians' rediscovery to an orthodox Christology was simplistic (29) though the now common opinion that it is in the area of eschatology that the clearest links between Jesus and early Christian belief are to be found (30) shows that their efforts contained a correct intuition. The dangers of this tactic were clear enough, and the modern churchman C. W. Emmet wrote The Eschatological Question in the Gospels (1911) in order "to remove the widespread impression that the position of Loisy and Scheitzer is somehow more compatible with a full and Catholic Christianity than is that of the Liberal Protestants" (p. viii). At least the latter "portray for us a Christ whom we can unreservedly admire and love, even if it is a little doubtful whether we ought to worship Him. The Jesus of eschatology it is difficult either to admire or to love; worship Him we certainly cannot" (p. 77).

A full consideration of English Christology and gospel criticism during this period would have to explore in detail the impact of catholic modernism. The best English contributions arose from the attempt to hold together the liberal protestant insistence upon the historical figure of Jesus and the catholic modernist recognition of the dogmatic element in Christianity (31). For present purposes it is sufficient to note that however much or little the eschatological question was considered, the result was nevertheless a confident historical picture of the ministry and passion of Jesus. This is what seemed to matter most for a Christianity which centred on the incarnation.

Even a straightforward liberal protestant like J. M. Thompson continued to speak of "the incarnation", and to assume that his position was compatible with orthodoxy. Whether the English modernists' understanding of the doctrine was in fact compatible with orthodoxy became an issue in the later controversy sparked off by the M. C. U. Girton Conference in 1921. The subsequent history of doctrinal commission (1976) upon doctrinal commission (1938) shows how little it was resolved.

Earlier in the century William Sanday was quite explicit that what he was trying to do was to combine the newer historical knowledge with the orthodox christological dogma. He recognized that "the German factor is the most important. What Germany is saying to-day, many circles in Europe and America will be saying tomorrow" (32). There was no evading the moderate historical conclusions which constituted the critical consensus of the day.

The only question was how to integrate these into one's Christology. For Sanday was perfectly clear that he did not want to follow the German liberal protestants into what he called their "reduced Christianity" based purely on the human historical Jesus. He had seen how far removed the liberal protestant Christology was from "the universal verdict of the Church and from traditional Christianity" (33). In both their rejection of the miraculous birth and resurrection, and in their deep reverence towards Jesus, "it might perhaps be said that the general position is like that which we associate with the better Unitarianism" (p.264). Having noted that Harnack "rarely speaks (about Church, Doctrine and Worship) without some disparaging epithet", he remarks, "One is almost inclined to suppose that there must be in Germany a sort of professorial religion which exists rather in the air, in a religious Cloud-Cuckoo-Town, and does not correspond to that of any actual religious body" (34).

The way in which Sanday hoped to get beyond this purely human historical Jesus and to recover an orthodox Christology was by starting with "an irreducible minimum" of historical data about Jesus, left behind after 150 years of criticism: "Grant us so much, and we shall recover what ought to be recovered in time ... what is now left us, we may be sure is built upon the solid rock; the gates of Hades itself will not prevail against it" (p.267).

Sanday's critically assured minimum "contains two things which I believe will be found to be the key to all the rest" which if not yet generally agreed, soon will be. These are "1) That Our Lord really believed Himself to be the Messiah, and 2) that he also believed Himself to be in a unique sense Son of God. There may be dispute over what we mean by 'unique sense'. It is allowed that our Lord Jesus Christ drew a clear distinction between Himself and all the children of men. That is the foundation stone of the Creeds. Grant us that, and the rest will follow. These two concessions are my second ground of hope. They are axioms which I conceive bar the way against any further fall. The Christian faith can, I believe, be reconstructed out of them" (35).

The vulnerability of such an approach is obvious. These were not axioms; they had in fact been challenged by Wrede's thesis that the belief in Jesus as Messiah was the product of Christian post-resurrection faith, and not rooted in Jesus' selfconsciousness. Sanday took Das Messiasgeheimnis in den Evangelien very seriously (36), and rejected it with uncharacteristic vehemence. He noted its "independece, its originality and the newness of the questions which it raises" But he "consider(s) it to be not only very wrong, but also distinctly wrong-headed" (37) "Wrede has directness and ability, and he never minces matters; as I have said, he belongs to no school and repeats the formulae of no school. But he writes in the style of a Prussian official. He has all the arrogance of a certain kind of common-sense. His mind is mathematical" (p.77). Sanday sees in him a symbol of what is bad in German criticism: "that unfortunate spirit of perpetual carping" (p.76 n.).

Wrede's hypothesis fared little better in Germany until Bultmann supported it (38). There was plenty of scope for disagreement (39). But more important for present purposes than Sanday's arguments against Wrede and the complacency with which Schweitzer's reply in The Quest of the Historical Jesus was generally accepted in this country, is Sanday's comment on the Messianic secret hypothesis: "Such was the way the early

Church glossed over the flaw in its own title-deeds"
(p. 74, my italics). Nothing less than Christianity itself was held to be at
stake. If the Christology of the Church was not rooted in the historical life
of Jesus Christian belief would be undermined.

Stated in this way few would disagree. Reimarus' explanation of the emergence of Christian belief as a fraud consciously perpetrated by the apostles
implied a massive "flaw in the title-deeds". Such a complete break between
Jesus and Christianity is incompatible with the traditional doctrine and
shows that the doctrine of the incarnation can (in principle) be falsified. But
the real question is how much and what kind of roots Christian belief needs
in Jesus. The question dominated German discussion in the 1950s and
1960s (40). We shall turn shortly to the German form of this question in
terms of "continuity" or identity (or not) between the Jesus of history and
the Christ of faith. What characterizes the more conservative English
scholars under consideration here is that their affirmation of the doctrine
of the incarnation discouraged them from starting with the historian's
distinction. They started with the Church's faith in Jesus as Lord and God
and sought to integrate the results of modern historical research into this.
Sanday saw that "the very grave problem which lies before the Church of
England at this moment (i.e. 1905) is how to appropriate and assimilate the
really valuable material in the writings of (the German liberal Protestants)
without relaxing our grasp upon our own fundamental beliefs" (41). This
naturally led them to be happier with historical conclusions about Jesus
more or less compatible with their traditional faith-image of him. This
faith image might be modified slightly in the process, as Gore had shown.
The Johannine picture of Christ might be replaced by a more Synoptic picture, but the historian's results and the believer's faith picture of Jesus
were expected to co-incide. Only if an equilibrium was achieved between
the historian's results and the believer's view of Jesus was the doctrine
of the incarnation considered safe. The gospels had provided past ages
with some such equilibrium between "knowledge" of what Jesus was like
and belief in him. Historical study was expected to secure this, not to
destroy it.

This attempt to maintain the doctrine on the basis of the historical evidence
was a continuation of Lightfoot's work. But in his case a conviction about
the essential historicity of the Fourth Gospel made the equilibrium between
the historian's and the believer's picture of Jesus relatively easy to maintain. One can see why a conservative such as Tholuck in Germany could
consider the apostolic authorship of the Fourth Gospel a matter of life and
death for Christian faith (42), and why Headlam continued to champion
"The Fourth Gospel as History" (43). Even today Christian apologists
grasp at the straws provided by the undoubted existence of historical traditions in the Fourth Gospel and argue for as early a date as possible,
even when they know that the christological heart of this work cannot be
defended as the actual words of Jesus.

Sanday's hope of moving directly from history to dogma, and finding "the Deity of Our Lord Jesus Christ as expressed in the Gospels" (44) was sustained by an attenuated idealism which presupposed a continuity between God and man: "when once we assume that our Lord Jesus Christ thought of Himself as Son, thought of Himself as T h e Son, thought of God as in a peculiar sense H i s Father, or T h e Father, all the essential data are before us" (p. 138). He found "little indications, strangely delicate and unobtrusive ... that in spite of the humble form of His coming He was yet essentially more than man ... It is the unclouded openness of the mind of the Son to the mind of the Father that was the essence of his being". Despite "these fundamental facts, so human in their divinity and so divine in their humanity" (pp. 141 f.), it is doubtful whether such a "unity of will" satisfies the orthodox dogma, and certain that it owes more to Johannine theology than rigorous historical research.

Sanday was at least aware of the threat to his position by a more sceptical gospel criticism; he entered into debate with Wellhausen (pp. 155-61) as well as with Wrede. The same cannot be said of A. C. Headlam who published T h e L i f e a n d T e a c h i n g o f J e s u s t h e M e s s i a h in 1923 without any reference to the Synoptic criticism of Dibelius, K. L. Schmidt and Bultmann. He described this book as part of an attempt "to put the case of the New Testament leading to a belief in a Divine Christ merely on the grounds of true history" (45). Headlam's simplistic view of the relation between history and dogma is particularly clear in his Preface to the second edition (1927). He recalls that he had concluded "that the Gospel narrative was trustworthy, and that it implied an estimate of the person and work of Jesus inconsistent with a mere belief in a humanity, however elevated. In fact an elevated and sinless humanity probably in itself implies a more than human nature. Jesus was not simply human" (p. xviii). Headlam seems to think that historical work will take him that far, because he goes on to say that "Such an investigation was a preliminary to discussing the more theological questions, 'What think ye of Christ, whose Son is He?'"

The incarnational presuppositions of Headlam's position become clear when he insists "that the Jesus of history was i d e n t i c a l with the Jesus of faith, that the conception of Christ expressed in the historical creed of the Christian Church was a t r u e i n t e r p r e t a t i o n of the Gospel narrative" - by which he means the historical reality of Jesus - "and that the foundation of the Christian Church as the great instrument for the salvation of mankind expressed the aim and purpose of Christ's ministry" (i b i d . Italics mine).

That the creeds give a true interpretation of Jesus, and that the Christian confession refers to the historical figure of Jesus is implied in incarnational belief. Whether this can be secured by modern historical research, much less proved (as Headlam seems to imply) is another question. Even if one thinks of divinity in terms of perfect humanity such a perfect humanity would be impossible to verify historically. Even that can only be a matter of belief (46). But the story of gospel criticism from Reimarus and Strauss to the present day, and especially the history of traditions research of the present century, underlines the difficulty of supporting a theological account of Jesus by appeal to the results of historical research. Even if one defines divinity in a way that is in principle open to historical observation, anything in the gospels which lends direct support to a Christian evaluation of Jesus is likely to be judged a product of such evaluation, the reflexion of the Early Church's belief rather than a historically accurate reminiscence of Jesus. The gospels are the product of Christian faith and were written to support Christian faith. They undoubtedly contain more or less historical information about Jesus, but this has to be dug out of sources whose intention and pre-literary history threatens their historicity at precisely the points most directly interesting to the Christian theologian. This is the basic weakness of the English apologetic considered above. The logic of historical criticism was working against it, and was bound to destroy it, even if this did not become plain until the 1960s.

The situation is particularly clear in the fulminations of Headlam. He had a long record of polemicizing against historical scepticism. His "method" was to identify this with "Baur and Tübingen" and to trade on the common English belief that Lightfoot had destroyed Baur, together with the general German awareness that subsequent research had corrected his results (47). He mostly ignored the more recent German scepticism, and asserted in his Preface to the second edition (1927) of The Life and Teaching of Jesus the Christ that "During the last fifty years almost every theory which was supposed to justify a sceptical attitude regarding the records of our Lord's life has been disproved. The historical character of the Gospel narrative has been vindicated and the record shown to be trustworthy" (p.xx). Even the miracles were vindicated. Only a prior conviction that Christ was merely human caused critical doubts. Headlam did not accept that so far as modern historical method is concerned this stance was inevitable, and episcopal duties left little time for keeping up with German scholarship. However, the translation of Dibelius' form critical work into English in 1934 called for action. He wrote a review article (48), and a new preface to a third edition (1936) of his own book.

Old age had not mellowed his style: "Dr Dibelius' book is the last of those which have been thrown at our heads by those English theologians whose idea of the attainment of truth is to accept without criticism the latest German book" (49). More interesting than his judgment on this "really quite worthless criticism" (p.283) are his thoughts on "the different mental attitude there is about the Life of Jesus in German critical circles and among ourselves. We are brought up to accept the life of Jesus revealed in the gospels as historical. We believe that it is true history unless the contrary is proved, and our religious position is built on that belief. The critical position which Dr. Dibelius clearly inherits is that no part of it is historically true unless it can be proved so. The religious position of the early Christians is based on the preaching of a gospel, and that gospel created the life of Jesus. What created the gospel is very hard to discover. Dr. Dibelius' work therefore, which to us seems destructive, would, we believe, in German circles be looked upon as

constructive. To most English readers he would seem to be devoting himself to destroy the credibility of the gospels. He would, I think, claim to
be supporting it" (p. 282. My italics).

This quotation shows Headlam's awareness of the underlying theological
differences between the two traditions. English Christianity was still
centred on the gospels; German theology since the First War owed more
to Paul. Behind the English interest in the gospels stood a belief in the incarnation which could still be thought to arise naturally from historical
study of them. Although German liberals of the previous generation had no
such interest, a theologian like Sanday could find common ground with them
because they were at least interested in the historical reality of Jesus.
English theology had, sometimes ungraciously, "given up much of what we
have held to be sacred and true" (50). Biblical scholars had settled for a
Jesus suspiciously close to that of the liberal Protestants, even where they
denied denying the miracles. Phrases such as "the divine Life" had long
since disappeared, even if the doctrine of the incarnation was still asserted.
But now the Germans were hopelessly out of step again. If they had once
known Jesus according to the flesh, yet knew they him so no more: "Dr.
Dibelius tells us that the Christian Church created the historical Jesus and
takes from us not merely the supernatural Christ, but the great teacher
who transformed the basis of human morality, and what Dr. Sanday called
'The sweet and blessed figure of Jesus of Nazareth'" (p. 282).

In order to see whether there is any justification for this remark it is
necessary now to turn to a very different German tradition, where sceptical historical criticism of the gospels appears to have caused no anxiety
about Christology.

III

Historical theology made a far more rapid advance in Germany than in
England. The century from 1831 to 1930 marks the period in which it made
its decisive impact upon Christian theology. Nowhere were the implications
of historical study for Christian thought more evident than in Christology.
The significance of Strauss and Baur in this context is that they connected
(in different ways) the approach to Christology typical of the Enlightenment,
in which historical and theological statements are sharply separated, with
their new and radical gospel criticism. Many of the past differences between German and English historical criticism of the gospels can be explained by the growth of the one out of Enlightenment rationalism and the
other out of ecclesiastical orthodoxy.

The Enlightenment critique of orthodox Christology and its preference for
a human historical Jesus led it to abandon not only the ecclesiastical dogma,
but even the traditional incarnational structure of Christianity, in which
Christian belief in God and Christian evaluation of Jesus are inseparable
and the latter also inseparable from the historical reality of the man from

Nazareth. Instead, German christologies in this tradition make a sharp distinction between the modern historian's Jesus and Christian evaluation of him. Whether the former or the latter is considered the "real" Jesus, this results in a separation which is precisely what incarnational Christology resists.

The Enlightenment approach to Christology in terms of this sharp distinction is a natural one for anyone whose theological thinking is shaped by modern historical critical study of the gospels. It has quite recently become commonplace amongst Anglican theologians (51), since the traditional classical training has been replaced by courses in historical criticism unsupported by metaphysical questioning. The argument of this section is that the Enlightenment type of theological response to the new situation in gospel criticism was perhaps inevitable in the nineteenth century, but that it was an unfortunate development and that English theologians would do better to recover what can be preserved of their own tradition of incarnational Christology instead of following the German liberals along a fateful path. Modern European rationalism almost destroyed Christian orthodoxy by means of a "divide and rule". It separated truths of history from theological statements and thus opposed the christological dogma. But when traditional Christian evaluation of Jesus is separated from the historical reality theologies based on one or the other are likely to prove fatal for Christianity. Anyone who accepts the basic truth of Christianity is therefore well advised to avoid them.

It is now two hundred years since Lessing evaded the censor and published the seventh and most provocative of the Wolfenbüttel "Fragments of an Unknown Author" (52). Albert Schweitzer called the work of Reimarus "perhaps the most splendid achievement in the whole course of the historical investigation of the life of Jesus" (53). This judgment has been more than justified by subsequent twentieth-century gospel criticism. Schweitzer praised Reimarus as "the first to grasp the fact that the world of thought in which Jesus moved was essentially eschatological" (op. cit.). But his even greater significance lies in the extent to which he adumbrated Strauss and Baur and even twentieth century history of traditions research by distinguishing very sharply between the early church's theology contained in the gospels and those elements of the biography of Jesus which could still be detected through the crust of subsequent Christian belief. He recognized that the gospels are like doubly exposed photographs in which the early church's faith-picture has been superimposed upon the historical reality of Jesus. The main programme of twentieth century gospel study has been to distinguish and separate these two (or more) pictures.

In comparison with his recognition of what Strauss was later to call "the Christ of faith and the Jesus of history" (54), and much twentieth-century theology the "historical Jesus and the kerygmatic Christ", Reimarus' mistaken account of how the Christian picture of Jesus arose is insignificant. The "fraud theory" of Christian origins had some plausibility at a time when the apostolic authorship of Matthew was accepted, on account of the evidently secondary account of the guard at the tomb. But this was a false tack and Strauss rightly abandoned it. Instead, he provided a more plausible account of the emergence of Christian faith and the development of "myths" about Jesus in which this found expression. Whereas both his supernaturalist and rationalist predecessors in gospel criticism presupposed the general historicity of what was related (whether or not they accepted it as miraculous), Strauss followed Reimarus in distinguishing clearly between the few historical elements in the gospels, and the material which was the product of Christian faith.

The extent to which modern historical study of the gospels has followed Reimarus, Strauss and Baur is interesting but less important than the various theological responses made to this radical historical criticism. It was bound to cause problems for an orthodoxy which did not distinguish very clearly between historical and theological assertions about Jesus. Orthodox belief distinguished between the "states" of Jesus - his earthly humility and his heavenly exaltation - but not between historical and theological statements concerning his earthly sojourn. Eighteenth century "proofs" of the divinity of Christ from prophecy and miracle depended upon accepting the gospel records as historically accurate and providing a kind of empirical verification of the dogma. Given this fusion of history and dogma, rationalistic historical criticism seemed to falsify the dogma when it cast doubt upon the history.

Those who thought that gospel criticism had destroyed orthodox belief in the incarnation by distinguishing between what Jesus was actually like and how the early Christians thought of him, faced the challenge of reformulating Christology on the basis of the historians' disjunction between the historical Jeus and the Christ of subsequent Christian faith. It was possible to reconstruct Christianity on a basis of the latter alone, or the former alone, or to clarify both of these and then seek to combine them. All three variants of this approach begin by holding apart "the historical Jesus" (i.e. the modern historian's reconstruction) and the "Christ of faith". Such a procedure is necessary in historical analysis of the gospels. Whether it is the appropriate starting-point for Christology is the question posed by contrasting English and German responses.

At the end of his critical analysis of the gospel material in The Life of Jesus (1835), Strauss appended a "Concluding Dissertation" in which he set out to "re-establish dogmatically that which had been destroyed critically" (p. 757). His tactic was to set aside the historical Jesus as irrelevant and build his Christology on the Christ of faith reflected in the mythical material in the gospels. He interpreted this with the help of Hegel's distinction between Vorstellung (pictorial representation) and Begriff (idea), but referred the "idea" not to the historical figure of Jesus, but to the human race. A more radical break with traditional Christianity could scarcely be conceived, and more traditional Christians declined to follow Strauss. But even if his particular interpretation of the Christ of faith was not accepted, his first step of constructing a Christology on the basis of the distinction which historical research makes within the gospel material (historical Jesus material and theology of the early church) has dominated German liberal and kerygmatic theology to this day. And his second step of choosing the Christ of faith rather than the Jesus of history as the basis for Christology was to find different kinds of followers, from kerygmatic theologians to Catholic modernists. Only his third step of interpreting the Christ of faith on the basis of his own left-wing interpretation of Hegel was to prove unpopular - even though it could reasonably claim to be the most consistent development of Hegel's thought.

In the same year, 1835, Strauss' former teacher F.C.Baur published D i e c h r i s t l i c h e G n o s i s in which he also began to develop his Christology in terms of the distinction which he had learned from Hegel between the human historical martyr Jesus and the Christ perceived by Christian faith in the Godman in whom the divine nature is revealed. This second "moment" of faith is mediated by the outpouring of the Spirit in the death and resurrection of Jesus (p. 712, cf. 693-8). Unlike Hegel or Strauss, Baur attempted to find a place for the historical Jesus as well as the Christ of faith in his own Christology (55), and his use of Hegel was very different from that of Strauss. But they both turned to Hegel in their dissatisfaction with Schleiermacher's attempt to identify his archetypal Christ with the historical figure of Jesus. They both considered that the price of a theology based on consciousness was a clear distinction between the Jesus of history and the Christ of faith, and the attribution of divinity to the latter only.

Schleiermacher's Christology is not our concern here. But in that its structure was incarnational in the sense used in this essay, it held together Christian evaluation and the earthly reality of Jesus, and was in this sense similar to the English theologians already considered. As a "theology based on consciousness" it was, of course, very different from that of the English conservatives. But its incarnational structure allowed his successors to develop it in a more traditional direction, even though at the cost of failing to accommodate the results of radical historical criticism.

The (different) uses of Hegel by Strauss and Baur, and their attempts to build their christologies upon his clear distinction between the Jesus of history and the Christ of faith, marks the point at which the German liberal tradition diverges from both Schleiermacher and the English theologians. By his insistence (against Strauss) upon the significance of the historical Jesus for theology, Baur provides a hint of how Hegel's new structure could be developed in a more orthodox direction. One senses the tension between his aim to remain orthodox and his fundamental distinction between the Jesus of history and the Christ of faith when he suggests that Jesus must "somehow" have been what faith took him to be (pp. 716 f., cf. 712 f.). Strauss, by contrast, develops Hegel in a clearly unorthodox direction, with his third step already mentioned. But all three are heirs to Lessing and the Enlightenment's "dirty great ditch" between truths of reason (including theology) and truths of history.

Schleiermacher's solution depended upon the fundamental historicity of the Fourth Gospel and fell victim to Strauss' gospel criticism. The Hegelian alternative of constructing one's Christology in terms of the distinction made by historical research within the gospels provided a neat solution to the problem posed by gospel criticism. Whether or not it was theologically satisfactory, it opened the way for historical research to proceed unfettered by the supposed requirements of incarnational dogma. This route was now pursued in different ways.

Hegelianism soon waned in Germany and subsequent liberal protestantism chose the opposite route to Strauss and built its Christology upon the Jesus of history. Apart from a more sophisticated use of the new historical methods, and an appreciation for religion, nourished by romanticism and a cult of personality, this path was a continuation of the Enlightenment view of Jesus as a noble teacher of morality. Jesus pointed men to God, but was not himself in any sense God incarnate. Whereas the christological dogma had held together Christian belief in God and Christian evaluation of Jesus, these now fell apart.

Wherever this path has been taken the so-called Jesuses of history have generally contained more of their authors' religion or anti-religion than has been admitted. Schweitzer showed this for the Jesuses of ethical idealism and the same is true of more recent revolutionary Jesuses. But all these new Christs of reduced faith, thinly disguised as the products of historical research, are united in their rejection of the christological dogma. The historian's distinction is here being used as a weapon of theological criticism, forged by rationalism and directed against orthodox Christian belief. The liberals' break with traditional Christianity was and still is religiously motivated by Christians who think that this is the best way forward for Christianity in a "secular" or anti-dogmatic culture. Whether any religion can long exist without dogma remains a question, but the novelty of the new proposal can be admired.

The most effective orthodox counter-attack against liberal life of Jesus theology took a fateful form. Martin Kähler's little book T h e s o - c a l l e d
h i s t o r i c a l J e s u s a n d t h e h i s t o r i c b i b l i c a l C h r i s t (1892, 1896[2] Eng. tr. 1964) a c c e p t e d the liberals' distinction but turned it against them by arguing that Christianity was concerned with the latter, not the former. He was himself a conservative theologian with no wish to dispense with the earthly reality of Jesus or the identity of this with the Christ of Christian proclamation (56). He disliked the "Byzantine" expressions of classical Christian dogma but unlike Strauss would have insisted that the earthly Jesus is the subject of the Christian confession, and that is the criterion of an incarnational Christology.

Kähler himself, therefore, was an incarnational theologian in the broad sense defended here, - as were Paul and Luther. It was only the modern historical reconstructions which Kähler questioned, not the significance of the earthly Jesus himself. But his kerygmatic formulations could be adopted in a Pauline-Lutheran theology of the word which was less interested in the earthly reality of Jesus. By his riposte to the liberal life of Jesus theology he actually sharpened the new nineteenth-century option of basing Christology upon the split between the Jesus of history and the Christ of faith.

This was a tempting option, not only because it was compatible with extreme historical scepticism about the gospels, but also because it coincides with a Pauline-Lutheran emphasis upon the preaching of the Gospel, rather than the Synoptic Gospels' picture of Jesus. If the pendulum had to swing, this was the natural direction for a Lutheran reaction against liberal Protestantism to take.

The kerygmatic theology of Bultmann and his successors was able to recover continuities with the thologies of Paul and Luther, and its orientation to proclamation brought renewal to church life even outside German Protestantism. Its sudden eclipse in the late 1960s, however, has revealed its limited appeal outside the narrow circle of theologians shaped by the combination of radical gospel criticism with dialectical theology. Headlam's irritation with Dibelius was not entirely without justification. Christian theology cannot long afford to sit light to the historical reality of Jesus.

This has been widely recognized over the past generation within kerygmatic theology. The consistency of Bultmann's view that the "mere that" of the historical Jesus is all that is necessary for theology has been successfully challenged. His successors have either given up the theological necessity of the historical Jesus altogether (57) or have recovered an interest in the "how" of what Jesus was like (58). In most of these newer developments the sharp disjunction posed by historical criticism between the historical Jesus and the Christ of faith has again been carried over into Christology. Whether modern theologians have followed Strauss and Bousset (59) in denying the importance of Jesus for faith, or whether they have built upon the historian's reconstructions in opposition to the church's doctrinal tradition (as Cupitt proposes), or whether like Käsemann, Ebeling and others they have sought to co-ordinate the Jesus of history and the Christ of faith, most theologians in this tradition have continued to build upon this distinction.

We have seen the necessity of making this distinction in critical study of the gospels. The 'historical Jesus' represents the historian's ideal: The reconstruction of Jesus of Nazareth as accurately as the historian can achieve it. This reconstruction can be no more than an approximation, especially where the evidence is so limited as here. But the "historian's Jesus" is also an interpretation and an interpretation of a quite particular sort. It is an account of Jesus which neither presupposes nor reflects Christian belief. As such it is bound to stand in an ambiguous relation to specifically Christian interpretations of Jesus. Nevertheless, it is a fact of the intellectual life of to-day that both Christians and non-Christians are interested in what Jesus was actually like, and that they pose the question in much the same way, and that they may well reach similar conclusions.

However, the uncertainty of the various reconstructions, some sympathetic and others antipathetic to Christianity, must also be recognized. All these conflicting interpretations of Jesus are less "hard" than was once thought. Certain aspects of Jesus' life, ministry and death, and of the emergence of the early church, can be discussed amongst historians regardless of their evaluation of Jesus, and a few of these questions admit of relatively certain conclusions. What can be known in this way has altered Christians' faith-image of Jesus, as we have seen. But it has not been sufficient to produce a "purely historical" alternative picture. Every fully fleshed-out picture of Jesus, whether Christian or not, involves more than hard historical facts. However rigorously based on historical probabilities, every historical synthesis involves metaphysical as well as historical judgments. Even where Christians have been deeply influenced by historical research, their pictures of Jesus have involved more than history. That was as true of the German liberal Protestants as of the English conservative theologians. This must be emphasised, because it was commonly thought that acceptance of modern historical methods necessarily implied a repudiation of any dogmatic view of Jesus. Because these methods could not recognize divine interventions they were held to imply an anti-supernaturalist view of the world. But our view of the world is not so exclusively shaped by modern historical and scientific method (as understood in the late nineteenth century).

Both the limitations of all historical reconstructions of Jesus and the phenomenology of Christian faith cast doubt upon the enterprise of doing Christology "from below", i.e. starting with a purely historical picture of Jesus and separating it entirely from Christian evaluation, before proceeding to this. There is a sense in which Christology naturally starts with Jesus, and a Jesus viewed historically. But this cannot be a complete picture of Jesus entirely abstracted from Christian or anti-Christian evaluation. And Christology has other starting-points. Our view of God, man and the world, shaped as this is by Christian tradition as well as contemporary experience, is present at the outset.

The attraction of this liberal approach to Christology lies not in the finality of its historical reconstructions, but in the widespread hostility to dogma. The historic Christ was pitted against the dogmatic Christ by men for whom the latter seemed incredible. In this essay we have seen how the evaluation of Jesus preserved in the dogmatic formula "truly God, truly man" has often remained closely associated with the patristic theology within which it first found expression. This particular metaphysical theology to-day seems remote and unhelpful to many who realize full well (against the Ritschlians) that there can be no serious Christology without metaphysics. But we have also tried to suggest that the dogmatic formula may be distinguished from the particular theology in which it was first explicated.

This distinction will seem unhelpful to the liberals who are fundamentally opposed to dogma as such, and not simply to the old Greek theology. But it may help pinpoint the central issue both in the recent English debate about the incarnation and in the past 200 years of liberal theology: whether or not Christianity must have a dogmatic element, and where this is to be located.

The liberals' non-dogmatic Christianity looked moderately plausible in an age when belief in God, and a rather Judaeo-Christian belief in God at that, seemed reasonable to most people. This is no longer the case, and it is arguable that the liberals will have to accept more of the Christian tradition in order to sustain what they wish to retain. Belief in God itself is scarcely credible outside the context (or influence) of a particular religious tradition. It requires something of a dogmatic stance, even though it is shared by various religious traditions. But there is no reason to anticipate its survival in isolation from particular religious traditions. So far as Christians are concerned the heart of their tradition lies in Christology. It is therefore here that the dogmatic element in Christianity may be expected.

The kerygmatic theology with its authoritative, proclaimed Christ itself preserves a dogmatic element in its Christology, if by "dogmatic" one means truths asserted but not accessible to reason. Other modern theologians, trained by modern gospel criticism to do Christology in terms of the distinction between the historical Jesus and the Christ of faith, also introduce a dogmatic element into their christologies when they assert the "identity" of these, or treat the resurrection of Jesus in quite traditional supernaturalistic ways. Against both positions it is possible to argue that the dogma of the incarnation provides a more satisfactory centre and basis for articulating Christian faith.

This dogmatic formula does not claim to explain, but rather to preserve the mystery of God in Christ. It recognizes that the truth about Jesus lies beyond all historical discovery and beyond all theological exposition. But it repudiates, as Christians have generally repudiated, the suggestion that what the historians conclude (even supposing they could agree) provides the deepest truth about Jesus. All the light that historians can shed is to be integrated into theology, but Christians have claimed access to a truth about Jesus beyond the limits of reason alone or anything dreamt of in the historian's philosophy.

The christological dogma does not preempt the theological task of making it intelligible by reference to reason and experience. But it insists that there is something "given" in Christianity, and it speaks of God. Against the Enlightenment and liberal instinct to separate its talk of God from its evaluation of Jesus, the dogmatic formula insists, as a basic rule of Christian theology, that these be held together. The necessity for this is all the more apparent where Christian belief in God can no longer be generally presupposed.

We have seen how certain ways of understanding the traditional dogma inevitably fell victim to modern rationalistic historical research. But the liberal hostility extends to the dogmatic formula as such. The basic objection to it lies in what is considered its insufficient rational justification, i.e. its dogmatic character. Historical investigation of its origins sets up psychological barriers to accepting its truth. But broadly incarnational language is found as early as Paul (and probably earlier) and the early history of Christian thought prior to the formulation of the dogma (and the formation of the cannon) can be understood as the initial period in which the Christian church gradually discovered its identity. In any case the truth of the dogma is not logically dependent upon the history of its formulation. Its truth is rather to be tested by its capacity to shape Christian experience.

The same test must be applied to the modern alternatives to incarnational belief - the christologies based upon the historian's distinction. It is difficult to prove anything here, but there are some indications that the modern alternative leads to a dissolution of the Christian tradition. The equanimity with which some liberals accept this suggests that, while finding much of value in the Christian tradition, they do not accept that there is here something "given" which has unique and final significance for mankind. Again, our vastly expanded vision of the universe makes such hesitations psychologically explicable (60). But it is hard to see how any religion can claim to speak of God without making universal claims. No doubt God is greater than any human account of him, but there is something paradoxical about any believer down-grading his own religion to one amongst others in "the universe of faiths". The perspective of the phenomenologist of religion is no substitute for a religious position.

Some modern Christologies based upon the sharp disjunction have been seen to involve a radical break with the Christian tradition by abandoning the historical Jesus altogether (Ogden) or the traditional Christian evaluation altogether (Cupitt). Such a drastic mutation is no doubt a possibility, but where so little store is set upon continuity with the past a new religion is virtually being proposed. There is no objection in principle to new religions. Japan has lots of them, and new religions always owe much to their matrix. But those who remain with older religions have to draw theological lines somewhere. The Christian community has to go on defining itself over against developments which it cannot accept. Amongst the recent developments it shows no signs of accepting are those which dispense with the historical figure of Jesus and those which abandon belief in God. The socalled secular theology had important emphases to offer, but Christianity remains a religion.

The most satisfactory theologies (from a traditional point of view) amongst those which begin from the historian's distinction, are those which (like Baur's) attempt to retain both the historical Jesus and the Christ of faith. This is not the place for a detailed critique, but it is generally clear that they find it difficult to bring the two sides together, and are often left with a kind of Christological dualism, in some ways analogous to the old Nestorianism. No doubt some will find this preferable to what looks suspiciously like a new form of monophysitism amongst conservatives who fail to distinguish sharply between historical and theological judgments about Jesus. But against both these natural tendencies the incarnational dogma directs theologians to hold together the constituent elements of Christian belief without confusing them. The Chalcedonian alpha-privatives can be reapplied to the new and necessary distinction between history and theology.

One book from the kerygmatic camp reaches out towards an incarnational expression of Christian belief. It is no coincidence that Günther Bornkamm's Jesus of Nazareth (1956 Eng. tr. 1960) is the one product of the Bultmann school which has gained unreserved theological approbation in England. It should be read not as a purely historical exercise, but as a subtle attempt to integrate his historical conclusions, reached on a basis of the historian's necessary distinction between historical and post-Easter theological elements in the Synoptic Gospels, into a Christology which holds together the Christian confession and the historical reality, and so respects one fundamental requirement of the incarnation dogma.

When Bornkamm concludes that "the secret of his being" (das Geheimnis seines Wesens) could "only reveal itself to his disciples in his resurrection" (p. 178) he is able to do justice to the historian's conclusions about the origins of Christology and yet respect the early church's belief that it was Jesus they were talking about. He is able to do justice to the gospel form and "understand why the traditional accounts of Jesus have woven record and confession into one. By this they show that they took Jesus himself, in all his words and even apart from them as the Word of God to the world (Jn. 1.1, 1 Jn 1.1)" (p. 189). The incarnational formulae here are appropriate. Jesus is no longer, as for Bultmann, merely "bearer of the Word"; he is the Word made flesh. And "the mystery of his being" is acknowledged to lie beyond the formulations of either historian or theologian.

Bornkamm's Jesus book shows how a modern kerygmatic theology can be integrated into a fundamentally incarnational structure through a refusal to tear apart the "historical Jesus" and the "Christ of faith". But few kerygmatic theologians have held together the historical reality of Jesus and Christian evaluation of him so effectively as Bornkamm. The historian's instinct is to hold these apart, and when that has been taken as a startingpoint it is difficult to bring them together. The tendency has been to speak of a "continuity" - theological as well as historical - between them (61). Even "new questers" as anxious as Bornkamm to find a theological role for the historian's reconstruction of Jesus within a kerygmatic theology have been left with a kind of "christological dualism" similar to that of Baur, in which the Jesus of history and the Christ of faith are never integrated. Baur thought that his Hegelian metaphysics provided a satisfactory account of their relationship, but despite the justified revival of interest in Hegel Baur has found no followers at this point.

It is common for theologians trained to distinguish between the historical reality of Jesus and early Christian interpretations of him preserved in the New Testament, to insist upon the "identity" of the Jesus of history and the Christ of faith. But this is an unhelpful formulation. It treats ambiguous and abstract phrases as though they were clear enough to be compared and identified. What is presumably meant is in the first place that the early Christian interpretations of Jesus referred to the human historical figure, (which is historically clear enough) and in the second place that some at least of these interpretations are true (which is an affirmation of faith). Attempts to make this affirmation of faith intelligible are surely doomed to failure if they approach this christological task by first reaching historical conclusions about the two terms "historical Jesus" and "Christ of faith", and then try to show how they are related, or can be "identified". Such an approach to Christology in terms of the Enlightenment "split" between the history and the Christian evaluation of Jesus can only bring them together again by sheer assertion. Against this, the dogmatic formula "truly God, truly man" presupposes the "identity" and makes no claim to demonstrate it. It can accept the possibility of historical conclusions (such as those of Reimarus) falsifying it, but within the limits of this negative historical control provides Christians with a guideline for their interpretation of Jesus as the saving revelation of God. Such a guideline is not incompatible with most modern historical conclusions about Jesus and the early Church, and despite the risk involved in accepting this new knowledge no conclusions destructive of Catholic Christianity have survived scrutiny.

The dogma of the incarnation is admittedly a dogma, not a rational conclusion. It goes beyond historical reason but does not contradict it. It is confirmed in Christian experience but not demonstrated by this. The alternative attempt to preserve continuity with the Christianity of the past by a sheer assertion of the "identity" of the historical Jesus and the Christ of faith cannot help but look arbitrary, because it will be natural for the "historical" Jesus to be thought of as the "real" Jesus (62) and the religious evaluation as merely a matter of personal taste. Against this, the incarnational formula insists that the mystery of Jesus for ever eludes our rational grasp. Christians are surely bound to assume that their interpretation of Jesus provides a fuller truth than the historian's method can offer. The latter will offer new insights which no theological account of Jesus today dare ignore. But when it claims to give "the real Jesus", in opposition to the Christ of dogma it is no longer a method offering new insights but a world-view in conflict with traditional Christian belief.

The starting-point of Christology is not historical research, but rather the Christian confession of faith reflected in such incarnational statements as that "in Christ God was reconciling the world to himself", or even such plainly mythological expressions as "for us men and for our salvation he came down from heaven". If it were necessary to choose between a "Christology from below" and one "from above" (which it is not) the latter would be preferable, because it insists that G o d is the ultimate subject of Christology.

In their own historically indefensible way the English theologians of the first quarter of the twentieth century maintained this traditional Christian insight. They preserved the possibility of a dogmatic, incarnational version of Christianity long enough for the Catholic Church to assimilate the new historical knowledge and find ways of integrating this

into the traditional faith. Their own attempts to combine a cautious historical criticism with patristic theology failed to do justice to the new knowledge.
For this reason the doctrinal and philosophical theologians who were less
aware of the new challenge, or less disturbed by it, provided more coherent
accounts of Christianity than Sanday or Headlam.

When Sanday chided Gore (63) for ignoring the achievement of German historical critics his colleague the Regius Professor, Henry Scott Holland
replied that "they are perilous witnesses" (64). "They offer us no Christ
whom we could dream of worshipping" (ibid). By presenting Jesus "as a
purely historical phenomenon ... they necessarily omit the heart and core
of the Christian Creed" (ibid). "They do but illustrate the limitations of
their critical methods which prohibit them from accounting for the religious
value and significance of the Lord Jesus Christ" (p. 131).

This line of argument could be pursued in different directions. Hoskyns and
others thought it provided a way of criticizing liberal Protestantism at a
historical level (65), and of reaching instead historical conclusions more
compatible with the Christian orthodoxy which in fact emerged. But this
was a return to seeking historical causes, if not proofs, for theological
beliefs. It led to a more exciting use of the New Testament, but not to more
convincing historical conclusions. It was theologically justified in holding
together history and dogma, but it hoped in vain to find support for this position in unbiassed historical research. The traditional dogma was maintained in the early part of this century not because such historical apologetic
is cogent but because its religious and philosophical reserves were strong
enough for it to survive the run on its historical credit brought about by the
assimilation of liberal Protestant life of Jesus research. But this threat
has become stronger, contrary to the optimistic forecasts of Sanday. If the
dogma of the incarnation is to be preserved a new tactic is necessary - one
which allows full rein to gospel criticism without abandoning the incarnational structure of Christology.

A more promising development of Holland's remarks on "the limitations
of (the Germans') critical methods" lies not in criticizing them for what
they share with most other historians, but in recognizing the limited scope
of historical work in theology generally. If Christians are to continue to
confess Jesus as divine to-day it will be in despite of the historian's frame
of mind, not thanks to his results. It will mean refusing to allow that historical research can yield the full truth about Jesus. What light it can shed
is not to be evaded. Faith cannot be insulated from the effects of historical
research so long as it remains a faith in God founded in the life, death and
resurrection of one who was a historical figure. There can be no question
of repeating the mistakes of Martin Kähler and Catholic Modernism and
separating faith from history. That would be to ignore the English witness
to what is necessarily involved in an incarnational Christology. But
Christology proceeds from the life, death and resurrection of Jesus.
The Christian belief in God's initiative is there from the outset. As Holland
insisted, "only by starting from the Resurrection does the Life, or its

record, become a revelation, a power, a religion. The criticism which would confine itself to the Life as lived condemns itself to spiritual bankruptcy" (p. 146).

An Englishman who has lived with the ghosts of Baur and Strauss in the Tübingen Stift and who like Sanday "agrees more often with my own countrymen but learns more from the Germans" (66) may be permitted to conclude by quoting from a deeply theological poem by the friend of Hegel and Schelling in that same Stift. After all, it is poets like Browning and (real) philosophers like Coleridge rather than the biblical scholars who have taught Englishmen the value and truth of the doctrine of the incarnation. So with Hölderlein in "Patmos":

> O give us wings of the mind most faithfully
> To cross over and to return.

Footnotes

1 Some Tendencies in British Theology, S.P.C.K. 1951, pp. 47 f.

2 In The Background of the New Testament and its Eschatology, ed. W.D.Davies and D.Daube, Cambridge, 1956, p. 216.

3 Journal of Religion 46, 1966, pp. 296-300.

4 Cf. F.Hahn "Der Beitrag der katholischen Exegese zur neutestamentlichen Forschung", Verkündigung und Forschung, 2/1976, pp. 83-98.

5 Tendencies, p. 29.

6 The title of A.M.Ramsey's useful survey, Longmans, 1960.

7 Cf. L.B.Smedes' The Incarnation: Trends in Modern Anglican Thought, J.H.Kok N.V.Kampen, 1954.

8 Gott als Geheimnis der Welt, Tübingen, 1977[2].

9 The Crucified God, (1972) Eng. tr. SCM Press, 1974.

10 Die Auferweckung des Gekreuzigten, Neukirchen, 1971.

11 Jesus - Die Geschichte von einem Lebenden, Freiburg, 1977[4]. Eng.tr.Collins. 1979.

12 Jesus the Christ (1974) Eng. tr. Barns & Oates, 1976.

13 In addition to the essays by Dr Dyson and Dr Rogerson, see S.W.Sykes, "Germany and England", also printed in this volume.

14 See L.E.Elliott-Binns Religion in the Victorian Era, Lutterworth, 1964[3], p. 182 for evidence of this.

15 An Historical Enquiry into the Probable Causes of the Rationalist Character of the Theology of Germany, London 1828.

16 Cf. J.B.Lightfoot's famous essay, 'The Christian Ministry' appended to his commentary on the Epistle to the Philippians (1868), and the chilly response in England to E.Hatch The Organization of the Early Christian Churches, Oxford, 1881.

17 Cf. R.W.Church's review of Renan Les Apôtres (1866) in Occasional Papers, Vol. 2, London, 1897.

18 The Apostolic Fathers Part II. Vol. 1, London, 1885, p.xv.

19 Essays on the Work entitled "Supernatural Religion", London, 1889, p. 2.

20 Biblical Essays, London, 1893, pp.1-198.

21 Foundations, London 1912, p.75.

22 The Life of Christ in Recent Research (1907), pp.161-71.

23 Appended to Outlines of the Life of Christ (1905), p.259.

24 The So-called historical Jesus and the historic, biblical Christ (1892, 1896[2] Eng. tr. 1964). It is not mentioned by Schweitzer in his Quest.

25 Die Idee des Reiches Gottes in der Theologie, Giessen, 1901.

26 See "The Eschatological Idea in the Gospels" in Essays on some Biblical Questions of the Day, ed. H.B.Swete, London, 1909.

27 Church Quarterly Review, 76, 1913, p.10. Cf. R.Knox Some Loose Stones, London, 1913, p.35.

28 Recent Research, p.88.

29 See Wernle's criticism of Sanday in Theologische Literatur-zeitung 34, 1909, Sp.98-100.

30 E.g. R.Bultmann "Jesus and Paul" in Existence and Faith, Fontana, 1964.

31 E.g. A.E.J.Rawlinson Dogma, Fact and Experience (London, 1915) for a critical reception of E. Le Roy's Dogme et Critique, and W.R.Inge on "Liberal Catholicism" in Faith & Knowledge, Edinburgh, 1904, pp.281-92, and O.C.Quick Liberalism, Modernism & Tradition, London, 1922, - to mention but a specimen Anglican historical, a philosophical and a doctrinal theologian.

32 "The Position in 1905", appended to Outlines, p.261.

33 Outlines, p.263. See also An Examination of Harnack's "What is Christianity?" London 1901. Mozley Tendencies, p.29 notes that Harnack's book was widely read and contained much with which Anglicans could agree: "But the breach with Catholic theology was too clear and too deep for it to be very influential".

34 "The Position in 1903", appended to Outlines, p.250. Cf. Inge: "the English Church is far from being content either with the individualism or with the truncated creed of professorial Protestantism" (op. cit., p.285).

35 Outlines, p.267. Cf. Recent Research, p.138.

36 Journal of Theological Studies, 4, 1904, pp.481-99.

37 Recent Research, p.69.

38 "Die Frage nach dem messianischen Bewußtsein Jesu und des Petrus-Bekenntnis", Z.N.W. 19 1919/20, pp.165-74.

39 For an account of the debate up to 1939, see H.J.Ebeling Das Messiasgeheimnis und die Botschaft des Marcus-Evangelisten, Berlin, 1939.

40 E.g. G.Ebeling Theology and Proclamation, 1962 Eng. tr. Collins, 1966; E.Käsemann New Testament Questions of Today Eng. tr. SCM Press, 1969, pp.23-65.

41 Outlines, p.273.

42 Cf. M.Kähler The so-called Historical Jesus, p.108.

43 The title of his last book, Oxford, 1948.

44 The title of his final Cambridge lecture in Recent Research.

45 In a letter to Fr.Rickaby (1923), quoted in R.Jasper's biography of Headlam, Faith Press, p.138.

46 Cf. S.W.Sykes "Christ and the Diversity of Humanity", The Modern Churchman, 1971, pp.182-91. Also D.E.Nineham's "Epilogue" in The Myth of God Incarnate, SCM Press, 1977.

47 B.g. "Bishop Lightfoot as Historian" in G.R.Eden and F.C.Macdonald Lightfoot of Durham, Cambridge, 1932, p.138. Also Art. "English Theology" in Theologisch Tijdschrift, c.1915, p.147. CQR, 91, 1921, p.329. Etc.

48 CQR, 119, 1935, pp.280-95. Art 'Formgeschichte'.

49 P.293. Cf. CQR 77, 1914, pp.30 f.

50 CQR, 76, 1913, p.168.

51 Contrast the earlier attempt to establish this perspective in The Hibbert Journal Supplement, 1909, Jesus or Christ?

52 Fortress and SCM Press reprint, ed. C.H.Talbert, 1970.

53 Quest p.23.

54 1865. Fortress Press reprint, Tr. and Ed. L.E.Keck, 1977. (The German has also been reprinted, Ed. H.J.Geischer Göttingen, 1971).

55 See Peter C.Hodgson The Formation of Historical Theology, Harper and Row, 1966. I have discussed this in a forthcoming essay, "F.C.Baur" in: Religious Thought in the Nineteenth Century. Cambridge, 1982.

56 Cf. H-G Link Geschichte Jesu und Bild Christi: Die Entwicklung der Christologie Martin Kählers. Neukirchen, 1975.

57 S.Ogden Christ without Myth, Harper & Row, N.Y. 1961.

58   E.g. G. Ebeling Theology & Proclamation, Collins, 1966, pp.54-81. J.M.Robinson A New Quest of the Historical Jesus, SCM Press 1959.

59   The Faith of a Modern Protestant, London, 1909.

60   The importance of this has been rightly emphasized by S.M.Coakley in an unpublished Hulsean Prize essay, Cambridge 1977.

61   Cf. the discussion of Bultmann's essay "Das Verhältnis der urchristlichen Christusbotschaft zum historischen Jesus" (Heidelberg, 1960), by Käsemann, New Testament Questions of To-day. S.C.M. Press, 1969, pp.35-65, and G.Ebeling op. cit.

62   Cf. C.G.McGown The Search for the Real Jesus, 1942 D.Cupitt "The divine Christ - or the real Jesus?" "The Times", 17 September, 1977.

63   Bishop Gore's Challenge to Criticism. London, 1914.

64   "Nature and Miracle". Reprinted in Creeds & Critics, London, 1918.

65   See "The Christ of the Synoptic Gospels" in Essays Catholic and Critical, Ed. E.G.Selwyn, London, 1926.

66   The Life of Christ in Recent Research, p.38.

ANGLICANISM AND PROTESTANTISM

by

S. W. Sykes

The problem with which this essay is to deal can be put as follows: Modern theological history has seen a number of attempts to define the difference between Protestantism and Catholicism in the form of antithetical principles. Very often these definitions have been the work of fully convinced Protestants or Catholics, who have felt no need to locate Anglicanism in the spectrum. The questions therefore arise: Does the Anglican Communion fit in relation to this antithesis as either mainly Protestant or mainly Catholic? Or does the very existence of the Anglican Communion mean that these antithetical principles are too highly abstract and general to be of any theological use or interest?

It is obviously wise to delimit one's aims in a single essay on so large a theme. To begin with the subject is of importance in the theological relations of England and Germany, in view of the prominence of Anglicanism within England and its absence from the German scene. A certain clarification of the ecclesiological stance of Anglicanism, especially in its relations with Protestantism, has, therefore, some value. Beyond that my intention is merely to offer a modest and preliminary introduction to the internal conflicts within Anglicanism - conflicts which play so important a role in its somewhat hesitant and always complex relations with other communions.

The three sections of this essay deal respectively with the Protestant-Catholic antithesis, with the continuously self-modifying process of the Anglican reformation, and with the wider implications for Anglican ecclesiology of that process.

I

The habit of setting out the difference between Protestantism and Catholicism in the form of an antithesis has a long and significant history. One of the most outstanding examples occurs in Friedrich Schleiermacher's 1831/2 Glaubenslehre where the following statement occurs:

> The former (ie Protestantism) makes the
> individual's relation to the Church dependent on
> his relation to Christ, while the latter
> (ie Catholicism) contrariwise makes the

individual's relation to Christ dependent on
his relation to the Church (1).

Numerous other examples occur in books on the "essence of Protestantism"
or the "essence of Catholicism", in which definitions of an even more
appraisive character than Schleiermacher's have barely disguised the contrast between the author's own chosen standpoint and that of its supposed
antithesis.

In relation to these ways of construing the religious situation the Anglican
Church can scarcely exist except as a curious anomoly. An example of this
occurs in an address given by Paul Tillich to the Fiftieth Church Congress
of the Protestant Episcopal Church in 1942. Tillich, manifestly at a loss
how to integrate his discussion of the revolutionary social changes lying
behind the world war to his audience's denominational allegiance, is asking
whether the Anglican Church ("and in a more remote way the Greek Orthodox Churches") would be of help in the process of a transformation of Protestantism which would not in any way involve the loss of "the Protestant
principles". Or, he continues, is "the middle way of the Episcopalian
Church a way of compromise, uniting the weaknesses of both sides" (2)?
The question is significantly unanswered.

Another major twentieth-century theologian appears to have a more positive
solution. Karl Barth, in the section of the Church Dogmatics where
he announces his claim that "Church" Dogmatics means for him Reformed
dogmatics, treats Anglicanism as a branch of Protestantism. He identifies
the Evangelical, or Protestant, church as that church which treats the
"Word of God" as the only possible norm and as distinct from three "heretical" movements, namely Neo-Protestantism, Roman Catholicism, and
Eastern Orthodoxy (3). The Evangelical Church is, according to him, itself
divided between the Reformed, the Lutheran and the Anglican branches,
the Anglicans and Lutherans being regrettably disfigured by certain over-
emphases or distortions. He adds:

> We do not understand the antithesis between Reformed
> and other Evangelical dogmatics in the light of an
> antithesis between Churches which confront each other as
> Church and non-Church or anti-Church. We interpret it
> rather as the antithesis between various theological
> schools or movements within the same Church and its
> basically agreed confession (4).

Barth's inclusion of the Anglican with the Lutheran and Reformed Churches
as belonging to the one, holy, catholic and apostolic Church is no more,
and no less, than an opinion of one major theologian. Barth does not show
himself elsewhere either deeply interested in, or exceptionally well-informed about, Anglican theological history. It remains, according to report,
one of the acknowledged lacunae in his synthetic theological achievement.

In the light of the success of the Oxford Movement's strenuous endeavours
to distance the Anglican Church from its Reformation origins, and set it in

a more profound relation to Roman Catholicism and Eastern Orthodoxy, Barth's unqualified categorisation raises suspicions. Once again, Anglicanism seems to be anomalous; but on this occasion an anomaly which Barth's instinct for tidiness prompts him to consign, without further discussion, to the least inconvenient pigeon-hole. The antithesis between Protestant and Catholic is still axiomatic; Anglicanism on this analysis belongs unequivocally to the Protestant side of the divide.

It is possible for the Anglican response to this history of categorisation to be rather patronising and disdainful. It could be said that it rests on sheer ignorance of the internal history of the communion. It has been frequently remarked that very few German-speaking theologians have any mature knowledge of Anglicanism. Cranmer, Jewel, Hooker, Butler and Maurice are scarcely known to them. Occasionally, when modern English theologians are referred to, it is evident that the writer has little idea whether or not they are Anglicans, or even whether they are English or American.

These complaints, however, rest on an unexamined assumption, namely that it is incumbent in some way for German-speaking theologians to familiarise themselves with Anglican writing. No one organises his reading on the principle of proportional representation. The fault must lie with the failure of Anglicans to create the kind of theological tradition which could not be ignored and which would create a demand for its translation. If Anglicanism does not fit the categories of Catholic and Protestant which have become axiomatic in the history of theology since the Reformation, then Anglican theologians ought by now to have validated their claim to be disruptively different.

Another more serious grounds for distain, however, may lie in the alleged English dislike of forms of theological disjunction. The Entweder - Oder mentality, supposedly characteristic of the supposedly existent "German mind", sees everything (or, at least, as much as it can) in great polar opposites (5). "Catholic" and "Protestant" is simply another such dichotomy; a way of over-simplifying the incredibly complex matter of interpreting divine revelation. Anglicans have, therefore, no grounds for concerning themselves with whether or not they are Catholics or Protestants, or a kind of anomalous hybrid, simply because there are no grounds for supposing that one must be either more one or another. Anglicanism simply exists on a spectrum which is not polarised in that kind of way.

This argument has great force. If one were to ask the question, Is the Anglican Church Protestant or Catholic?, one must first establish that there are some grounds for supposing it must be one or the other, and that the terms "Catholic" or "Protestant" are mutually incompatible designations of a Christian communion.

On the face of it there seems to be a fundamental objection to this kind of polarity. How, if this dichotomy is set up, is one to interpret Eastern Orthodoxy (to which Tillich also referred when discussing the significance of Anglicanism). The phenomenon of Christianity does not display itself as divided into two incompatible interpretative systems, but into a more bewildering and kaleidoscopic variety. Protestantism and Roman Catholicism are primarily Western forms of Christian faith, and it would be typical of Western arrogance and myopia for Western theologians to organise fundamental polarities on the basis of their own ecclesiastical divisions.

This objection, powerful though it is, need not be fatal. What is at issue is the contrast, not between Roman Catholicism and Western Protestantism, but between Catholicism and Protestantism conceived of as theological, or ecclesiological principles. The question whether Anglicanism is Catholic or Protestant is not the same thing as the question whether Anglicanism is more focussed upon Rome or belongs to some imaginary Pan-protestant federation. Rather, it could be argued, what the terms "Catholic" and "Protestant" connote is a basic choice facing those considering Christian faith and its ecclesial character, such that one could only not clearly opt for one or other side by being seriously confused about what it is to belong to the Christian Church.

A political analogy may make the latter argument clearer. A state may be faced with the choice of either going to war with a neighbouring state which is oppressing a minority group racially related to its citizens, or of condoning genocide. No third possibility exists which does not in the end lead either to one or the other. The secret smuggling of arms to the oppressed group, or the provision of sufficient funds for them to mount effective resistence, would certainly lead to a declaration of war by the opposing state. Mere protests to the United Nations would imply a willingness to take the matter no further if that body were powerless to intervene. In such an extreme and polarized situation it might be said that the political reality of the matter exhibited itself as imposing a choice between two mutually exclusive courses of action, such that one could only not opt for one or the other by being seriously confused about what it means to be politically involved.

That, I believe, is the kind of case which could be made in defence of the polarization of religious commitment into "Catholic" and "Protestant" camps. But fortunately it is not essential to decide the question for the present purposes. Here all that is necessary is to treat the matter hypothetically in the following way: Let us suppose that it is antecedently probable that Catholicism and Protestantism are mutually incompatible and antithetical ways of construing what it means to be the Christian Church, and then let us ask whether this view provides us with a plausible and illuminating way of interpreting Anglican history and theology, and of understanding its future task. I concede that this is to rest the essay upon uncertain, or merely hypothetical, foundations. It does, at the same time, lead us to an interesting conclusion.

We turn, secondly, to consider the standpoint of the Anglican church, facing at once a highly controversial question. With reference to what are we to consider its standpoint? At once we are apparently faced with three quite different classes of prescriptive theories:

(i) Theories which see Anglicanism as a form of "undifferentiated Catholicism" - that is, as relying upon and appealing to the beliefs and structures of the primitive and undivided church.

(ii) Theories which insist on the status of the Anglican reformation or reformations, as reconstituting the English church on the basis of pure Apostolic doctrine, and which accord primacy of place to the Scriptures as normative.

(iii) Theories which regard Anglicanism as simply Englishmen (and honorary Englishmen in other countries) going about their religious business as seems right and proper from time to time.

The choice between these three classes of theories only becomes urgent when it occurs that one or other of the different types are simply denied as containing appropriate matter for consideration; as, for example, when it is denied by the ones belonging to groups (i) and (iii) that reference to the events of the Anglican Reformation carry any weight whatsoever. At this stage in the argument it is necessary to establish no more than the fact that it is relevant to the interpretation of Anglicanism that we should consider the events of the Reformation. Here we are assisted by the fact that we are interested primarily in a view of Anglicanism which makes clear the nature of the situation in which it finds itself today, especially viz-a-viz Protestantism. Prescription for that situation is not the immediate goal.

Thus, whether or not Bishop Henson was right in his view that "the key to a right understanding of the modern Church of England lies in a just appreciation of the unique character of the English Reformation" (6), it is to the Reformation that we first turn. Here we are confronted by a further difficulty in delineating the period of time occupied by the Anglican Reformation. In his book entitled The English Reformation, Professor Dickens has reviewed the period 1529 to 1559 (7); the story is taken further by Professor Haugaard in his work Elizabeth and the English Reformation (1968) (8); and it would be a bold man who would deny that in the seventeenth century the Anglican Reformation was yet once again decisively modified. There is, in short, no single event, person or period which as the right unchallengeably or unambiguously to claim to be "the classical period" for the formation of doctrine in the Anglican church.

In this situation the correct course to take seems to be to view the Reformation as a continuously self-modifying process, rather than a single event or series of events. Accordingly my picture embraces the whole period of Anglican history in five major sections:

(i) The grounds and tendencies of the Henrician reformation as furthered by Cromwell and Cranmer, and its relation to the Lutheran reformation.

(ii) The settlement attempted under Elizabeth.

(iii) The 1662 Act of Uniformity, and the Book of Common Prayer annexed to the bill.

(iv) The development of a triadic conflict between latitudinarians, evangelicals and anglo-catholics in the eighteenth and nineteenth centuries.

(v) The impact of biblical criticism and liberal theologies.

What is in view here is the identification of certain leading characteristics of the Anglican reformation, and the history of their subsequent development and qualification. Heavy emphasis must therefore be placed on the fi rst two of the five components which will receive longer treatment than the following three.

(i) The Henrician reformation. In an outstanding recent work which gathers together more than a decade of research, Professor Geoffrey Elton again powerfully argues for two theses; that Henry's reformation was rooted in a distinction between things necessary for salvation and things indifferent (so-called a d i a p h o r a), and that it was essentially a lay reformation, signalling the triumph of the laity in the realm of religion (9). The first of these theses is demonstrated by reference to the crucial work of Thomas Starkey who wrote in 1535 A n e x h o r t a t i o n t o t h e p e o p l e i n - s t r u c t i n g t h e m t o u n i t y a n d o b e d i e n c e (published in the following year at Thomas Cromwell's insistence). Starkey, who had trained in the humanistic atmosphere of Wolsey's college in Oxford and of the University of Padua, was made a chaplain of Henry VIII. The theological position which he developed to be of service to his royal master involved the identification of papal authority as a matter of indifference since it was not expressly commanded in Scripture. Basing himself on Melanchthon he argued that there existed a field of jurisdiction distinct from laws of God and of nature, though growing out of them. In this area it was for the sovereign to make regulations from time to time, subject always to the word of God. At this stage, of course, there is no intention of going the whole way with the German reformation, on whose troubles Starkey offers some rather negative comments. There is, rather, a middle way by which the English nation, under Henry, will "avoid this dangerous division grown in among us, by the reason whereof, some are judged to be of the new fashion, and some of the old" (10). (This concept of the v i a m e d i a is, of course, highly unstable, and subject to varying content, according to what is deemed essential. Nonetheless it became the principle tool of Anglican apologetics in, among others, Jewel, Hooker and Whitgift). Starkey (for whose name we search in vain in the O x f o r d D i c t i o n a r y o f t h e C h r i s t i a n C h u r c h) is, in some respects, the real hero of Elton's picture of the Reformation.

Elton's second thesis is scarcely less interesting, namely that the Henrician reformation, though on the face of it a spiritualization of the authority of the king in substitution for the authority of the Pope, was in fact only consolidated by the act of a lay Parliament. Thus his headship of the church could be controlled, or at least reinforced, by the same means as his secular authority. "Henry might claim to be a lay bishop inheriting the position occupied by Constantine the Great, a claim which effectively spiritualized kingship; in reality he and his subjects behaved as though authority in the church had fallen to a layman" (11). Cromwell and Cranmer saw more accurately than Henry himself that Luther had provided the correct theological interpretation of the actual state of affairs by his doctrine of the priesthood of all believers. It is, therefore, a mistake to treat the Henrician revolution as a mere act of state without theological content, though it was a content only capable of expression in broad terms. Cranmer and Cromwell were clear that the faith of the church should be formulated closely upon scriptural authority, be established by the King in Parliament, and not made the subject of theological quibbling (12).

On both these points Elton deserves very careful consideration. Many writers have recognised the importance for the Anglican church of the idea of few essential articles of faith to be found in scripture. The fundamental articles tradition was used repeatedly by apologists up to and including Newman in his last Anglican writing, The Prophetical Office of the Church. Though the term via media came to be redefined (again by Newman and the Tractarians) as between Papacy and Protestantism, rather than (as by Melanchthon and the sixteenth-century Anglicans) between Papacy and Anabaptism, the conscious moderation of Anglicans in matters apparently involving theological precision has remained both to help and to inhibit it. Further the importance of the laity in Anglicanism, though it did not lead until our own century to the participation of the laity in synodical government, is more deeply rooted than a cursory examination of its doctrines and practices might lead one to suspect. Dickens is amply justified in his comment on the non-implementation of Cranmer's plan to hold annual diocesan conferences attended by laymen as well as clergy, that "it may reasonably be argued that the Reformation failed to break with the feudal character of the bishop or bring him out of his isolation into regular exchange with his flock" (13).

(ii) The Elizabethan settlement. Melanchthon has left an indelible imprint on Anglicanism, not merely in his importance for Starkey's fundamental distinction, but also by means of the contribution of the 1530 Confessio augustana to the formulation of the 39 Articles, via the Wittenberg Articles (1536), the Thirteen Articles (1538) - both of which were the direct result of negotiation between Lutheran and Anglican theologians - and the 42 Articles of 1552 (14).

The reason why the Lutheran character of the Church of England did not receive further reinforcement is largely political. With the death of Luther in 1546 and the defeat of the Schmalkaldic League, German Lutheranism lost such international interests as it had previously (15). The experience of a Mary weaned the exiles of uncritical royalism, and Calvin's influence began to grow. By the 1550's Calvinists of Zurich were evidently anxious to prevent any return to, or growth of, Lutheranism in England. The evidence suggests that it was Elizabeth herself who insisted on modifying the 1552 book in a conservative direction, against further Calvinist influences (16). The outcome of the complex struggles of Elizabeth's reign is a rejection of the totalitarian aspirations of strict Calvinism, and a channelling of the formidable elements of Puritanism which contributed to the English Reformation into practical channels. Haugaard comments on Elizabeth's achievement:

> Elizabeth's solution depended heavily on the ability and
> commitment of the sovereign but, in her hands, the church
> fared well. She refused to allow the clergy to become
> sole arbiters of moral, political, and religious questions
> as both papist and presbyterian would have had it. She
> insisted that an outward liturgical and clerical
> discipline be maintained to protect congregations from
> dissident clerics. She reminded the highest councils of
> the church that ecclesiastical decisions must take account
> not only of 'principle' but also of human reality measured
> in political and social terms. At its worst this could
> mean a Christianity captive to worldliness and political
> expediency. At its best, it could ensure the recognition,
> sometimes absent in religious circles, that the so-called
> 'secular' orders of human life possess an integrity of
> their own. A church which ignores that integrity either
> retreats into irrelevant pious sentimentality, or
> attempts to impose a demoniacal clerical tyranny (17).

(iii) It is hardly necessary to mention the fact that within the restoration, the previous decades of civil and political conflict played a major role. The alliance of episcopacy with the Stuart monarchy in Scotland led, after the fall of Charles I, to a demand from the Scots for an end to episcopacy (18). The resentments created by the overthrow of episcopacy in the Commonwealth period contributed directly to the amendment in the Ordinal, passed by Parliament in 1662, requiring episcopal ordination for any one to be "accounted or taken to be a lawful Bishop, Priest, or Deacon in the Church of England", and the draconian terms of the Act of Uniformity. Professor Norman Sykes commented:

> This statute thus laid down the same conditions for ministers
> of the foreign reformed churches as for Protestant dissenters
> at home wishing henceforth to exercise the ministry of the Church
> of England. No Lutheran or Reformed pastor might be admitted to
> Anglican benefices, with or without cure of souls, until he had
> received episcopal ordination. The Act marked indeed the
> parting of the ways (19).

Commonly this moment in the history of the Anglican church is discussed in relation to the doctrine of apostolic succession, which it is supposed to support. But its true significance is broader. Article 36 and the Elizabethan Ordinal had ratified episcopacy, without stating whether or not this form was an integral part of the catholic church (20). Now a step had been taken which differentiated any episcopal ordination from any non-episcopal ordination. This clearly required some theological justification; and the only justification possible would be one which attributed to the fact of ordination by a bishop a power separable from that involved in the ordination of, for example a Lutheran minister. Only by reason of such an account could one distinguish between the "effectiveness" of the episcopal ordination of a Roman Catholic or Eastern Orthodox priest and the insufficiency of the rite of a non-episcopal church.

The significance of this development for Anglicanism is enormous. It is no longer possible to regard this aspect of the question of church order as part of the a d i a p h o r a , or things indifferent. Although it was by means of that concept that papal supremacy had been ended and a lay reformation begun subject only to the judgement of the word of God, now it h a d to be argued that episcopacy a t l e a s t did not belong to the a d i a p h o r a ; that it was, in fact, enjoined upon the church by unalterable divine law made manifest in the scriptures; and that those churches which failed to maintain this order, howsoever they might claim to model themselves upon the word of God, were in serious breech of divine law by failing to maintain, or to acquire, the blessing which alone accrued from episcopal ordination.

(iv) The development of a triadic party conflict. It is not to be wondered that this new element in Anglicanism speedily contributed to profound internal conflict. The adiaphoristic strand in Anglicanism developed rapidly into a movement, looking for toleration and an end to religious controversy. John Locke, picking up the term "the essence of Christianity" from Hooker, redefined it so as to exclude the controversial doctrines of justification by faith. The latitudinarian of the seventeenth and eighteenth centuries stood loose to the more heatedly debated matters of theological controversy, and also to ecclesiastical order and liturgical practice. The desire for a liturgy broad enough to be acceptable to dissenters, and even to theological convictions of a unitarian variety, gave rise to a number of proposals for reform of the 1662 book (21).

On the other hand, the Puritan tradition of the English reformation received a great stimulus and further development in the evangelical impact of Wesley and Whitefield. The question of the ecclesiological status of dissent once again became crucial, and with that question the real condition of Anglican ecclesiology again became apparent. At the close of the eighteenth century Anglican Evangelicals were able to join with dissenters in founding the London Missionary Society, with its fundamental principle the design

> not to send Presbyterianism, Independency, Episcopacy,
> or any other form of Church Order and Government (about
> which there may be differences of opinion among serious

persons), but the glorious gospel of the blessed God
to the heathen (22).

We come, finally, to the Oxford movement. Obviously enough, part of its
platform would be, in Pusey's own analysis of Puseyism, a "high estimate
of Episcopacy as God's ordinance", a view for which there was, by now,
long Anglican precedent (23). More significant and more decisive in the
creation of a new climate of opinion in the Anglican church was its explicit
re-evaluation of the Reformation. To quote Pusey's outline again, the sixth
feature of the movement was

> reverence for and deference to the ancient Church, of which
> our own Church is looked upon as the representative to us,
> and by whose views and doctrines we interpret our own Church
> when her meaning is questioned or doubtful; in a word,
> reference to the ancient Church, instead of the Reformers,
> as the ultimate expounder of the meaning of our Church (24).

As Professor Owen Chadwick remarks, the implied antithesis between
Reformers and the Fathers made a momentous difference to the "temper of
mind" characteristic of the Oxford Movement. Froude's vilification of Protestantism ("Really I hate the Reformation and the Reformers more and
more") (25), Newman's conscious desire to disconnect the Church of England from continental Protestantism (26), and his negative portrait of
Luther has made a lasting impression on the Church of England. Writing in
1932, H.D.A.Major, in an introduction to the Conference edition of the
Modern Churchman (the Conference subject was "The Reformation: Old and
New"), stated:

> Today Martin Luther, the greatest protagonist of the
> Reformation, is viewed as a vulgar, violent and mistaken
> man as hostile to humanist culture as he was to social
> democracy. And the Reformation he achieved is regarded
> as the parent of a malign progeny which shattered the
> religious unity of Western Europe and gave rise to a
> multitude of
>> Petulant, capricious sects,
>> The maggots of corrupted texts (27).

If the situation has altered today, it can only be as a result of the work of
two English Methodists, Professor Gordon Rupp and Dr. Philip Watson.
An experienced Lutheran observer of the English scene has written:

> It is significant that in Anglo-Catholic circles, where
> the greatest hostility to Luther has been expressed,
> there has not been any major re-study or re-valuation
> of Luther such as has been carried out by Roman Catholic
> scholars on the Continent. In fact, it may be said that
> the creativity of Anglo-Catholicism as a whole is minimal at
> the present time; in seeking renewal in liturgy and moral
> theology ... Anglicanism is having to learn from the

avant-garde of Roman Catholicism rather than from its
own Catholic wing (28).

The achievement of the Oxford Movement is amply reflected in the importance attached in the contemporary Anglican communion to the Reports of
the Anglican - Roman Catholic International Commission on Eucharistic
Doctrine, Ministry of Ordination and Authority in the Church, and the corresponding lack of interest in the Report of the International Conversations
between Anglicans and Lutherans, held from 1970-1972 (the Pullach Report),
and the fact that the Church of England did not participate (for whatever reason) in the Leuenberg Concordat of reformed churches in Europe (1973).

(v) The impact of biblical criticism and liberal theologies. That a new era
opened for Anglicanism in its slow and protesting reception of biblical
criticism in the nineteenth century, and the ambiguous (and, I believe,
ultimately disingenuous) position accorded to liberal dissent by the Report
on Doctrine in the Church of England, is becoming increasingly clear. The
latitudinarianism which appealed to a plain reading of the clearest parts of
scripture is by no means the same phenomenon as the proposals of the
more radical of the authors of Christian Believing or the Myth of
God Incarnate (29). The position accorded to Scripture by the Anglican
reformers, in agreement with their continental predecessors, remains at
the root of the doctrinal position of the Church of England as set out in
Canon A5 (30).

The position accorded to Scripture in Articles 6, 8, 19, 20, 21, and 34,
in the Book of Common Prayer and in the Ordinal is unambiguous. The notion of what constitutes the scriptural "proof" of a doctrine is, and always
has been, extremely complex, and the chief characteristic of the modern
period of Anglicanism has been the death of certain acute simplifications of
the problem. The doctrine of the inerrancy of scripture, for which Anglican
evangelicals fought in the nineteenth century, has had to be abandoned,
losing its ultimate character as the methodological prolegomenon to an
evangelical dogmatics.

The Anglo-Catholic has also suffered at the hands of biblical criticism.
The ecclesiology of the 1662 Preface to the Ordinal, to which reference
has been made, contains the assertion:

> It is evident unto all men diligently reading Holy
> Scripture and ancient authors, that from the
> Apostles' time there have been these Orders of
> Ministers in Christ's Church; Bishops, Priests,
> and Deacons.

Despite the efforts of the contributors to K.E.Kirk's Apostolic
Ministry (1946), it must be said that no such thing is in any way
"evident" (31). Chiefly responsible for this change is the widely accepted
late dating of the Pastoral Epistles - a change which separates us even
from J.B.Lightfoot's cool evaluation of the evidence (32). The Anglican
argument for episcopacy now appears to rest on its speedy and uncontro-

versial adoption by the second century (33). But such an argument can only be said to entail the words "by divine providence", if Anglicans are willing to take a similarly hospitable view of other relatively speedily and uncontroversially adopted developments; and in this case the status of the Scriptures as an instrument of reformation becomes acutely problematic.

The modern liberal theologian, by contrast, walks naked into a sea of possibilities. Deprived by historical criticism of the latitudinarian's optimistic belief in a relatively simple and uncontroversial basic truth in the Bible, he tries to maintain his life in the Church by denying the cogency or satisfactoriness of what others believe. As proof of his bona fides he offers the statement that he "takes the classical tradition very seriously", and offers as theological substance massive programmes of reconstruction which, he alleges, will make the faith more credible. What he is reluctant to do, however, is to specify how and why what he proposed is appropriately called Christian, since what is Christian is necessarily related to Christ and necessarily involves the use of scripture.

As I have briefly depicted it in its five principle components the Anglican reformation poses the contemporary Anglican church with an acute dilemma. The dilemma can be put thus: the Henrician reformation was a lay reformation against clerical domination, bringing to an end not merely the jurisdiction of the Bishop of Rome but, in Cranmer's liturgical work, the intercessory functions of the clergy. The Restoration, however, incorporated a wholly incompatible element into this fundamentally Lutheran picture, by attributing to the act of episcopal ordination a potency separate from the reformed conception of the ministry of word and sacraments. Anglicans clergy now might claim "something" unexplained and ambiguous, found equally in Roman Catholic and Orthodox priests, but not found in Lutherans or the Reformed ministers.

The most obvious way of interpreting this "something", which the whole dramatic nature of every ordination reinforces, is that a force of some kind passes through the fingers of the ordaining bishop (34). It is Anglicans who are committed to defend something of this kind since they alone are obliged to identify what it is that distinguishes their orders from those Protestants who share every other aspect of apostolic doctrine in common. When Roman Catholic theology abandons the cruder notions of a mechanical conveyance of sacramental "character" in ordination it leaves the Anglican high and dry. For the Roman Communion the fundamental question is the total relationship of the apostolic gospel and apostolic order. This is excellently illustrated in Lutheran-Roman Catholic Statement on the Eucharist and Ministry emanating form the U.S.A. (35), which contains the following significant observation from the Roman Catholic side:

> It may be objected that while the Lutheran communities do
> constitute churches, they are defective churches in an
> essential note that has ramifications for the Eucharistic
> ministry, namely, apostolicity. This charge is true if
> apostolicity is defined so as necessarily to include

apostolic succession through Episcopal consecration. However it is dubious that apostolicity should be so defined. In the first two centuries of Christianity, apostolic succession in doctrine (fidelity to the gospel) was considered more important than simple succession in office or orders. The lists of bishops that appeared late in the second century were intended to demonstrate more a line of legitimised teachers than a line of sacramental validity. Undoubtedly apostolic succession through episcopal consecration is a valuable sign and aspect of apostolicity, for in church history there is a mutual interplay between doctrinal integrity and the succession of those who are its official teachers. Yet, despite the lack of episcopal succession, the Lutheran church by its devotion to gospel, Creed, and sacrament has preserved a form of doctrinal apostolicity (36).

If some Roman Catholic theologians are able to envisage the possibility of recognising the validity of Lutheran ministries, notwithstanding their non-episcopal character, the position of the Anglican who insists on the implications of the 1662 Ordinal, and enshrined in Canon C1 of the Church of England (37), would be both untenable and absurd.

III

The concern of this essay has been to locate the Anglican communion in relation to Protestantism. The analysis of the doctrinal history of the Church of England rested upon the hypothesis that there exists a fundamental antithesis between Protestantism and Catholicism, conceived of as theological or ecclesiological principles. In terms of that antithesis the Church of England began as an unmistakably Protestant body, insisting that it was possible to distinguish essentials from inessentials in the corpus of received traditions and advancing lay persons to a position of great prominence. That these constitute Protestantism cannot be seriously doubted. The fact that, for centuries, Anglicans used the essentials/inessentials distinction specifically in polemics with Roman Catholics is historical confirmation of the underlying tendency of Protestantism to place the onus of judgement in matters of the truth squarely on the shoulders of the whole community. A comparatively conservative judgement, such as was made in the very early days of Henry's reformation, somewhat misleadingly retains the appearance of Catholicism; but the reality is quite otherwise. For the distinction between essentials and inessentials is quite unstable, and subject to varying content. But once invoked, it casts into doubt the integrity of the tradition, catholicity as received and practised in the whole church. If separate parts of that whole begin to make decisions about what does, and does not pertain to the truth in its essential demand on the believer, then the believer himself may be faced with the necessity of judging for himself. And in the reign of Mary and subsequently such was the experience of many.

Similarly, and even more obviously, is the advancement of lay persons a clear characteristic of Protestantism, closely connected to the previous principle. The evidence in early Anglicanism lies primarily in the position of King and Parliament in relation to the enactment of Reformation; but it is strongly supported in the nature of Cranmer's eucharistic liturgy and in the social readiness of England for the diminution of clerical power. Cranmer's own arguments against the sacrifice of the mass rest heavily upon the undesirability of the power it bestows upon the clergy. The principle that the layman, through his access to and knowledge of the scriptures read in his own language in the church, may hear the gospel and respond fully to the grace of God manifestly and significantly alters the position of the ordained minister, no matter how high the doctrine of the ministry, or how conservative the doctrine of the sacraments, may be.

However, in relation to the ministry we are in sphere of relative degrees of power and influence. There are more ways than one in which a clerical caste can maintain a central position in the church. One is by means of confining access to the benefits of salvation via its own ministrations; other is by the control of theological education. Power lost in one way may be regained another. The fundamental factor is the necessity of leadership. Leadership entails authority, and authority can be validated and justified in a diversity of ways.

It is not, therefore, to be wondered at that the Anglican church, having set so clear a Protestant course in its early days, introduced in the seventeenth century a quite different principle into its understanding of ministry. It is quite intelligible why the Anglican Church at this point enacted as a piece of practical legislation about entry to its ordained ministry something which reinforced the position of the episcopate. Unfortunately it does so in a way which, intelligible enough in a fully Catholic context, is simply unintelligible in a Protestant one. That is the principle that, to a bishop in the Catholic church is given Catholic responsibilities, i.e. responsibilities in relation to the one united church. What this principle presupposes is that there is one united church. It is impossible that there should be rival, but validly appointed, Catholic bishops pursuing independent courses of action. That, however, was precisely what the Anglican adoption of the regulation about episcopacy entailed. It entailed the supposition that any Roman Catholic or Orthodox bishop ordained priests for ministry in the church in such a way that that ordination effected the essential transformation of status required for Anglican ministry; but that Lutheran or Presbyterian ordinations did not. In the context of a united Catholic church the claim that only ordination deriving from the Catholic bishop made sense. Even the concept of a national church, part of a Catholic church, made a certain sense, provided that the status of those ordained in other countries could be satisfactorily resolved with reference to basic types of agreement. What made no sense however was to elevate any episcopal act of ordination over any non-episcopal act irrespective of the lack of unity between the respective bishops.

The admission of this antithetical principle provoked in the eighteenth and nineteenth centuries gross internal conflict. Not surprisingly German Protestants, observing the scandalous and unedifying disputes of the late nineteenth century, concluded that their cause was the inadequately Protestant character of the Anglican reformation (38). In this they were not, however, strictly accurate. It would be more accurate to argue that the Anglican church, in the course of the long history of its reformations, incorporated into its basic documents an internal contradiction between Protestant and Catholic principles. There seems nothing to protect us from the conclusion that Anglicanism as it now exists is founded on an incoherent doctrine of the church; and that its attempts to resolve or conceal this gross internal antinomy has repeatedly led it into a series of chronic conflicts from which it barely escapes with any integrity.

The adoption of so negative a conclusion, calmly though it might be contemplated by any non-Anglican, ought to provoke Anglicans to some rigorous thought about the doctrine of the church. Our investigation seems very markedly to confirm the view that Anglicanism is something anomalous, even absurd, among the churches of Christendom. Two consequences follow from this study, though both are well beyond its scope. The first is the long acute question of Anglicanism's future, particularly in the light of the participation of Anglicans in locally negotiated united churches. What is the Anglican communion for as a whole, in the context of the ecumenical movement? Does its anomalous or absurd character entail its swift demise, or has it tasks still to perform? The second consequence leads directly from the first. What is the final significance of the hypothetical tension set up between Catholic and Protestant principles at the start of the essay? Can there be a systematically satisfactory resolution of the antithesis? What is the relation between a doctrine of the church, and the kind of willingness to tolerate pluriformity which seems increasingly to be the only conceivable modus vivendi for a modern church?

Footnotes

1 F.D.E.Schleiermacher, The Christian Faith (ET, Edinburgh, 1928), p.103.

2 P.Tillich, The Protestant Era (Chicago, 1948), p.248.

3 K.Barth, Church Dogmatics 1/2 (ET, Edinburgh, 1956), p.829 f.

4 Op. cit., p.832.

5 See, on "alternative" patterns of thought, the essay of Professor Dietrich Ritschl in this volume.

6 H.Hensley Henson, The Church of England (Cambridge, 1939), p.7.

7 A.G.Dickens, The English Reformation (London, 1964).

8 W.P.Haugaard, Elizabeth and the English Reformation (Cambridge, 1968).

9 G.R.Elton, Reform and Reformation (London, 1977).

10 Cited in W.G.Zeeveld, Foundations of Tudor Policy (Cambridge, 1948), pp.154 f. But see, in qualification of Zeeveld's argument that Melanchthon's adiaphorism is the origin of Starkey's views, J.F.McConica, English Humanists and Reformation Politics Under Henry VIII and Edward VI (Oxford, 1965).

11 Elton, op. cit., pp.196-199.

12 Dickens, op. cit., p.179.

13 Dickens, op. cit., p.251.

14 See further, C.Hardwick, A History of the Articles of Religion (London, 1851), p.11, E.C.S.Gibson, The Thirty Nine Articles of the Church of England (London, 1896), I, p.8, F.E.Brightman, The English Rite (London, 1915), I, lvi, F.Preuser, England und die Schmalkaldner (Leipzig, 1929), p.139, E.Doernberg, Henry VIII and Luther (London, 1961), p.114, N.Tjernagel, Henry VIII and the Lutherans (St.Louis, 1965), p.188, Dickens, op. cit., p.251 f, and Haugaard, op. cit., p.258 ff. A general review of the evidence, with bibliography, is found in Carl S.Meyer's helpful article, "Melanchthon's Influence on English Thought in the Sixteenth Century", Miscellanea Historiae Ecclesiasticae (Louvain, 1967), II, pp.163-185.

15 Dickens remarks that it was the inhospitality of the Lutheran states to the Marian exiles which inhibited further development in a Lutheran direction, op. cit., p.286.

16 See Haugaard, op. cit., pp.109 and 341.

17 Haugaard, op. cit., p.341.

18 See N.Sykes, Old Priest and New Presbyter (Cambridge, 1956), pp.114-117.

19 Sykes, op. cit., pp.116-7.

20 See Haugaard, op. cit., p.272, where the author gives his opinion that the majority of the Bishops who framed Article 36 (not 35, as in the text) would have held the view that the form of the ministry was a matter of indifference provided that some public discipline regulating the call to office were established.

21 See Horton Davies, Worship and Theology in England, 1690-1850 (Princeton, 1961), Ch.iv, and G.J.Cuming, A History of Anglican Liturgy (London, 1969), Ch.8.

22 T.Haweis, An Impartial and Succinct History of the Rise, Declension, and Revival of the Church of Christ (London, 1800), Introduction, p.x; cited by Sykes, op. cit., p.173.

23 H.P.Liddon, Life of Pusey (London, 1893), ii, p.140; in O.Chadwick (ed), The Mind of the Oxford Movement (London, 1960), p.51.

24 Ibid.

25 Cited from Froude's Remains by O.Chadwick, The Victorian Church (London, 1966), I, p.175.

26 See a letter of Newman to Rickards, 30 July 1834, cited by G.Faber, The Oxford Apostles (London, 1933), p.114.

27 The Modern Churchman, Vol XXII (1932), p.225.

28 F.Sherman, "A Lutheran in an Anglican Environment", Lutheran World, Vol XII, No 3 (1965), p.254.

29 For a discussion of the differences see my The Integrity of Anglicanism (London, 1978), Ch 2.

30 "The doctrine of the Church of England is grounded in the holy scriptures, and in such teachings of the ancient Fathers and Councils of the Church as are agreeable to the said Scriptures. In particular such doctrine is to be found in the Thirty-nine Articles of Religion, the Book of Common Prayer and the Ordinal".

31 K.E.Kirk (ed), The Apostolic Ministry, Essays on the History of the doctrine of Episcopacy (London, 1946). Among the many replies to the arguments of the authors K.M.Carey (ed), The Historic Episcopate (2nd edn; London, 1960) remains the most interesting.

32 In his commentary on Philippians, (London, 1900), p.45 f.

33 See the article, preparatory for the 1978 Lambeth Conference, by Henry Chadwick, "Episcopacy in the New Testament and the Church", Today's Church and Today's World (London, 1977).

34 At the justification offered by the Archbishops of Canterbury and York in their reply to Apostolicae Curae, the Encyclical of Pope Leo XIII (13 September 1896) condemning Anglican Orders as invalid. The reply contains the argument that the Anglican reformers "concentrated the parts of the whole rite as it were on one prominent point, so that no one could doubt at what moment the grace and power of the priesthood was given", Anglican Orders (London, 1932), p.54.

35 Text in Modern Ecumenical Documents on the Ministry (London, 1975), pp.51-86.

36 Op. cit., p.70.

37 A more modern example makes this clear. Bishop Charles Gore (1853-1932), regarded in the early twentieth century as a leading Anglo-Catholic, was rightly seen by both a nonconformist and a Roman Catholic critic to be operating with a principle of "private judgement", even in his defense of ostensibly "catholic" theological and ecclesiological positions. See J.Carpenter, Gore (London, 1960), p.144.

38 The literature is cited in my article "Deutschland und England", Z. Th.K. (1972) 4, pp.439-465, esp pp.446 f and 456. An English version of this article appears in this volume,

HOW I SEE GERMAN THEOLOGY

D. Ritschl

Let me preface my remarks by drawing your attention to the significance for German history and German thought of today's date - the 20th of July. When reporting and reflecting on German theology - and this is what I am asked to do today - it is perhaps appropriate to remember the representatives of the best of German tradition who, in the dark age of German history, risked and gave their lives in the final, belated and abortive attempt on Hitler's life on July 20th, 1944. After millions of Jews and other unwanted human beings had already been murdered, and after thousands of Christians, members of the army and the aristocracy, socialists and trade union leaders, had been persecuted, imprisoned or executed, the Catholic Count Stauffenberg acted on behalf of the rest of the resistance movement in making the unsuccessful attempt. And it was after this dark day that the finest of the members of the movement were slaughtered too, among them, as you know, Dietrich Bonhoeffer. The participation of Christians and churchmen in the resistance movement is, of course, not the only reason why the 20th of July is theologically significant. The question is whether German theology has been shaped by this event and to what extent it has succeeded in reinterpreting its own history in the light of this unique experience. An added aspect of our interest is the question whether there is a noticeable difference between German and Swiss theology since, with the exception of French speaking Switzerland, theology there is tied to the German language and to German intellectual history as well.

May I offer yet another preamble to this lecture? I would like to indicate why I am not really ready to do justice to the assigned task of reporting and critically reflecting on German theology. Not that I neglected to do my home-work. I tried my best between the end of the semester in Mainz and the beginning of a preaching mission in New Jersey this coming Sunday. But precisely here lies the problem: I am still living in two worlds, I am oscillating between German and English-speaking theology and church-life. The danger is that I am no longer at home in either of them. After twenty years in the English-speaking world (six in Scotland, fourteen in the United States and many months in Australasia), I feel in many ways more at home in English-speaking theology, Presbyterianism and ecumenical endeavours than in my own Swiss church and German university traditions. With my return to the German-speaking world some years ago I experienced many severe disappointments. The university no longer is what it used to be - so it seems at least, compared with what I remember and perhaps idealize in retrospect. The church in Germany seems to have moved away from what I remember it to have been immediately after the war. I am, therefore, undoubtedly prejudiced. I hope you will nevertheless trust me as your travel guide when I now invite you on a sight-seeing tour of some typical developments and aspects within post-war German theology. I will try to refrain from exaggerated value judgements and will take as my heuristic device, as it were, the maxim that in whatever we say about another part of the church or about other theologies we should try to be ecumenically responsible. By this I mean that we should above all be interested in what builds and preserves the unity of the church in the honest search for mutual understanding and ultimately for the truth of God for us. Allowing this maxim to shape my inquiry, and your way of perceiving it, I would like to make five points.

I. Different concepts of theology

What does theology mean in the phrase "German theology"? I want to make it clear that our theme is not German church-life nor recent church history. "Theology", it seems to me, is not clearly defined in contemporary ecumenical circles such as ours here today, nor is there anything like an agreement among German churchmen and theologians on what "theology" stands for. In the interest of clarity I would like to introduce a more or less external typology which, if I am not mistaken, covers the ways in which people use the term theology. Theology can be conceived as:

(1) the sum total of the churches' or their spokesmen's rationally communicable utterances in matters of faith, love, hope, ethics, the meaning of life, etc. This would then include all preaching and teaching, all public declarations and manifestos, all personal Christian witness and counselling, i.e. activities which are often (if not always) situation-bound. This understanding of theology is widespread in English-speaking churches and is also found in German-speaking countries. It is, in my opinion, a rather meaningless concept of theology.

(2) The thematic concentration on certain aspects of the Christian faith in relation to specific situations and periods in history, themes which then serve as heuristic principles for the interpretation of the rest of the Bible and the later tradition. Such 'mono-thematic' theologies have often existed in the history of the church (if not also in the New Testament) and are today manifest in movements such as 'liberation theology', 'black theology', 'feminist theology' and also liturgical and eucharistic theologies. These types of "theology" are typical of trends in American theology but they are deeply rooted in German theological tradition (think of the monothematic Lutheran emphasis on justification!) and are still found in Germany today, e.g., in the emphases on exegesis, on history, on hermeneutics, on political ethics, and so forth.

(3) The search for the inner logic of that about which Christians and Jews and other interested groups think and speak in reference to God and to human thoughts and actions related to him. Theology would then be related to the church as grammar is to language; it would not be a 'container' in which the 'treasure' of faith, love and hope rests, nor would it be a heuristic principle in the form of a single theme with which to get hold of all the rest of Christian thought. It would serve the purpose rather of testing as well as stimulating the believers' (and within limits also the unbelievers') thinking about God and themselves, their prayers, memories, hopes and plans for action. Theology would be concerned with - and ultimately consist of - 'regulatory' or 'regulative' sentences in their relation to ancient and modern creeds, to today's problems and tasks, and to the different emphases in the ecumenical church as well as the Synagogue. In short, it would be theology as theory - as that kind of theory without which one cannot be practical. Such enterprise is not the exclusive task of professional theologians or ministers, nor is what they do automatically theology in this third sense.

I do not see much point in using the term theology in the sense of categories No. 1 and No. 2. Not that I fail to understand the intention of those who use 'theology' in these senses: No. 1 aims at avoiding an isolationist and exclusively scholarly concept of theology; No. 2 stresses the concreteness and pointedness of such broad understanding, it strives to overcome an 'objective', impersonal and scholastic approach to the lively, beautifully dangerous and excitingly relevant things of God and of mankind. Nevertheless, I think that No. 1 offers much too broad a concept which in fact is no concept at all but merely the name of a very wide field of activities, while No. 2 narrows down the number of approaches and perspectives for the understanding of the gospel and the church's task to a very few tasks, important as they may indeed be.

A typology is of course not a description of reality. We should be cognizant of the fact that the three types of theology are mutually interwoven and at times not sharply distinguishable. Nevertheless, I will focus my report on German theology with a special interest in type No. 3. A simple way of formulating our question would perhaps be this: what is it that makes German theology tick, what is it that controls it, stimulates and corrects it?

It is perhaps helpful to draw attention to another distinction between types of theology. I am thinking of the difference between the claim that theology has a hermeneutical task over against the other possibility that it is an analytical enterprise. This distinction may not mean too much to you at this point. I will come back to it later when describing certain specific features of post-war German theology. The point is that the general tendency in German theology was - perhaps no longer is but certainly was until recently - an emphasis on the hermeneutical task of theology. This emphasis is a faithful expression of theology's adherence to the tradition of Augustine and Luther, a highly problematical way of doing theology, it seems to me. It implicitly supports a faith-centered, ultimately a man-centered kind of theology, i.e., a way of centering on the problem-loaded question: how can I get a gracious God? If this Augustinian-Lutheran quest is permitted to stand forever at the center of the theological enterprise, something will happen to theology and to the church that is rather unfortunate. I hope I will succeed in making this clear.

II. Tendencies in German theology since 1945

Leaving aside the historical question whether German theology prior to World War II or even prior to the turn of the century was always hermeneutically oriented, it is certainly correct to say that the interest in hermeneutics has shaped German theology during the fifties and sixties. The main question was how to u n d e r s t a n d the ancient message and what to think and say about its s i g n i f i c a n c e for us today. This approach, which at first sight looks quite natural and familiar to all of us, is actually perpetuating the embarrassing and perhaps fruitless controversy on 'how to make relevant' ancient texts to modern people. This ambition is typical of Billy Graham as well as of Bultmann, the only difference being that the latter employs a much heavier scholarly apparatus than does the former. The question, however, is the same. Now, I hope not to be misunderstood: the question as such is not to be denied or ignored altogether. Of course there is justification in asking theological questions along the line of what we may call a 'forward direction', i.e. from earlier to later times, from the Bible to today. But if this remains the only direction of asking, if one neglects the emphasis on the believer's p r e s e n t state in the church, in worship and prayer, in encountering the presence of God now, then the one-sidedness of the 'forward directed question' becomes obvious. Worship, life together in the church, prayer, enjoying and praising God now, serving him and our fellow men now - these are as important points of departure for theology as is the Bible. What good do the ancient texts do if their content meets us in the middle of nowhere, in an ecclesiological t a b u l a r a s a situation, as it were?

I have made these deliberately provocative remarks in order to prepare the ground for understanding the typically German theological preoccupation with exegesis. But before commenting on this I would like to attempt a classification or a typology of the various high-points in theology in the development since 1945. And mentioning this magic date, let us not forget that in all probability the other important year, 1918, the end of World War I and with it of the ancient monarchies in the German countries (the end of the nineteenth century, culturally speaking), marked a cultural shock of even greater importance than the year 1945. The end of the Second. War was for many citizens, in some ways for everybody, a liberation, a relief, a

new chance. Thus the post-war years after the Second War were markedly
different from the famous 'Twenties'. What the population in general and
the Christians in particular saw when looking back to the thirties and to the
years of the war was a combination of horror, guilt, personal loss of home
and of loved ones (10 million), and of admiration for those parts of the
church that had resisted the ideological pressure and had made the good
confession. This admiration was shared by many who themselves had not
been active church members or who had sympathised with the Nazi doctrine
at least during its early years. In other words, the church (I am not speaking of the resistance movement, the assessement of which remained ambiguous in some segments of the population) enjoyed an enormous prestige
after 1945! In a sense this was also true of neighbouring countries such as
Switzerland and the Netherlands, Denmark, and - in a different way, of
course, in accordance with the history of its résistance - France. Even
though the actual number of ministers and church members who had been
active members of the Confessing Church was rather small, this wing of
the church, and of course its theological position, was often taken to have
been the vicarious church or the true representative of the best of ancient
German and Christian tradition. I do not want to enter into analyses and
arguments about this claim. Here it suffices to observe that the Confessing
Church itself was more interested in preserving its integrity than in
changing the situation. This judgement in retrospect sounds harsh. It is
not meant to be that. Most scholars who have gone into detailed studies of
the years 1933-1945 seem to agree that even the finest spokesmen of the
Confessing Church were theologically more concerned with the p u r a
d o c t r i n a and the freedom to let the v i v a   v o x   e v a n g e l i i be heard
than with a theologically grounded attempt at constructing something new.
We must acknowledge, perhaps, that German theology at that time was not
capable of doing more than it actually did. And we may add that, in all
likelihood, British, American, French or Scandinavian theology would not
have been in the position either, to construct or to demand what we today
would have wished them to have, had they been in the same situation. If
this is true, then we must conclude that nineteenth and early twentieth
century theology simply did not equip sufficiently the theologians and churchmen of the thirties to do more than call for the preservation of the integrity
of the church in a time of danger. I do not appreciate our younger, Marxist
oriented theologians on the Continent who belittle the achievements of the
Confessing Church during the Nazi time, merely by drawing attention to the
fact that then the church 'only interpreted the world rather than changed it'.
It does not take much courage to say this today in a situation of wealth and
security. And yet, there is truth in this criticism.

The following changes in the development of theology since 1945 can perhaps
be recognised:

(1) 1945 until approx. 1955 almost exclusive emphasis on e x e g e s i s;

(2) 1955 until approx. 1965 emphasis on hermeneutical and m e t h o d o l o g i -
c a l questions, a growing interest in ethics;

(3) 1965 until approx. 1975 a f r a g m e n t a t i o n of the theological endeavour into socio-political ethics vs.
conservative trends.

Period No. 1 was characterised by an almost obsessive concentration on
Old and New Testament exegesis. The lecture halls of the famous biblical
scholars, Gerhard v. Rad, Günther Bornkamm, Ernst Käsemann, Walther
Zimmerli, Claus Westermann, and many others, were crowded four times
a week with several hundred students. Candidates for the ministry were
expected to sight read almost any chapter from the Old Testament and certainly any New Testament book. They had to know the intricacies of the apparatus, the main steps in the history of scholarly exegesis and the theological implications of such problems. Church history was selectively
studied, with the main stress on Reformation and nineteenth-century theology. Patristic studies were neglected, ethics was hardly taught. Practical
theology was taken very seriously but seen almost entirely from a biblical-
exegetical point of view. Dogmatics (today more frequently called Systematic Theology) was taught by Barth and his theological followers (e. g. Otto
Weber, H.-J. Iwand, W. Kreck, H. Gollwitzer, H. Vogel, H. Diem) as well
as by outspokenly Lutheran theologians (e. g. W. Elert, P. Brunner,
H. Thielicke, W. Trillhaas), but it can fairly be said that exegesis determined the students' minds more than did dogmatic theology. (Karl Barth's
impact may have been an exception; many students moved to Basel to hear
him for at least some semesters). Philosophy was hardly looked at, and if
it was, then only because of a general cultural interest of the good student,
not really as a conversation-partner of theology. Psychology was despised.
Sociology was not known.

Period No. 2 showed the typical marks of the beginning of scholasticism.
'Barthians' and 'Bultmannians' defended their positions, Lutherans
rediscovered classical confessionalism and international Lutheran connec-
tions. Heidegger's ontology and philosophy of language - very different
from any Anglo-Saxon language philosophy - began to be welcomed by the
theologians; Gadamer's philosophical hermeneutics reached their desks
too, historical and exegetical studies gradually gave way to a new interest
in ethics. Bultmann's enormous impact on New Testament exegesis was
slowly transformed into an increasingly dogmatic preoccupation with
hermeneutical method (the names of G. Ebeling and E. Fuchs should be
recalled in this connection; one may also think of the Faculty of Divinity in
Glasgow and of Drew University, New Jersey, or of Claremont in California).
This emphasis was combined with what Ernst Käsemann and James Robinson
called the "New Quest" for the historical Jesus. It is possible that there
were hidden connections between this scholarly interest and the newly discovered significance of Jesus in political ethics, e. g. in Martin Luther
King's non-violent ethics which certainly had its outreach into German
church circles. Period No. 2 was also the time when 'academic theology'
climbed to the highest aspirations and again expected a degree of excellence
from its students and younger lecturers which certainly matched that of the
great period of historicism at the end of the nineteenth century. No one re-

ceived a teaching position or was appointed to a chair who had not published several substantial books and a great number of learned articles. Academic theology began to be more and more isolated from practical church life, although an increase of ecumenical and political concerns is also typical of this period.

Period No. 3 is so close to us that an objective characterization appears to be more difficult. To be sure, the traditional negative assessment of the Eastern European Marxist regimes gradually gave way to a more differentiated view among Western European intellectuals and churchmen. The Vietnam war and developments in the Third World led to increasingly anti-American sentiments, especially in West Germany. Responsible (as well as irresponsible) peace movements had glued together many Eastern and Western theologians, young and old, and a genuine concern for political ethics, more precisely, for social justice, became the typical mark of the majority of theologians in the late sixties. However, a very unfortunate polarisation partly destroyed what at first seemed to have been a conversion of the German academic theologian to questions of social and political dimensions. Strong groups of students and younger lecturers attempted to dominate theological faculties and local churches by turning the discussion on any conceivable subject into a more or less dilettante seminar on political-economic theory, often of a Marxist-Leninist persuasion. Older professors who had experienced a certain waning of enthusiasm about their lectures soon joined forces with the very young colleagues and thus tried to find their luck and academic success once more. The atmosphere was often tense and unpleasant, academic standards went down rapidly, examinations were endangered by the political-ideological positions of examiners as well as of students, and the local churches hardly understood what was going on; and if they did understand, they certainly did not appreciate the kind of training their future ministers were receiving. The most lamentable result of this period is perhaps the fact that a good number of able and promising theologians have moved to the 'right' in anger over the decay of the university and the antichurch and frequently atheistic positions of their students. This 'new conservatism', as it is called with reference to the youngest generation, is in part the fruit of useless and exaggerated attacks on the middle generation by the radical students of the early sixties. This may be one explanation which should not be overdone, however. I have observed manifestations of a new conservatism in the United States as well as in Australia and New Zealand, although the students in these countries have never been as radical as the West Germans. There seems to be a general conservative 'back-lash', as the Americans call it.

The most recent developments in German theology, however, are not merely to be seen in the light of the 'new conservatism'. To be sure, theological students today are much more conservative - or better, they are a-political - than were their older brothers and sisters some years ago. But academic theology has its own way of proceeding, it does not exhaust itself in reacting to situations (This is good, perhaps). After the Barth-Bultmann controversy, which lasted from about 1945 or 1950 until

1960, and after the more dogmatic or scholastic debate on hermeneutics, German theology has once again moved into the territory of methodological questions by taking up the themes of philosophy of science, or Wissenschaftstheorie, in its possible application for, or original enrichment by, theology. This time the systematicians are leading the discussion, not the systematically interested exegetes. The exegetes are clearly in the background. Wissenschaftstheorie is also the concern of large sections of contemporary philosophy and the philosophy of social science and of sociology. Thus most recent German theology has entered into some sort of dialogue - it is not yet a very intense exchange of thoughts - with analytical philosophy in the English-speaking world and with language philosophy. Heidegger's philosophy of language, which had never been in touch with British or American philosophies of language, has clearly been pushed to the periphery, and the younger German authors begin to study the same philosophical books which are read in Britain and in the United States. In addition, they are concerned with the so-called positivism-controversy which was connected with the names of the social philosopher, J. Habermas, and the philosopher of science, Karl Popper. It is too early to judge whether these theological-methodological endeavours will bear fruits and what kind of fruits these will be. There are at present not too many authors at work whose concern is with what one may call substantive theology. (While W. Pannenberg and especially G. Sauter are mainly concentrating on questions of method, E. Jüngel may be mentioned as an author who attempts to penetrate into the great classical themes, cf. his new book on 'God as the secret of the world'; and Gerhard Ebeling will shortly publish his three-volume Dogmatik des christlichen Glaubens). Some Roman Catholic authors, too, try to go beyond mere questions of prolegomena, method or strategy. (Walther Kasper and Karl Lehmann should be named as representatives of the middle generation, and Karl Rahner, of course, as an author of the old generation).

III. Is there anything new in today's German theology?

To phrase the question in this way is of course partly misleading. Theology need not be 'new'; it should be helpful to those who are in the church (the synagogue) as well as to some other interested people. Who are we to know which theology performs this service? Moreover, much theology today is done orally and never finds its way into published books or articles, at best it appears in mimeographed form. This is certainly true of theology in the Third World, but most likely also of theology in our industrialized countries. Much contructive work is done by teams of authors, no longer by individual writers. This applies to German theology as well as to ecumenical study groups. The time of the 'great theologians' - for such a long time typical of German theology in particular - is quite obviously over. They seem to have died with the Barths, the Bultmanns and Tillichs. So, what then is 'new' in German theology today? What is exciting, unique and deserving attention? Frankly speaking, I think, very little indeed. Or, to put it differently: the whole enterprise, though not being new or exciting or unique, certainly deserves some attention from the ecumenical church. Much solid work is done (in part perhaps more solid than elsewhere), many interesting books and essays are published, many students are instructed (in fact, there was never a time in one and a half thousand years in Germany when there were as many theological schools in operation, seminars taught and lectures delivered!), many sermons are well prepared, much competent counselling is offered - and yet, there does not seem to be too much life and joy in it. Here is not the place to analyse this most strange and also complex phenomenon. It is, of course, part of the general cultural, intellectual, spiritual and socio-psychological situation in the extremely busy, active, industrious and wealthy German Federal Republic. However, it is noteworthy that theology in East Germany as well as in German-speaking Switzerland does not seem to show greater signs of joyful life and creativity than does West German theology. Is this so because of the leading position of the West German theologians? Hardly so. The East Germans are producing quite some remarkable pieces of work, and so do most certainly the Swiss (as well as some Austrians). The Germans - in this case the West Germans - no longer occupy a leading position. If this is so, then there are reasons for suspecting that the general atmosphere in Western Europe seems to have affected the work of the theologians. It is also possible that theology is experiencing an interim period, finding itself today in a 'holding pattern', as it were. In suggesting this I do not think primarily of the gravity of the legacy of the 'great theologians' of the middle of the century, rather of a series of unprecedented challenges to the task of theology. Criticism from Marxism, even more severe and serious critical attacks from churches in the Third World, new findings in anthropology, psychology, in medicine and biology, new patterns of thought and new issues in the social sciences - all these and many additional challenges prevent theology - and with it German theology - from producing decisively successful and sparkling new results. It is certainly fair to say that many of the influential concepts of earlier theologians would not have made much impression had they been propounded today. All of us who do theology find ourselves in a new and very challenging situation today. Much speaks in favour of being less confined to one's own denomination or to a certain theological school. This is a new situation, to be sure. It calls for tolerance as well as for a new sense of responsibility towards one's own tradition, and it requires of us more sensitivity in interdenominational and transcultural communication as well as a greater readiness for participatory ways of doing theology. A new style of theology is called for.

Nevertheless, without invalidating the above observations, it is not quite meaningless to ask what theology in a certain geographical and cultural territory has to offer to other segments of the same enterprise. In attempting an answer I would like to suggest that contemporary German theology -

not unlike American theology - is experiencing the tension between what we called above theology No. 2 and No. 3, and that this tension in itself could conceivably give birth to something new, or at least to something helpful. Monothematic theologies are in combat with theologies of the third type. Typical of the former is the direct or hidden claim that theology can and must show a correspondence between God's actions and our tasks (e.g. in J. Moltmann's or H. Gollwitzer's writings), whereas the characteristic mark of the latter is - denying such insight into a direct correspondence - the much more limited claim that theology is no more than a regulative, correcting and stimulating enterprise, providing, as it were, the rules for the dialogue of those who talk about God. Mono-thematic theologies (No. 2) are perhaps the out-growth of the typically German preoccupation with hermeneutics and its quest for 'relevance', whereas the more scientific and more academically oriented theology (No. 3) is shaped by analytical thought. The tension between these two seems to me to be a meaningful point of departure for further theological investigations which might do justice to the complex challenges of our time. Some truly helpful thoughts have already grown out of this controversy. Useful studies in ethics have appeared in recent years and the whole complex of ecclesiological questions is beginning to shape theological thought. This is partly due to the impact of Protestant-Catholic or Protestant-Orthodox consultations on questions concerning the Spirit, church offices, the significance of teaching and of doctrine, etc. It is to be hoped that these kinds of theological projects will in the long run temper the minds of some of the obviously exaggerating monothematic theologians, such as the representatives of 'atheism', of an exclusive emphasis on social action, or of anti-ecumenical or conservative protestant propaganda.

If this analysis is not too optimistic, one would have to say that German theology is no longer entirely shaped and guided by its exegetical tradition and its adherence to Reformation (or, in the case of German Catholics: of counter-Reformation) theology. Analytical, phenomenological and generally philosophical thoughts have once again started to influence German theology. However, it would be a gross overstatement to say that analytical philosophy and the modern social sciences mean for theology today what Kant and Hegel meant for nineteenth theology. I do not think that this will ever be the case. Philosophical and theological pluralism is too deeply rooted today ever to allow the growth of a uniform approach to the task of doing theology.

German theology, it seems to me, is gradually moving closer to the themes and partly also to the methods used in theological work in other parts of the world, if only by participating in the widespread thematic and methodological pluralism typical of more recent ecumenical thought. This may not be the case with respect to older members of the theological community, however, nor to those who stick to ecclesiastical provincialism or a narrow interest in their personal careers. But the climate, on the whole, is open to participation in trans-national theological work. By the same token this means, I am sure, that German theology has lost its claim to a leading position or monopoly in the world-wide theological endeavour. Only provincially minded theologians who overestimate the importance of classical historical, exegetical and editorial work still dream of the international superiority of German academic theology.

IV. What are the typically 'German' features in German theology?

If one wants to shy away from profound cultural analyses or speculative comparisons of the character of European peoples - and this we should certainly do - much is gained by the simple reference to the characteristic structure of German academic training and research. It is noteworthy that all theological training in Germany is taking place within the context of the university. (Switzerland, the Netherlands and Scandinavia hold the same system, partly because their university tradition was strongly affected by the German university structure and its reforms in the early nineteent century). (There is a very small number of church-owned training centers, but those that provide a full theological education, as in the case of the Kirchliche Hochschule in Berlin or of some Roman Catholic institutions, have full university status). The main point of interest for us here, however, is not the importance of this external structure (which, incidentally, would also be true of the Scottish tradition), but rather the fact that theology is read by the ministerial student as a first degree. To be precise, there are no 'first degrees' as distinct from degrees or diplomas for special studies such as theology or law. Any subject such as theology, law, forestry, architecture, languages, history, medicine etc., is offered in the university as a discipline in its own right and is studied by the students for a period of at least five years. There may be intermediate examinations in some disciplines, e.g. in medicine and in the natural sciences, but the main emphasis is on the preparation for the final examination in the sixth, sometimes even the seventh year of university training. Students can change university during these years, and they frequently do as often as two or three times. The idea behind this system is that all universities are ranked equal and that students should be free to follow their interests by chosing to study under certain professors whose specialties or whose positions appeal to them. This system of equally ranking universities (including the Swiss universities) goes back to the university reforms after the Napoleonic wars. And it was since that time that theological students used to change from one city to another, depending on whom they would like to study under in a certain field. Thus, in the last century, the intellectually alert student would have tried to spend at least some semesters with Harnack, with Wellhausen or with Gunkel. This tradition remained unchanged until very recently. Students would have liked to hear the grand old men in the Biblical field, in theology, in history, and would have gone, therefore, to Heidelberg, Basel or Göttingen, or would have followed the professors when they moved to other places, as they often did. This situation is beginning to change today for reasons which need not be fully explained here. The number of students has increased rapidly. It is difficult to find housing. Many students are married and one of them has at least a part-time job. Thus the tendency is not to change university too often or not at all. But the old system is still valid in this that it is insignificant where a students takes his degree. All universities are considered to be of equal rank, and besides, many ministerial students sit their final examinations with an examining board of the church and not of the university (although there they would find university professors as examiners). Doctoral degrees, of course, are university degrees, but they are taken by very few students. But even then it does not matter where the degree is taken.

This brief sketch should equip us to point to some characteristic features of German theology. Some of these may have their parallels in some American or British university departments of theology, although the similarities exist on the surface only, it seems to me. The following typical marks may appear to be no more than part of the external structure, they are however, I would propose, very deeply rooted in these structures which, in turn, are the expressions of the cultural, ecclesiastical and academic self-understanding of classical and perhaps also of contemporary German theology. I should like to single out and enumerate the following:

(1) Theology is done within the context of the secular university. Since there are no colleges and only very few separate seminar and office buildings for theological faculties in German universities, i.e. since the theologians use the same lecture halls as do the lawyers, philologists or the historians, the physical integration into the university is more complete than in any other university system I know of. It is obvious that this has both great advantages and drawbacks.

(2) Academic theology is, therefore, cut off to some degree from the church. Theological training is not organically connected with worship and prayer. Whilst the students for the ministry have to go through a two-year practical training as assistant ministers after their university years, the students who aim at teaching in secondary schools (by combining theology with one other discipline) do not have the advantage of such exposure to practical church life. Moreover, many professors never had practical experience in a parish, or only the two required years as assistant ministers.

(3) Since all universities are state universities and all theological faculties established or legally defined by concordats between the official majority churches (or the Roman Catholic church within the territory) and the respective state, the Protestant and Catholic theological faculties seem to be separated forever even if its members were interested in a much greater degree of cooperation or even fusion. The bureaucratic structure of the universities also leaves its marks in other areas of theological activity, although academic freedom is fully guaranteed.

(4) The classical German university was professor-centered. This encouraged the formation of 'schools' around one scholar and his assistants. This, in turn, enhanced the danger of tensions and hostilities between professors. However, the situation has radically changed during the past few years. German professors (in all disciplines) now have much less authority than British or American 'heads of departments'. Students, assistants and also secretaries participate fully in the decision-making-processes, including the appointments of professors. (The tensions - including court cases - over this development have been dramatic).

(5) Since for theological studies there are no clearly defined curricula or fixed sequences of courses, students tend to feel lost at least during their early years. They very much appreciate personal guidance or counselling, but it is hardly possible to do justice to this expectation since the numbers of students have gone up so rapidly (e.g. over 700 in Mainz, and over 1000 in Göttingen, Heidelberg, even more in Tübingen and Münster, to name but a few places). The old German university system was designed for very small and élite student bodies including frequent contact with the lecturers and professors. This ideal situation came to an end already at the turn of the century, and the recent and much belated university reforms have not at all succeeded in overcoming the difficulties. (The student-faculty ratio in disciplines other than theology is even less fortunate). Academic standards are consequently going down, obviously in theology, perhaps in other fields too. Hebrew, Greek and Latin are still required of all theological students (for Roman Catholics, Hebrew is at places optional, likewise for those who prepare for teaching in secondary schools). But the old idea that these languages are taught in secondary schools and can therefore be presupposed for the study of theology, has, with some exceptions, become an illusion. Thus there has disappeared within a very few years not only the traditionally considerable exegetical skill of the theological students but also their joy in doing exegetical or historical work. With the relative absence of philosophy as a possible alternative for a solid 'backbone' of theological studies, there is not very much left at the present time. This is way many - not only of the older generation - are rather pessimistic about the state of German theology. Excellent doctoral students and splendidly trained scholars as teachers do not really make up for what seems to be lacking.

V. An attempt at comparing German and British theology

I am now tempted to do what I said should not be done. But, hoping that you will not take too seriously what is proposed in these concluding remarks, it might be justifiable to attempt a summary of our observations by exaggerating some points. It will be obvious, of course, that the comparisons are based on vast generalizations (such as, for instance, the use of the term 'British' theology).

(1) German theologians tend to think and argue in a l t e r n a t i v e patterns of thought, whereas British theology has a preference for a d d i t i v e patterns. The former present and defend a position, the latter add points to a story or stones to a mosaic. Positional and alternative patterns of thought are fruitful in research and undoubtedly promote ongoing discussion and further investigations; additive patterns are useful ecumenically and do not allow much of a tension between academic theology and the work of the church.

(2) Despite the relative absence of a discussion between theology and philosophy in Germany, German theology conceives of itself as an enterprise which is responsible to the academic world, the secular university. British theology, despite its moderately intense contact with philosophy, feels more directly responsible to the church. (This is externally manifest in the use of ecclesiastical titles, e.g. 'Canon', or designations such as 'the Rev.' or 'Very Rev.', by British academic theologians, a custom quite unknown to German theologians since the time of the Baroque).

(3) German theology, even in its more conservative quarters, attempts to be 'modern', up to date, even progressive with regard to results of research or new publications on certain subjects. The tendency is - despite the interest in historical research - to be suspicious of older books, especially in the Biblical fields and in dogmatics and ethics. In Britain, on the other hand, there seems to be a greater sense of respect for earlier positions and a certain feeling of distrust of obviously new thoughts or innovating suggestions. Even academic theologians in Britain disregard not infrequently the results of research in other countries (the Continent as well as America) or publish as their own discoveries thoughts or opinions that had been discussed elsewhere long before. A recent example of this would be the heated discussion in England as well as in Australasia on the book T h e   M y t h   o f   G o d   I n c a r n a t e , the theses of which were discussed on the Continent many decades ago.

(4) German theology bears the marks of provincialism and of a certain degree of ingrown, academic self-sufficiency, although all lecturers and most students read one or two languages other than German very well indeed. German church officials are often more ecumenically minded and informed than are their counterparts in the academic world. British theological teachers and authors, on the other hand, being part of a very much smaller theological, academic establishment, are, it seems to me, more open to worldwide problems and to ecumenical tasks. This difference may partly be due to Germany's international isolation after World War I and the absence of any ties to other parts of the world such as are provided within the Commonwealth.

144

(5) German theology has always been 'bi-denominational', i.e. it was academically manifest in its Protestant and Catholic forms. And Protestantism exists only in two traditions, the Lutheran and the Reformed - a distinction, incidentally, which today is almost ignored in academic theology. Anglicanism is not represented on the Continent, and the Methodist and Baptist churches are so small that they were never noticed in academic theology, nor, for that matter among the members of the majority churches. This historically conditioned situation has enhanced preoccupations with certain theological themes typical of these major traditions, e.g., the Lutheran focussing on justification, on faith and grace, on the unhappy doctrine of the 'two realms' (hence the enormous emphasis on Romans 13!), or the Roman Catholic interest in natural law and natural theology, and the Reformed or Calvinist critique of Lutheranism and of aspects of Catholicism. The difference from British theology is obvious. There is a much greater confidence in the usefulness of the search for a common denominator, noticeable perhaps in the traditional interest in patristic studies.

(6) However, the traditional German setting is changing more rapidly than the British, it seems to me. The great numbers of permanent or temporary immigrants from Greece and Yugoslavia, as well as the refugees from some Eastern European countries have caused the Orthodox Church to grow into the third largest denomination in West Germany. Universities begin to have lectureships in orthodox theology. The ecumenical advantage of this is already noticeable. In Britain, on the other hand, immigrants from the Commonwealth countries have caused many social problems but have not affected the denominational structures.

If one considers all of these differences, and adds to them the observations that there is much more money available in German theology and German church life and that the authority structures are much more severely challenged in German schools, universities, the churches and public life than they are in Britain or even in America, one may wonder whether the theological enterprises have anything in common at all. I think they still have, and they will have more as we approach the end of the century. Not only is there infinitely more exchange between the two countries on almost every level, but - and that may have an even more immediate effect - the industrialized countries are moving closer together because of the sheer force of economic and political pressure and of common tasks in relation to the poorer countries. The churches, and with them theology, will unquestionably be affected by these developments. It is to be hoped that we, who have our share in the theological enterprise, will be able to preserve a useful measure of pluralism and at the same time participate in the common ecumenical task. The differences between the various traditions seem small in the light of the magnitude of our common tasks.

GERMANY AND ENGLAND:

AN ATTEMPT AT THEOLOGICAL DIPLOMACY (1)

by

S. W. Sykes

In this essay I propose to concentrate on the question of the mutual relations between non-Roman Catholic theologians in Germany and England in
the problems of fundamental theology (2). I am not, therefore, primarily
concerned with ecumenical relations nor with co-operation in historical
research. Indeed my starting-point is the observation that at a time when
ecumenical relations appear to be good and the exchange of ideas in biblical and patristic studies at least as fruitful as at any time in the last 100
years, it would still not be possible to say that in fundamental theology
there is anything like a mutually profitable engagement (3).

A cursory glance at the principal German language periodicals of the last
fifteen years reveals the fact that books of fundamental theology written in
England are very rarely noticed. Furthermore, personal contacts suggest
that there is a widespread feeling in German-speaking protestantism that
English theology is so highly idiosyncratic that it can only be doubtfully
relevant elsewhere. In England on the other hand, while modern German
theology has established a firm foothold in the theological curricula of the
Universities, there is plenty of evidence of a sense of the foreignness of
some of its basic themes (4).

Two explanations of this situation are popular. One derives the divergence
in theological writing from the respective ecclesiastical traditions,
Anglicanism, Lutheranism, and Calvinism. The other points to the
diverging traditions of philosophy. Both make valuable points, particularly
the latter. In so far as theology is influenced by the dominant philosophy of
the time, our recent philosophical histories could scarcely have been more
calculated to inculcate mutual misunderstanding and rivalry (5).

Important though such considerations are, I am convinced that they neither
explain, nor begin to remove the barriers. On the contrary. The repetition
of the allegedly fundamental divergencies of view-point and the use of the
ambiguous and inexact terms of ecclesiastical and intellectual history
(Anglicanism, idealism, etc.) has the general effect of perpetuating isolation. Moreover, what has to be explained is not, in fact, the m u t u a l
ignorance of each other's fundamental theology, but rather the fact that
while German theology is read but mistrusted in England, English theology
is simply not read in Germany. I have accordingly set myself two tasks.
First, to explore some of the further reasons for the apparent separation

of our theological traditions; and secondly, to comment on the significance of nationality for theology.

I have called this a study in theological diplomacy. Being myself an Englishman it may not unreasonably be thought that my motive in writing is to "sell" English theology. My view is, however, old-fashioned though it may be, that a diplomat is not a salesman. I wish to exclude entirely the question of the inherent value of our respective theological traditions and to concentrate on an interesting aspect of recent theological history. I recognise the possibility that the theological work of even a large nation or ecclesiastical tradition could be seriously defective for various reasons, and that judgments to this effect have played a large part in the period of history under review. Thus although it may be important that the contiguous nations of the enlarged European Community so understand and respect each other theologically that their Christian thinkers will be enabled together to make a contribution to its moral future, in the long run it only matters that German read English, Dutch read Belgian, and French read Italian theology, and v i c e v e r s a , if the theology in these languages contains good material.

Accordingly this essay is diplomatic in the sense of being propaedeutic to the more difficult task of sound theological judgment.

                                        I

One of the best statements of the gulf which we are to examine comes from the year 1902 and from the pen of the English translator of Harnack's Das Wesen des Christentums , T.B.Saunders. We must recognise that the turn of the century was a time when public opinion in both countries, poisoned by the events of the Boer War, was in a nervous and negative frame of mind. Professor Max Müller observed in his autobiography that the prejudice against Germans was greater at the time of writing (1901) than at the time of his first arrival in England (1846) (6). The historian, Erich Marck's brief but much admired pamphlet, Deutschland und England , published simultaneously in both countries in 1900 gives ample evidence of the prevailing sense of an inevitable clash of interests, which must nonetheless be prevented from breaking out into open conflict.

Despite this generally unfavourable background, Saunders gives a remarkably fair description of the situation in theology, the more so because he is engaged in defending Harnack from his Oxford critics:

> There is a popular impression among us that the German inquirer
> is unresponsive to the subtler promptings of the religious spirit;
> that he has an inadequate sense of its mystery; that he pays small
> attention to the deep significance of religious institutions and the
> moral aspect of their continuity. He is said to be too destructive in
> his criticism; too ready to disprove the authenticity of whatever he
> is reluctant to accept; too eager to accept a natural explanation of

phenomena which, as we are told, would lose their force and even their meaning if they were so explained. On the other hand the English inquirer is said to inquire too little; to interpret the documents of his creed not in the light of research, nor with any allowance for the psychological element in history, but with a paramount regard for tradition; and, if he attempts any criticism at all, to ignore its results by trying to blend them with the very ideas which they destroy (7).

We should notice that this comment concerns the boarderlands between biblical criticism and systematic theology, into which Harnack had strayed while claiming the immunity of the impartial historian. That is to say it concerns an attitude to historiography, which as I shall hope to show is of prime importance for our topic.

We are obliged, however, to go back another hundred years in time if we are seeking the origins of the radical divergence of English and German theology. In 1799 Schleiermacher complained in his speeches On Religion of the Anglomania which he found prevalent among his contemporaries and the "miserable empiricism" which he felt characterised the British attitude to religion.

This latter complaint has to be seen against the background of the considerable literature in German philosophy and theology arising out of English deism and the work of Locke. Because English was a less familiar language than French there is evidence of a substantial activity in translating English works into German, in which indeed Schleiermacher had himself taken part. What is more important is the influence of empirical and critical thinking evident throughout the work of a figure like Semler (8). In the problems which he tackled and the methods which he used, Semler shows himself to be a member of that international theological circle inspired by Locke's critical philosophy. The very independence of his contribution, which eludes most the categories into which eighteenth-century thought is usually fitted, is unthinkable without the impulse of the English enlightenment.

Schleiermacher's revolt from the "empiricism" of English philosophy was no side-issue in the development of his theology. In the Erläuterungen to the speeches of 1821 he admits that he had expressed himself somewhat rhetorically, but believes the original complaint to be justified. Particularly emphasised is the criticism that English thinkers are uninterested in Wissenschaft for its own sake, as distinct from its usefulness, and the fact that even the celebrated piety and practical Christianity of the British are put to the service of national self-interest (9). It is of great significance for the future that this rejection of what is regarded as the leading characteristic of English thought is accompanied in Schleiermacher's other work by a theological justification of patriotism and an attack on "cosmopolitanism" (10). Wichern likewise, a pupil of Schleiermacher, though strongly influenced by the examples of practical Christianity he found in English Church life, insisted on "earnest opposition" (ernsten Widerstand) against the inroads of the English spirit into Germany (11).

I am at the moment confining myself to producing examples of conscious rejection of English religious life and thought in the early nineteenth century, and am making no attempt to estimate how widespread such a view was. This is an important qualification, because it is all too easy to create a "general impression" by the quotation of selected examples. With the same qualification one can refer without difficulty to instances of an equally strong determination in England to resist German influences, especially in the field of biblical criticism. Although Herbert Marsh, Lady Margaret Professor of Divinity in Cambridge from 1807-16, had translated Michaelis's Introduction to the New Testament into English in 1801, adding to it his own not uninteresting theory of the literary relation of the four gospels, there was a body of opinion which regarded "Germanism" with deep suspicion. The root of this fear was, as Connop Thirlwall made clear in his long introduction to his translation of Schleiermacher's Kritische Versuch über das Lukas evangelium, the problem of the compatibility of biblical criticism with a doctrine of biblical inspiration. Here it must be remembered that the critical work of the English enlightenment had occurred for the most part outside the Universities of Oxford and Cambridge and that until 1871 every University teacher within them was obliged to subscribe in writing to the Thirty-Nine Articles (12). Thus orthodox divines, who thought that the battles of "rationalism" were behind them found themselves faced by a much more professionally competent critical movement stemming largely from Germany.

Since German was not one of the languages of polite society and in the absence in the early nineteenth century of translations of German works of philosophy and theology the impression was easily put about and not easily refuted that German theology was unsound. Matters were brought to a head in 1825 when H.J.Rose published four lectures attacking the alleged rationalism of German theology. The lectures were at once translated into German and created great offence (13). Their importance, however, derives from the fact that they called forth from a young English biblical scholar studying at the time in Bonn, E.B.Pusey, one of the few really able studies of the German theological enlightenment to appear in English. Pusey's work was by no means a defence of "rationalism", but the trouble he took not to misrepresent the views of those with whom he disagreed incurred him in suspicion (14). When we consider how thoroughly versed he was in German biblical criticism (he had even translated long extracts from Lessing for his friend John Henry Newman) and how warmly he expressed his admiration of Schleiermacher, it is all the more illuminating that in a letter of 1826 when the possibility of a tutorship had arisen at Oriel College, Oxford, he felt impelled to remark: "I hope that I need not say that I should introduce no German Theology into my lectures" (15).

In the course of the nineteenth century the position changed in several respects. A growing number of publishers translated German works, and the older generation of scholars was replaced by those who had worked at German universities. Gradually concern for a literally infallible scripture lost ground, and historical methods came to be assumed as proper in theological study. But there is still evidence of a felt gap, even amoung those one might expect to have been most sympathetic. Maurice, for example, in a long letter to a pupil early in 1848 expresses the view that "we must always be, to a certain extent, unintelligible to each other, because we (i.e. English and Germans) start from exactly opposite points; we, naturally, from that which is above and speaks to us; they, naturally, from that which is within them and which s e e k s for some object above itself". He then proceeds to complain that they allow philosophy to dominate everything, and to outline his own view of the proper relation of philosophy and theology (16). Maurice is, of course, too individual a thinker to be a reliable guide to the relations of nations, particularly since his knowledge of German was defective, on his own admission.

Perhaps still more revealing are the numerous asides, even from writers on biblical subjects where the relationship was probably closest (17). These require some explanation in addition to the probable legacy of mistrust from earlier decades. A contributing factor may well have been the failure of the English liberal movement to establish a native theological achievement of the breadth and impressiveness of Schleiermacher's; or again, many commentators rightly point to the success of the Oxford movement, which already in 1868 a German theologian with a long-standing interest in English church life was referring to as "falsch-anglikanischen Romanismus" (18).

These observations, however, remain a little on the surface of things. The deeper reason seems to me to lie in the perplexing history of historiography since the eighteenth century. A recent work has reminded us again of the exceptionally wide ramifications for the history of ideas of the rise and fall of historicism (19). By historicism Iggers understands the main tradition in German historiography from Wilhelm von Humboldt and Leopold von Ranke until the recent past. The term signifies the assumption of "a fundamental difference between the phenomena of nature and those of history", and the doctrine that the study of history alone provides the means for the understanding of the human situation. Iggers asserts that three sets of ideas play a leading role in the development of the historicist position, a concept of the state as an end in itself, a philosophy of value which rejects the idea of thinking in normative terms, and a theory of knowledge which broke with the natural law belief in the rational substructure of human existence (20).

It has been realised for some considerable time in theology that the critical situation in the Christian understanding of history expounded and exemplified in the post-war writings of Ernst Troeltsch needed to be overcome before any advance could be made. But it has also become clear that some of the early and enthusiastic claims for a new historical methodology resting on the work of Dilthey, Collingwood and Heidegger were exaggerated (21). Not the least useful feature of Igger's work is that it suggests to the theologian, who may well be somewhat weary of the inbred nature of the debates about "the historical Jesus", that he should take a broader view. In particular Iggers invites one to consider the significance for this period of the history of historiography of the process of divergence from and transformation of European traditions emphasising a common human nature or the theory of natural law. In this process the work of Herder plays a crucial part at the end of the eighteenth century (22).

In emphasising the significance of the divergence from natural law traditions Iggers is pointing to a theme which Troeltsch himself regarded as fundamental. In a lecture of 1922, at a time when the principles of historicism were under fundamental attack from the neo-Kantians, Troeltsch adopted as his starting-point the fact that the opposition between German and West-European thought lies in their different view of humanity (23). For typically 'western European' thought society is conceived, according to Troeltsch, in natural law terms as a rationally ordered grouping of equal beings for mutual advancement. Such thought emphasises human rights, is optimistic, supports national self-determination and the League of Nations, and takes an interest in backward and enslaved peoples. Typically German thought, on the other hand, rejects natural law, and is based rather on the ideas of the Romantic counter-revolution which erected for state and society the organic ideal of a group mind (Gemeingeist), "an ideal half-aesthetic and half religious, but instinct throughout with a spirit of antibourgeois idealism" (24).

Such fundamentally different viewpoints have a vast range of potential ramifications for philosophy, theology, historiography and politics. History is seen as subject to mysterious forces which from time to time mould out of individuals a "spiritual whole". Man may be valued less for himself than for his contribution to that whole. Further a new theory of community can be developed, namely as an expression of a Volksgeist, and the world-process can be pictured as the mutual struggle of a hierarchy of qualitatively different cultures, "where from time to time the leading nation surrenders the torch to the following one, and where originally all together represent in mutual complementarity the totality of life" (25). Historical study turns naturally to Geist in its individual and communal expressions, to biography, particularly of the great national heroes, and to the state, particularly the history of diplomacy and the struggle for national hegemony. Thus it may become intelligible how Otto Pfleiderer can write in a revealing essay on "The National Traits of Germans as seen in their Religion" (1892) that in Germany "highly organised religious belief, as well as mode of life in Church and Theology, stands in such close relation to political affairs that all changes and alterations of spirit or form of politics exert an influence upon the religious life and the ecclesiastical community", or looks forward to the day when the German element in Protestantism will triumph over every particle of foreign admixture (Roman, Greek and Jewish) (26).

And quite apart from the various ramifications for the relations of theology and culture, important consequences emerge in estimations of the value of generalized conceptual thought. From Schleiermacher on (though he himself was a good deal more sophisticated and careful than many of his disciples and commentators) a strong tradition developed which devalued the achievements of classical metaphysics in handling the common themes of human experience. Understanding, it was said, must free itself from the encumbrance of conceptualization if it is to confront the historical in its individuality. What originated as a protest against the dry formality of a particular dogmatic tradition became a prejudice against any form of metaphysical enquiry whatsoever (27).

In fairness to Troeltsch it must be said that he does not envisage all these consequences, and qualifies many of those he does envisage. But the qualifications do not detract from the basic premiss of his writing, that a fundamental divergence of thought emerged with the romantic movement, though having an earlier basis. The question immediately arises whether this portrayal of the divergence has any permanent validity. There is no doubt that Germany produced that movement in intellectual history which we call "historicism", and that it dominated intellectual life in Germany in a manner without parallel in other West European countries. The question is whether that movement's self-portrayal as a phenomenon in some way natural to the German Geist has any justification. I propose to examine this question by reference (i) to the notion of national character, and (ii) to Troeltsch's own proposals for overcoming the isolationist tendency within the German view.

(i) It is reasonably clear that the idea of referring to a nation's character, if not the actual use of the phrase "national character", is as ancient as the practice of speaking of a nation in personal terms. However the emergence of a theory of national character involving not merely the detailing of characteristics derived from and received in that nation's history, but the postulation of a suprapersonal Kraft directing its development, is distinctive of German romanticism, and particularly connected with Herder. From the start this theory directed attention to the phenomenon of language as the expression of fundamental cultural unity. Language, according to Schleiermacher, embodies a mode of thought which is not expressible in the same way in any other language.

This view introduces us at once to some of the complexities of the notion of nationality and the nineteenth-century phenomenon of nationalism. The notion of a nation's identity is by no means the imaginative creation of the German romantics. Acute patriotic feeling, according to the principal American writers on this topic, was primarily a product of eighteenth-century England with its self-conscious and not a little smug appreciation of its linguistic, political, economic and religious identity (28). The subject of national character was evidently a favourite one for coffee-house discussions. Nonetheless in Hume's essay of 1748 on the subject we find a firm denial that the English possess any distinctive national character (29). This was an early stage in the formulation of the notion. What transformed it was the more comprehensive theory of national character which emphasised the spiritual autonomy of each nation's cultural forms, beginning with its language. The view that nations, like individuals, change very little was very widely accepted and had important consequences for the practical handling of discussions of national life (30). From the statement that another nation's cultural achievements might be difficult to understand it was but a short step to the assertion that they were necessarily impossible to understand, or that one's national identity was threatened by their effect.

Such views were naturally not the sole property of German romantics. Examples can be found of Anglo-Saxon writers who claimed that "German thought" was necessarily opaque to them. One of the first Englishmen to take an interest in German literature, Henry Crabb Robinson (1775-1867), spoke of the "inherent and essential diversity of our English and your German m o d e s of contemplating the great matters of religious philosophy" (31). But although it ought, on the strict interpretation of romantic nationalist principles, to be sufficient to say "I do not understand German thought because I am English", in fact we suspect Robinson of a measure of intellectual laziness. Moreover it should be noted that the customary remark from German intellectuals about English thought is not that it is incomprehensible, but that it is superficial, by which is clearly meant not merely a habitual but also a culpable state of the English mind (that is, one capable of being prevented by the proper effort).

In fact the principle phenomenon giving rise to the impression of a great gulf separating English and German thought in the early nineteenth century, namely the neglect by British philosophers of German idealism, is capable of explanation without the aid of the "national character" school. Indeed there were instances where the challenge of idealism was accepted and seriously discussed. In one case where the predictable charge of "Germanism" was flung at the one English philosophical theologian of the nineteenth century to base his work explicitly on that of Schleiermacher, J.D. Morell (1816-1891), he responded to it by sharply distinguishing German phraseology from German "modes of thought". He wrote: "if the term is intended to indicate any distinctive mode of t h i n k i n g, then it would be instructive for us to have this mode clearly expounded instead of denounced ... for there can certainly be nothing in German thinking which is inaccessible to the laws of reasoning, or rules of evidence" (32).

This common sense conviction persists in the frequently repeated observation that statements about national character have rarely any academic, as distinct from pedagogical or propogandist, significance (33). There is, it is said, an important distinction between the legitimate popular function of national character studies as a means of self-criticism, reassurance, or the relief of racial tensions in myths, stories or jokes, and the use of national generalisations for 'serious' publications. In the case of the former everyone recognises their purpose, and, except in totalitarian regimes, no one is intended fully to believe them. Serious problems of verification arise, however, when selective features of the intellectual history of a nation are decked out with the trappings of academic scholarship and are promulgated with solemnity as the more or less fixed configuration of the intellectual processes of thinkers of that nationality (34).

The principal and most effective criticism of such works consists in a denial of the "objective" status claimed for them. Their weakest feature is the manner in which evidence is selected. Only more rigorous statistical procedures could support their argument, and social scientists are aware that work of this kind is only just beginning to emerge. The situation is not that the notion of "national character" is necessarily devoid of meaning, but that in order to give it anything more than the popular status of a roughly acceptable generalisation the appropriate methods are those of the social scientist rather than the intellectual historian. For the most part it is sufficient to explain a nation's interest in its own character by reference to geo-political pressures. Isolation of a nation or a social group can both accentuate its customary social or legal methods and give rise to the need for internal reassurance.

Troeltsch's basic idea that there exists a fundamental difference in viewpoint corresponding to a national "spirit" has, accordingly, been subjected to thorough and successful criticism by those who have pointed out that it rests on an arbitrary selection of evidence (35). Particularly crucial for the criticism is the fact that Troeltsch failed to integrate in his theory the significance for British thought of the neo-Hegelianism which was predominent from the late nineteenth century and still influential at the end of the 1930s (36). To be sure, Troeltsch realised that idealism of one kind or another was prevalent throughout Europe, but felt that it was not a thoroughgoing philosophical movement outside Germany since Anglo-Saxon social philosophers preferred the superficial democratic notion of "civilisation" to the German idea of "Kultur" (37). But here again the close examination of the evidence, such as the study of the political philosophy of the nineteenth and early twentieth century idealists, Green, Bradley and Bosanquet reveals that the differences which exist are by no means fundamental oppositions in manner of approach or of thinking (38). Nor can it be argued that we are dealing here with a few minor details of a total picture which a theory of "ideal types" cannot be expected to take into account. It is the leading features of the intellectual scene of these years which do not cohere with Troeltsch's hypothesis, and the criticisms lead to the conclusion that what is at fault is Troeltsch's method of dealing with the phenomena of the history of ideas.

Although this objection touches on a fundamental point in Troeltsch's argument, his development of what he regards as the distinctively German view of humanity shows that he is well aware of its dangers. He clearly sees that the more one stresses the qualitative differences of separate cultures, the more prone one is to national introspection and cultural isolation.

In order to overcome this he urges, first, with respect to the study of history, a return to the universal-history enterprise, a restoration of a teleological viewpoint, and a more resolute handling of a "harmony of cultures". This can be aided, he believes, by a reinvestigation of the classico-romantic age (1770-1800) before the development of the full romantic nationalist myth. Secondly, with respect to ethics, he wishes for a greater emphasis on the autonomy of personality, and the idea of "an indestructible moral core", in our ordering of our relations with others on an individual and national level.

By pointing to the period when the challenge of the Enlightenment was being formatively handled in both countries, and in a manner which sharply differentiates England and Germany from France, Troeltsch reminds us of the fundamental determinant of the modern age both in history and in theology, and in their interconnection (39). A similar point is made by a modern German historian, Fritz Fischer. "Modern historical science ... is a child of the Aufklärung, the century in which the attempt was made to overcome confessional contradictions and to cross the boundaries of christian Europe" (40). The deep change of viewpoint which Fischer asserts is taking place in German historiography, under both western and Marxist influence, is thus of fundamental significance for future intellectual relations. For it heralds the possibility of a return to a situation in which, as in late seventeenth and the eighteenth centuries, Anglo-Saxons (both Puritans and Anglicans) worked with Lutherans on the common problems of faith, feeling and reason, and the rationalist challenge.

If, as I have suggested, there might be diplomatic value in a re-examination of the challenges of the enlightenment to theology in its European context, there is a further task suggested by the fundamental revision of the historicist's viewpoint in its specifically German form. This concerns the relative significance of the reformation for the cultures of England and Germany. The theory of national "spirit" when joined with the unquestionable fact of the influence of Luther on the development of the German language and culture frequently produced the thesis in German historiography that "Germanic has signified Protestant just as Roman signified Catholic" (41). We can even find an example of a German Catholic writer addressing himself seriously to the thesis that Catholic and German are contraries (42).

The idea that Protestantism constitutes a distinct and definable entity in the religious world continues to attract adherents and its proper relationship to the enlightenment continues to be discussed. But when applied to the character of the English reformation and enlightenment this way of thinking runs into difficulties. Which is the normative form of Protestantism and which the normative response to the enlightenment? The fact that normative questions are not supposed to be asked in this tradition does not prevent them from emerging under pressure, as the following quotation illustrates:

> The enlightenment did not undermine the substance of religion
> nearly so deeply in Germany, nor did it produce that flat,
> superficial and life-destroying materialism and utilitarianism
> which is typical of the English and French enlightenment. The
> sole reason for this is that Germany experienced and assimilates
> the religious depths of the reformation; whereas England, instead
> of this, took over a reorganised church and state, nourished out
> of other, impoverished sources, and France suppressed and

eliminated the reformation in a persecution conducted with
unparalled cynicism (43).

This view of "the" reformation as a specifically German event was an essential part of the outlook of those who in the late eighteenth and early nineteenth century were consciously setting out to create a distinctively German culture. The fact that there are important theological judgements to
be made about the work of the different reformers in the different lands is
indisputable; but the abbreviation of these judgments by means of national
typologies confuses rather than clarifies the issues. So also does the assumption that Protestantism constitutes a type of religious life, about which
it is appropriate to speak in normative, as distinct from merely descriptive
terms (44). I believe, therefore, that it is a consequence of the re-examination of the late eighteenth century that the relative significance for England
and Germany of the reformation will need to be reassessed. In particular
the damage done by the subsequent accentuation of national divisions, which
the cosmopolitan outlook of the enlightenment attempted to overcome but on
an inadequately formulated basis, needs an appraisal freed from the influence of national typologies and capable of the sensitive evaluation of the
theological histories of countries other than one's own.

II

In this second part of my essay in theological diplomacy I propose to deal
with the problem of the significance of nationality for questions of theology.
As the previous section has demonstrated, there is abundant evidence that
English and German writers have been conscious of their national identities
over against each other, particularly since the rise of historicism. But
nothing is served by pretending that differences do not exist. Accordingly I
wish to show that these can be successfully and diplomatically handled
without the aid of that theory of nationality which has had the effect of
perpetuating divisions.

If we look right to the start of the period which saw the rise of the divergencies in their most accentuated form, we encounter the little known, but
most interesting and perceptive work of Karl Heinrich Sack, A n s i c h t e n
und Beobachtungen über Religion und Kirche in England
(1818). Sack paid a three-month long visit to England in 1817, returning to
a chair in Theology in Bonn in 1818. It was here that Pusey met him on his
second visit to Germany in 1826, and there began a correspondence which
persisted long after Pusey had abandoned his interests in German theology
for the cares and concerns of the Oxford Movement. Thus it was to Sack
that Pusey applied for a reasoned German view of J.H.Rose's incompetent
attack on German theology, and Sack's reply was printed in translation in
the first volume of Pusey's work.

Sack's interest in England clearly is based in the peculiar character of
English Evangelicalism, which, as Hirsch has noted, in its closer rela-

tionship both to orthodoxy and to practical Christianity has important points of contrast with German pietism (45). Thus we find Sack drawing particular attention to William Wilberforce's Practical View (1791), at the time in its eleventh edition, to Wesley's works, to Thomas Chalmers and to Simeon on the liturgy. The evident sympathy with which he views these movements is visible in his depiction of the principle characteristic of the English "a strong common-sense and a deep and powerful feeling. Both seem to tend in them, according to their initial inclination, more toward a concerted activity, to life itself, than to a onesided training and perfection" (46). The theme of practicality reoccurs in his description of the absence of separate theological faculties in England. The proper study of theology, he notes, is a private activity and "a kind of individual consultation and communication between old and young" ... a reference to the tutorial system at Oxbridge (47). Having seen, as he believes, the liveliness of the intellectual life thus produced, he believes that it is no bad thing that the English do not attempt to emulate Germans in their more purely academic (wissenschaftlich) activity.

As a matter of fact the theme of the commonsense practicality of English judgement in religious matters re-occurs with a somewhat tiresome regularity throughout the nineteenth century, and becomes one of the suspect generalisations of the "national character" school. Even Hare, who had more German theology (perhaps 3,000 works) on his shelves than any one of his contemporaries, liked to refer to "practical, statesmanly judgement" as the "peculiar spirit of the English mind", and to "practical Christianity" as "the very thing to keep their (i.e. German) theology from excesses" (48). Less valueless as an observation is the fact that none of the English Church parties of the early nineteenth century could be said to have neglected as a whole the practical expression of Christian faith in social action.

The obverse of this phenomenon is the often noted lack of speculative interest in English theology. Sack was quite prepared to believe that the pursuit of church history, patristics and reformation history was carried on in a lively way, and even that in symbolics, dogmatics (sic!) and moral theology the tradition was more lively in England than in Germany. But he felt bound to say that "interest in real scientific activity, whether in empirical or in speculative matters, has generally vanished a long time ago" (49). Even in Scotland, which at this time had a more lively philosophical tradition, German visitors were apt to be unimpressed. B.G.Niebuhr wrote from Edinburgh in 1799 that "the famed ascribed by Jacobi to the philosophical sense of the English is quite misplaced and founded upon ignorance" (50).

These views reflect both a temporary and a more permanent feature of English theology. The lack of close co-operation between philosophy and theology came to an end with the rise of idealism in Oxford in the late nineteenth century. But the attempt to use philosophy in the task of radically reconstructing and re-expressing Christian doctrine has not been a pronounced characteristic of English theology. Thus the philosophically trained theologians of the Lux Mundi (1889) school in Oxford understood themselves to be working within the framework of the Catholic creeds, and not on a reconstruction of Christian theology. The sometimes uneasy juxtaposition of liturgical and philosophical activity has played a major role in a theological tradition for so long dominated by Oxbridge Anglicanism. Sack himself noticed the importance of the liturgy to Anglicanism and the fact that it played a bigger role than preaching in the English Church. Bunsen whose influence on the English Broad Church movement was great, repeatedly said that he thought the English liturgy to be the most Christian order of worship he had encountered (51). The normativeness of the liturgical faith of the Church was effectively criticised from within Anglicanism only by the few 1920 modernists, who created a storm of opposition by daring to suggest the need for a new creed. When Sack observed that in England the church ruled theology, whereas in Germany the reverse was the case, he was making a point of some importance (52). The modernists, though they gained a victory in principle, were by no means popularly successful. Histories of the Church of England refer to "the fall of Modernism" and "the eclipse of Liberalism" in the inter-war years (53).

The disinclination to depart from confessional orthodoxy, which has characterised English theology virtually to the present, has been further prolonged by the basically linguistic interests of recent English philosophical theology. In itself, such an activity assumes that o t h e r people make statements of Christian faith for the philosophers to examine. But by itself it is unable to initiate any fundamental reconstruction of theology. It can, of course, take the traditional language and "translate" it into other language; as, for example when van Buren offers to re-express Chalcedonian orthodoxy in "secular" language. Or, more helpfully, it may sort out confusions in theologians' use of words - as when Ian Ramsey investigates the language of Gregory of Nyssa or John Robinson. The collection of essays, Prospect for Theology (1966), illustrated remarkably clearly the dominance over doctrinal theology achieved by theologians primarily trained in philosophical techniques (54).

One of the accidental, historical reasons for this phenomenon is the academic position of theology in the modern English university. For when the theological faculties were initially set up in Oxbridge in the nineteenth century, dispute between theological factions was at its height. Hence the study of doctrinal theology was unacceptable alike to protagonists and agnostics, as too susceptible to party spirit. What did become acceptable in the course of time was a philosophic engagement with basic theological themes. Hence when C.C.J.Webb opened his lectures in Religious Thought in England from 1850, he made clear that by religious thought he meant philosophy of religion (55). In England, doctrinal theology or systematics has not been developed at the University level on anything like the German scale. Expositions of Christian doctrine on the basis of the creeds, and monographs of a strongly historical nature on doctrinal themes have certainly been published; but few of these have a fully developed method at their base. It is doubtful, indeed, if a theological faculty in the contemporary secular university is the place from which such a theology could now be written (56). In this respect German and English institutions are very unlike each other.

This brief presentation of some of the commonly appreciated differences between German and English theology has stressed the fact that contingent historical factors of shorter or longer duration may create conditions which favour the development of certain kinds of theological activity, and may inhibit others. The importance of this type of explanation is that those who feel that what their own traditions have favoured is defective will not feel obliged to defend them as expressions of the national genius, but rather challenged to alter the conditions which produced them.

Thus Sack at the close of his study, which for so young a scholar is marked by a critical discernment and temperence of statement beyond his years, pleads for the binding together of German and English virtues in the further-ance of mutual understanding. And he expresses the wish that such connec-tions will flourish not merely between these two, but between all peoples (57). Sack's wish has probably been repeated frequently, and indeed seemed briefly to flourish in the inter-war years, which saw the publication of M y s t e r i u m   C h r i s t i (London, 1930), jointly edited by Deissmann and Bell (58). Interconfessional theology, however, is not necessarily the same thing as international theology, and if the latter is to be the aim the impulse must come from theologians in the Universities, rather than from Church leaders (59). An international theology will spring from the determined vision of the individual theologian as he makes his choice of reading matter. He will, of course, need to recognise the differences of tradition and culture which divide him initially from his foreign colleagues; but he will want, nonetheless, to set himself the standards of the ancient u n i v e r s i t a s . In doing so he will, today, face formidable obstacles. The loss of a com-mon language, the forces of nationalism (which economic prosperity per-versely strengthens) and the growing cultural gaps between not merely rich and poor countries but within these countries too, create about him a theo-logical babel which endangers the future of Christianity. Naturally the temptation is to resort to the anachronistic revival of theological imperialism, the arrogant assertion of one individual, church, nation or culture to provide the 'decisive' guidelines for the future. But the answer is more difficult.

It first consists in the preparedness of each language group and cultural tradition to make available to itself in academically reliable translation the best products of theological scholarship known to it from the whole Christian world, and to make these texts fundamental for the further devel-opment of its theological education. This is not an inconsiderable task. Newman's G r a m m a r   o f   A s s e n t , for all its influence outside England, has only recently been well translated into German, several attempts had to be made before parts of Kierkegaard were satisfactorily rendered into English, and the recent past has seen numerous careless translations of important works from German Catholic and Protestant theologians. The most useful texts often pose the greatest problems. We have to recognise that for all their past achievements and services, publishing houses in capitalist economies are in a most vulnerable position. Only a persistent academic determination to engage in a fundamentally international study of theology is likely to provide the drive to overcome the formidable problems of communication between nations.

The second requisite is fundamental works of historical scholarship probing the bewildering assemblage of facts and fantasies which underlie confessional and cultural divisions. There can be no objection to the application of Christian doctrines to particular local cultural or ecclesiastical situations. But by themselves such theologies may actually perpetuate divisive situations - a serious enough error in politics, but a blatant denial of Christ in theology. The linguistic confusions, muddles and sheer wrongheadedness which have helped to divide Christians from themselves and from others can be solved neither by careless indifference, nor by the coining and repetition of theological slogans.

The contemporary theological scene, while superficially internationalist in appearance, betrays many features of a deeprooted nationalist emphasis. The use of "novelties" of foreign origin in religious publishing merely encourages the latent xenophobia of the anticipated reaction. From the point of view of the publisher, particularly during the current recession of public interest in religion, both the novelty and the reaction are good for trade. Indeed it may be claimed that ephemeral works are justified by the other, "serious" publications which the profits permit. But in the long run this course has cumulatively deteriorating consequences. Divisions are accentuated, defensive positions are manned and theology becomes sloganised with a swiftly following public reaction.

The rejection of merely rhetorical novelties is by no means a rejection of new methods of study in theology, from whatever country of origin. This was indeed the mistake of many Englishmen when faced in the nineteenth century with novelties from Germany. No doubt the new freedoms were not then invariably exercised with care, but we do not need the help of the national character hypothesis to justify caution (60). It is doubtless true that the human sciences provide theological study with a fresh range of methods and constructive work. But, as in the nineteenth century so in ours, balance in the judicious application of new methods does not come easily and intellectual imperialisms of national and disciplinary origins raise their arrogant heads.

It was not the function of this essay to argue for the correctness of the "internationalist" case, nor to indicate the steps by which a coherent notion of "humanity" might be developed to be of service in theology. That I would want so to argue will be sufficiently apparent. But lest this should be thought to be merely the superficial assumption of an Englishman unrepentently perpetuating a natural law tradition, I quote with full agreement the position in this matter of Karl Heinrich Sack in his mid-nineteenth century work on the Church of Scotland:

There is little or no point in observing the characteristics and differences of peoples, if one fails to realize or acknowledge how slight these are in comparison with that in which they are fully alike ... So, in other words the reference to the Church of Christ and to the animating and purifying spirit proceeding from the Lord is the sole factor complimenting and reconciling the comparative stury of peoples; and no exaggeration of purely human mental properties, no high-minded maintenance of patriotic ideas, no criterion of morality or politics taken in itself can replace that perspective which issues from the recognition of Christ and his divine kingdom of truth (61).

Footnotes

1   An early draft of this paper was read at a meeting in the Theological
    Stift in Tübingen, on Thursday, 28 October, 1971, the day of the
    debate and vote on the Common Market in the British House of Com-
    mons. It was subsequently revised, and published as "Deutschland und
    England. Ein Versuch in theologischer Diplomatie", in the Zeit-
    schrift für Theologie und Kirche, 69. Jahrgang 1972 Heft 4
    (December 1972), pp. 439-465. The English version is here published
    with the generous consent of J. C. B. Mohr (Paul Siebeck), Tübingen.

2   By fundamental theology I mean the investigation of the methods,
    sources and norms of dogmatic theology.

3   I am not proposing to consider the relatively independent production of
    theological writing in Scotland, which has preserved closer relations
    with continental protestantism.

4   Cf. "Christian Doctrine in the 1960's" by M. F. Wiles, The Church
    Quarterly, Vol. II (1970), pp. 215-221, where the author expresses
    puzzlement about the full force of those theologies which make the idea
    of the Word of God central. Robert Morgan's reply, "The Word",
    Theology, Vol. LXXIV (1971), pp. 213-222, is an interesting clari-
    fication.

5   Thus English theology worked in the early nineteenth century largely
    independently of philosophy. It then took up a neo-Hegelianism just as
    Ritschl and his school was coming into prominence. In the twentieth
    century, as existentialism grew in influence on the continent, English
    philosophy turned slowly from idealism to realism and eventually to
    logical and linguistic analysis. Two contemporary British philosophers
    who clearly recognise the need for, and possibility of, fruitful dialogue
    are R. Bambrough, "Philosophy" in C. L. Mowat (ed.), The Shifting
    Balance of World Forces, 1895-1945 The Cambridge
    Modern History, Vol. XII , pp. 655-6, and B. Magee, Mo-
    dern British Philosophy (London, 1971) p. x. I am grateful to
    Mr. J. P. Clayton for these references.

6   My Autobiography. A Fragment (London, 1901), pp. 19 f.
    German translation, Aus meinem Leben, Fragmente zu
    einer Selbst-biographie (Gotha, 1902), p. 17.

7   Professor Harnack and his Oxford Critics (London,
    1902), pp. 11-12.

8   Between 1774 and 1784 Semler had a hand in the translation of seven
    English theological works, having earlier been involved with English
    biographies and histories. For a list of the more important works of
    philosophy translated into English between 1740 and 1790 see M. Wundt,
    Die deutsche Schulphilosophie im Zeitalter der Auf-

162

klärung (Tübingen, 1945), pp.270 f. G.Hornig, Die Anfänge der historisch-kritischen Theologie (Göttingen, 1961), discusses the extent of English influence on Semler.

9   Such opinions are based on two clear - but temporary - facts about English life, namely the hostility to speculative philosophy characteristic of Benthamite utilitarianism, and the existence of the Christian missions in the lands being colonised. Connop Thirlwall, Schleiermacher's English translator, was also in 1821 bewailing in a letter to Bunsen the dominance of the commercial spirit (Letters, Literary and Theological of Connop Thirlwall, ed. J.J.Perowne and L.Stokes (London, 1881), pp.59-60).
The idea that the English as a race are hopeless at philosophy passed into popular self-portraiture in the nineteenth century. E.g., "When we are not occupied in making machinery, we are (mentally speaking) the most slovenly people in the universe", a remark regarded as a French criticism of the English in Wilkie Collins, The Moonstone, Collins Classics edition (London, 1953), p.51.

10 Cf. the sermon "Wie sehr es die Würde des Menschen erhöht, wenn er mit ganzer Seele an der bürgerlichen Vereinigung hängt, der er angehört" (1806), in Sämtliche Werke, Predigten, Vol.I (Berlin, 1834), pp.223-238. The gentle defence of patriotism in this sermon had developed by 1813 into the theory that God has given a special character to each nation, as well as boundaries and tasks, and that the incursion of something foreign was to be resisted in the name of God. Predigten, Vol.IV (Berlin, 1835), pp.43. On Schleiermacher's nationalism, see J.F.Dawson Friedrich Schleiermacher, The Evolution of a Nationalist (Austin, Texas, 1966).

11 Quoted by R.Kramer, Nation und Theologie bei Johann Hinrich Wichern (Hamburg, 1959), p.97.

12 Article VI of these, while not explicitly teaching a doctrine of the infallibility of Scripture, nonetheless lends itself to one. But see Thirlwall's interpretation in A Critical Essay on the Gospel of St.Luke, by Dr. Friederich Schleiermacher, with an Introduction by the Translator, containing an account of the controversy respecting the Origin of the Three First Gospels since Bishop Marsh's Dissertation (London, 1825), p.xix.

13 English, The State of Protestantism in Germany described (London 1825); 2nd ed. with an appendix (1829); German, Der Zustand der protestantischen Religion in Teutschland (Leipzig, 1826).

14 E.B.Pusey, An Historical Enquiry into the Probable Causes of the Rationalist Character lately predominant in the Theology of Germany (London, 1828); but cf. especially Part II of this work, Containing an Explanation of the Views misconceived by Mr. Rose, and further

Illustrations (London, 1830), where he defends himself against
the charge of disbelief in biblical inspiration. In subsequent correspondence with Rose, Pusey indicated that he did not disagree with
him on fundamentals. Pusey in fact said that he regretted having written and requested that the works should not be reprinted - a request
that has unhappily been observed. His regret derives more from a
feeling that he gave currency to views he had always regarded as
erroneous, than from his subsequently more infallibilist interpretation
of biblical authority.

15   Quoted in H.P.Liddon, Life of E.B.Pusey (London, 1893),
     p.102

16   Quoted in Frederick Maurice (ed.), The Life of Frederick
     Denison Maurice, Vol.I (London, 1884), p.468. The tendency to
     generalise on the basis of a selection of examples also occurs in the
     controversy between Karl Barth and Reinhold Niebuhr on the discrepant
     viewpoints of "anglo-saxon" and "continental" theology, in K.Barth,
     J.Daniélou and R.Niebuhr, "Amsterdamer Fragen und Antworten",
     Theologische Existenz Heute (München, 1949). As Klaus
     Dockhorn points out in "'Angelsächische' und 'kontinentalische' Theo-
     logie", Evangelische Theologie (1949) pp.501-515, Barth's
     reading of early twentieth century English theology is defective, and
     he overlooks the extent to which his own theology creates the alleged
     discrepancy. But we note also the irony of the fact that Niebuhr accuses
     Barth of following that theological method which Maurice believed was
     characteristically English.

17   For instance a footnote in F.J.Foakes-Jackson's essay, "Christ in
     the Church: the testimony of History", in Cambridge Theologi-
     cal Essays, ed. H.B.Swete (London, 1905), p.476, where another
     work is cited contrasting the width of English speculation with the
     narrowness engendered by German specialisation.

18   Karl Heinrich Sack, Richard Hooker von den Gesetzen des
     Kirchenregiments im Gegensatz zu den Forderungen
     der Puritaner (Heidelberg, 1868), p.vi. In the opinion of more
     than one German writer in the early twentieth century the dominance
     of the "high-church" movement in Anglicanism spelt the end of hopes
     for good church relations with German Protestantism. Cf. Heinrich
     Boehmer in an essay of 1916, "Die Kirche von England und der Pro-
     testantismus", Gesammelte Aufsätze (Gotha, 1927), pp.69-
     128, especially p.93 where he explicitly declines to accept the liberal
     Anglican view that Anglo-Catholicism was a temporary phenomenon;
     and Albert Hauck, Deutschland und England in ihren
     kirchlichen Beziehungen (Leipzig, 1917), which speaks of the
     "Entprotestantisierung" of the Anglican Church, and asserts that it is
     most unlikely that close relations could be re-established. These
     wartime estimates naturally reflect somewhat the tensions of the mo-
     ment. Klaus Dockhorn in "Das protestantische Selbst-verständnis der

Kirche von England", Zeitwende: Die neue Furche, Vol. VII (1960), pp. 451-461, argues that the Church of England is an essentially protestant body, more Lutheran than Calvinist. But his view that the Oxford movement did not in the end bring about a great alteration in the Church of England seems to me, though partially justified, to underestimate the marked internal disagreements on the doctrine of the ministry and sacraments which still persist and create great difficulty when "anglicanism" has to be represented in ecumenical discussions. See now my essay, "Anglicanism and Protestantism", in the present volume.

19   G. Iggers, Deutsche Geschichtswissenschaft, 1971. This is a translation into German, with alterations and additions. of The German Conception of History (Middletown, Connecticut, 1968). References are to the German edition.

20   ibid, pp. 13-23

21   Cf. the able criticism of J. M. Robinson's views in Van A. Harvey, The Historian and the Believer (New York, 1967), pp. 164-203.

22   Iggers, p. 50 ff. See also the detailed and sensitive presentation of F. M. Barnard in Herder's Social and Political Thought (Oxford, 1965), a revised edition of his Zwischen Aufklärung und Politischer Romantik (Berlin, 1964). It is important to note the shift in Herder's thought from the early emphasis on the diversity of peoples, to a greater interest in universal unity and the sensus humanitatis in his later writings.

23   "Naturrecht und Humanität in der Weltpolitik", in Deutscher Geist in Westeuropa (Tübingen, 1925); translated into English in O. Gierke, Natural Law and the Theory of Society, 1500-1800, Vol. I (Cambridge, 1934), Appendix I.

24   Troeltsch, op. cit. pp. 6 f.

25   Troeltsch, op. cit. p. 15

26   International Journal of Ethics, iii (1892/3), pp. 38 f.

27   Cf. Iggers, p. 20 f. In controversies about the relations of theology and metaphysics in the nineteenth century and even today it is often far from clear what is meant by the word "metaphysics". A number of commentators have pointed out that attempts to undermine metaphysics, such as those of Kant or the early Wittgenstein, themselves require a meta-metaphysics. Cf., for example, D. M. MacKinnon, "Metaphysical and Religious Language" (1954) in Borderlands of Theology (London, 1968), pp. 207-221.

28   See C. J. H. Hayes, The Historical Evolution of Modern Nationalism (New York, 1931) and Nationalism: A Religion (New York, 1960). Also H. Kohn, The Idea of Nationalism, a

Study of its Origins and Background (New York, 1944), followed most recently by L.L.Snyder, The New Nationalism (New York, 1968). These writers refer above all to Bolingbroke (1678-1751), who, though spoken of as the "high-priest of the cosmopolitan enlightenment", argued that governments should vary in different lands according to the divinely-given spirit of each nationality, and went to characterise the national genius of Britain.

29 In "Of National Characters" reprinted in Essays, Moral, Political and Literary (London, 1963), p.212. But Hume was a Scotsman who thought little of the English.

30 Cf., for example, Karl Hillebrand, "Zur Entwicklungsgeschichte der abendländischen Weltanschauung", Zeiten, Völker und Menschen, Vol.VII (Berlin, 1887), pp.1-25, and his highly interesting discussion (with an Englishman) of English religious life, ibid, pp.245-309. Another historian who believed in the fixity of national types was Döllinger. Cf. Lord Acton, "Döllinger's Historical Work", The English Historical Review, Vol.V (1890), p.743.

31 Diary, Reminiscences and Correspondence, Vol.III (London, 1869), p.91.

32 The Philosophy of Religion (London, 1849), p.vii.

33 E.g. L.W.Beck, "German Philosophy" in The Encyclopaedia of Philosophy (New York, 1967), III, pp.291-308, esp. "The Genius of the German Philosophy", pp.306-8 and bibliography.

34 For a recent example of what is being criticised here see Herbert Cyzarz, "Versuch über den Nationalcharakter", in Was Bleibt. Wesen, Wege und Werke des Deutschen (Graz, 1962), pp.297-353. Many of the studies of British national character were undertaken by Sir Ernest Baker, the translator of Gierke and Troeltsch. See National Character and the Factors in its Formation (London, 1927; 4th ed. rev. 1948), and the collected work The Character of England (Oxford, 1948); also his lecture Christianity and Nationality (Oxford, 1927).

35 Two studies by Klaus Dockhorn are fundamental, Der deutsche Historismus in England (Göttingen, 1949) and Deutscher Geist und angelsächsische Geistesgeschichte (Göttingen, 1954). Cf. also M.Messerschmidt, Deutschland in Englischer Sicht (Düsseldorf, 1955), and two essays by P.E.Schramm, "Deutschlands Verhältnis zur englischen Kultur nach der Begründung des neuen Reiches", in S.A.Kaehler (ed.) Schicksalswege deutscher Vergangenheit (Düsseldorf, 1950), pp.289-319, and "Englands Verhältnis zur deutschen Kultur zwischen der Reichsgründung und der Jahrhundert Wende", in W.Konze (ed.), Deutschland und Europa (Düsseldorf, 1951).

36 For this criticism see C.C.J.Webb, A Study of Religious Thought in England from 1850 (Oxford, 1933), p.97.

37 "Der Geist der deutschen Kultur" in O.Hinze (ed.), Deutschland und der Weltkrieg (Berlin, 1915), p.59.

38 K.Dockhorn, Die Staatsphilosophie des englischen Idealismus; ihre Lehre und Wirkung (Bochum, 1937). The English idealists were clearly embarrassed during the First World War by the fact of the extent of their dependence on German philosophy. J.H.Muirhead initially argued in German Philosophy in relation to the War (London, 1915) that recent German thought (especially the "philosophy of militarism" in Nietzsche, Treitschke and von Bernhardi) had perverted the teachings of Kant and Hegel. Subsequently he developed the view that the revival of idealism in England was less a foreign importation than the continuation of a long-standing tradition, in The Platonic Tradition in Anglo-Saxon Thought (London, 1931).

39 Cf. Dockhorn, op.cit., pp.22-33.

40 "Aufgaben und Methoden der Geschichtswissenschaft", Geschichtsschreibung, hrsg. von Jürgen Scheschkewitz (Droste Verlag, Düsseldorf, 1968), p.7.

41 E.Marcks, Deutschland und England in den großen europäischen Krisen seit der Reformation (1900), p.12.

42 E.Przywara, "Deutsche Frömmigkeit I: Das katholisch Deutsche" (in Was Bleibt, see footnote 34), pp.359-378.

43 Hanns Rückert, "Die Bedeutung der Reformation für die deutsche Geschichte" Deutsche Theologie, Vol.VIII (1941), p.100. The view that the German experience of the Reformation was "deeper" (by which is meant not merely more radical, but also more profound and satisfactory) is found also in Wilhelm Dibelius's influential book, England (Stuttgart, 1925), 4th ed., Vol.II, p.79, and derives ultimately from Hegel. See K.Dockhorn, Deutscher Geist und angelsächsische Geistesgeschichte, pp.7-17.

44 A recent example is to be found in F.W.Kantzenbach's Protestantisches Christentum im Zeitalter der Aufklärung (Gütersloh, 1965), where the author asserts, "What is meant by the protestant tradition is not only a complex of purely profanely determined powers, but the expression of a specifically religious life-force", p.15. But these, of course, are not the only alternatives open to the theologian. One also notices the fact that this and other books with the word "Protestant" in the title or subtitle concern themselves solely with German Protestantism.

45 E.Hirsch, Geschichte der neuern Evangelischen Theologie, III, (Gütersloh, 1951), pp.250-252.

46 Sack, Ansichten und Beobachtungen über Religion und Kirche in England (1818), p.3 f.

47 He also notes that "professors obviously stand in an extremely lax and unsatisfactory relationship to their students"! ibid, p.52.

48 "Thou shalt not bear false witness against thy neighbour", A Letter to the Editor of the English Review (London, 1849), pp.53-55.

49 Ibid, p.51 (see note 46). This continues as a theme of criticism into the twentieth century. Otto Baumgarten, Religiöses und kirchliches Leben in England (Leipzig, 1922) remarks on the lack of philosophical depth in the following way: "A radical either-or between a scientific and a religious world view is missing" (p.28). Other commentators are less sure that this is in fact a defect. Karl Clemen, for instance, in an outstandingly well-informed study, "Der gegenwärtige Stand des religiösen Denkens in Großbritannien", Theologische Studien und Kritiken, Vol.65 (1892), No.II, pp.513-548 and No.IV, pp.603-714, indicates the importance for late nineteenth-century British theology of the proper grasp of the methods of the natural sciences, and of the thorough philosophical grounding and justification of religious belief in the face of strong anti-religious propaganda.

50 Lebensnachrichten über Barthold Georg Niebuhr, Vol.I (Hamburg, 1838) p.223.

51 W.Höcker, Der Gesandte Bunsen als Vermittler zwischen Deutschland und England (Göttingen, 1951), p.54.

52 Sack, op. cit., p.53.

53 RLloyd, The Church of England 1900-1965 (London 1966), ch.12. For myself I believe that there are striking resemblances in method between the modernist theologian, Bethune-Baker, in 1921, and John Robinson in 1971. See my essay, "The Theology of the Humanity of Christ", in reply to Robinson, and his reply in Christ, Faith and History, ed. S.W.Sykes and J.P.Clayton (Cambridge, 1972), pp.39-52 and 53-75.

54 Ninian Smart and Donald MacKinnon were the important exceptions, in two essays tackling the fundamental methodological problems of modern doctrinal theology. But neither could primarily be called a systematic theologian.

55 (Oxford, 1933), p.3.

56 The setting up in the new University of Lancaster of a Department of Religious and Atheistic Studies and the subsequent advertisement for a Professor of Religious Studies "of any religion or none" indicated the intention of that University not to give preference to religious solutions of the problems of theology. Cambridge's change from the title "Theology" to "Theological and Religious Studies" indicates a less radical move in the same direction. The stressing of the analytic over the systematic is indicated by the fact that in most English universities where

theology or religious studies is taught there is a substantial measure of cooperation with departments of philosophy and sociology.

57 Sack, op. cit., p.153.

58 This flowering of contacts followed the 1925 Stockholm Conference. Anglo-German theological consultations were arranged at Canterbury (1927), Eisenach (1928) and Chichester (1931). The common experience of the conferences was that such differences as emerged were individual rather than national. See, R.C.D. Jasper, George Bell, Bishop of Chichester (London, 1967), pp.65-8. One of the German participants at some of meetings, Professor Wilhelm Vollrath, published in 1928 his useful Theologie der Gegenwart in Großbritannien (Gütersloh). Cf. also the view of another of the participants Heinrich Frick, in his Geleitwort to M. Dietrich, Theologische Ontologie im modernen Anglikanismus (Berlin, 1936).

59 A recent example of an expressly ecumenical work, but bearing the significant title, Towards an American Theology (New York, 1967), illustrates the fact that no assumptions can be made about modern theologians engaging in theology as an international enterprise. Particularly revealing is the fact that in the preface to the English edition, the author, H. Richardson, contents himself with the assertion of the "fact" that German Protestant hegemony in theology is passing away, and that henceforth Anglo-Saxons need no longer take their theology second-hand from German sources. In the preface to the American edition, however, the author's real intention emerges. Modern creative theology, he states, must be "effected by American theologians working out an American theology" (p.ix). His theory is that theology has a "spatial centre", and that this has moved from Latin Europe to Northern Europe, and is now to be located in America (does he mean North America?), the land of the "decisive engagement" with "sociotechnic culture". This is full of difficulties. One can make sense, perhaps, of the idea of temporary "foci" of theology, which might be determined by careful historical research rather than the crude manner which the author suggests. But does theology have "decisive engagements?" If so, would anyone care to identify its decisive engagement with scientific thought, with historical criticism, with Marxism or with Freudianism? The suggestion is riddled with difficulties. First, since the Enlightenment, is there such a thing as "Christian theology", as distinct from theologies of differing characteristics and varying centres of interest making them more or less capable of coping with their differing intellectual tasks? Secondly, can the notion of a "decisive engagement" be helpfully differentiated from that of change or development in one or other of those theologies? The distinction between a change and a "decisive" change would be more probably rhetorical than clear.

What, indeed, the whole of the author's suggestion resembles is that intellectual imperialism which, in theological history, is more readily intelligible from psychological or social factors than from intellectual ones. It seems to overlook the possibility that a national group of theologians might be presented with a problem by their cultural circumstances which they disastrously fail to solve. There have been such engagements in recent history.

60 Cf. Connop Thirlwall, who by that time had become a bishop, to the Germanophile Roland Williams, commending "our English caution and reserve, even though it be strengthen by a bias in favour of antiquity, which leads us to supend our judgement upon these novelties, and not to treat them as if they had already decided an important question". C.Thirlwall, A Letter to the Rev. Roland Williams, D.D. (London 1860), p.68.

61 Die Kirche von Schottland, I. Teil (Heidelberg, 1844), pp.4 f.

STUDIEN ZUR INTERKULTURELLEN GESCHICHTE DES CHRISTENTUMS
ETUDES D'HISTOIRE INTERCULTURELLE DU CHRISTIANISME
STUDIES IN THE INTERCULTURAL HISTORY OF CHRISTIANITY

Herausgegeben von/edité par/edited by

Richard Friedli   Walter J. Hollenweger   Hans-Jochen Margull
Université de Fribourg   University of Birmingham   Universität Hamburg

Band 1   Wolfram Weiße: Südafrika und das Antirassismusprogramm. Kirchen im Spannungsfeld einer Rassengesellschaft.

Band 2   Ingo Lembke: Christentum unter den Bedingungen Lateinamerikas. Die katholische Kirche vor den Problemen der Abhängigkeit und Unterentwicklung.

Band 3   Gerd Uwe Kliewer: Das neue Volk der Pfingstler. Religion, Unterentwicklung und sozialer Wandel in Lateinamerika.

Band 4   Joachim Wietzke: Theologie im modernen Indien - Paul David Devanandan.

Band 5   Werner Ustorf: Afrikanische Initiative. Das aktive Leiden des Propheten Simon Kimbangu.

Band 6   Erhard Kamphausen: Anfänge der kirchlichen Unabhängigkeitsbewegung in Südafrika. Geschichte und Theologie der äthiopischen Bewegung. 1880-1910.

Band 7   Lothar Engel: Kolonialismus und Nationalismus im deutschen Protestantismus in Namibia 1907-1945. Beiträge zur Geschichte der deutschen evangelischen Mission und Kirche im ehemaligen Kolonial- und Mandatsgebiet Südwestafrika.

Band 8   Pamela M. Binyon: The Concepts of „Spirit" and „Demon". A Study in the use of different languages describing the same phenomena.

Band 9   Neville Richardson: The World Council of Churches and Race Relations: 1960 to 1969.

Band 10   Jörg Müller: Uppsala II. Erneuerung in der Mission. Eine redaktionsgeschichtliche Studie und Dokumentation zu Sektion II der 4. Vollversammlung des Ökumenischen Rates der Kirchen, Uppsala 1968.

Band 11   Hans Schoepfer: Theologie der Gesellschaft. Interdisziplinäre Grundlagenbibliographie zur Einführung in die befreiungs- und polittheologische Problematik: 1960-1975.

Band 12   Werner Hoerschelmann: Christliche Gurus. Darstellung von Selbstverständnis und Funktion indigenen Christseins durch unabhängige charismatisch geführte Gruppen in Südindien.

Band 13   Claude Schaller: L'Eglise en quête de dialogue.

Band 14   Theo Tschuy: Hundert Jahre kubanischer Protestantismus (1868-1961). Versuch einer kirchengeschichtlichen Darstellung.

Band 15   Werner Korte: Wir sind die Kirchen der unteren Klassen. Entstehung, Organisation und gesellschaftliche Funktionen unabhängiger Kirchen in Afrika.

Band 16   Arnold Bittlinger: Papst und Pfingstler. Der römisch katholisch - pfingstliche Dialog und seine ökumenische Relevanz.

Band 17   Ingemar Lindén: The Last Trump. An historico-genetical study of some important chapters in the making and development of the Seventh-day Adventist Church.

Band 18   Zwinglio Dias: Krisen und Aufgaben im brasilianischen Protestantismus. Eine Studie zu den sozialgeschichtlichen Bedingungen und volkspädagogischen Möglichkeiten der Evangelisation.